THE '98 READER

The '98 Reader

Edited by
Padraic O'Farrell

THE LILLIPUT PRESS
DUBLIN

First published 1998 by
THE LILLIPUT PRESS LTD
62-63 Sitric Road, Arbour Hill,
Dublin 7, Ireland.

A CIP record for this
title is available from
The British Library.

ISBN 1 901866 03 3

*The Lilliput Press receives financial assistance from
An Chomhairle Ealaíon/The Arts Council of Ireland.*

Set in 11 on 13 Lapidary by Sheila Stephenson
Printed in Ireland by Betaprint of Dublin

Contents

Foreword

Simply to read the list of contents could be the best introduction to this remarkable, and most moving and informative anthology. It treats only of one year in our Irish history, but that was a momentous and significant year and Padraic O'Farrell allows it to speak, and to sing and recite for itself. I bow before the research he has done, and the wisdom and lucidity with which he presents his findings.

He sets out from the Church of Dungannon. He gives us the declarations and resolutions made and signed by Wolfe Tone. It is good to look again on that vision and, in this year, to brood over all that went wrong. And if you are a Tyrone man you know that you, or somebody belonging to you, was around for the Battle of Diamond. Then, aided by Teeling, off we go to Bantry and fail, sadly, to encounter Hoche.

There are so many people all around us, the Bold Belfast Shoemaker, and John and Henry Sheares and Napper Tandy. And we pass by the Battle of Prosperous and may meditate on quiet lovely green places that once were bright with steel and dark-red with blood. And these pages give us the comment of the time, much of it wise, much of it fatal.

But the most moving moment for me in this great book was when I came to a series of poems of, or related to, the period. The procession begins with Florence Wilson's 'The Man from God Knows Where', which when I was a boy I recited, every word of it, at a concert in Omagh Town Hall. Fond memories. I survived. Then comes 'A Song of the North' by Brian na mBanban, who was Brian O'Higgins, father of the Abbey actor, and he and all his family were dear friends of mine. Then comes James Orr's 'Donegore Hill', and P.J. McCall's 'Henry Joy', and Ethna Carbery's 'Roddy McCorley', and Alice Milligan, great lady, meditating on that same fatal year.

And I recall the day, say sixty years ago, when a notable Ulster clergyman, Fr Paul Mckenna, brought me from Omagh town to an old mansion on the fringe of Mountfield village. And he stood at the door and called: 'Alice, where art thou?' And the aged poetess came forth. And I, being middling young, felt I was back in 1798.

Benedict Kiely

Preface

Just a few weeks of actual combat. Some of the engagements were mere skirmishes, others fierce and bloody. Yet the rebellion of 1798 has inspired more song, prose and poetry than many more significant and strategically conclusive campaigns.

The songs are most remembered. Rural Irish people now in late-middle or old age learned them as children. They did not stop to think of their bloodthirsty lyrics. Fertile young imaginations grasped the imagery of each stanza with fervour. Young arms plucked ash-plants from hedges and fashioned make-believe pikes. Every stream was the Slaney, every high rise was Vinegar Hill. Kelly the Boy from Killane and Father Murphy, each scarcely four feet tall, fought their way across bracken and heather. That was because Wexford had the most stirring selection of ballads.

Only in later years, when history had become a school subject, did they learn about the rising in the North, about Humbert in Killala. Then they remembered their fathers and mothers singing songs or reading poems about those episodes too: 'Henry Joy' or 'The Men of the West'.

The Second World War, with Vera Lynn and her White Cliffs of Dover and Jimmy going asleep in his own little room again, pushed the airs of '98 aside. 'The Shores of Tripoli' opened the way for American songs. They are still with us.

The prose and poems included here give a more sober view of strife and warfare. Some are included with reluctance, even apprehension, because they tell of sectarian atrocities the like of which are still occurring in part of Ireland, sometimes of similar nature and in the same locations. Because they are of an era in which warfare and violence were acceptable methods of securing rights, they incite and call for continuing strife.

They remind us that no account of the rebellion is complete without

starting long before 1798 and ending some years after. A chronology, therefore, supports this collection. It begins with the formation of the Volunteers in 1778 and ends with Michael Dwyer's surrender in 1803.

Padraic O'Farrell

Acknowledgments

I thank Antony Farrell of Lilliput Press for accepting this idea and going through with it. Thanks also to his editor, Brendan Barrington, publicist, Siobán O'Reilly, and Vincent Hurley, who assisted greatly in suggesting material and advising on sources. I am most grateful to Benedict Kiely for his generous foreword. I wish to thank the librarians and staffs of the National Library of Ireland and the county libraries of Westmeath, Wexford, Meath and Kildare for continuing assistance; the Department of Irish Folklore at University College Dublin and *Béaloideas* for permission to quote the account of the 'swearing-in' of Larry Byrne (see 'Of Wicklow') and of 'The Battle of Ballinamuck' (see 'Of Humbert'); Gearóid O'Brien and Seán Ó Rioghbardáin for their interest and help; my daughters, Niamh and Aisling, for word-proccessing, and my wife, Maureen, for proofreading.

Of Stirrings

A heady awareness of French-inspired republicanism fomented resentment to government brutality and opened the path to bloody and dramatic rebellion. The English radical Thomas Paine (1737-1809) wrote *The Age of Reason* (London 1794) and defended the French Revolution in *The Rights of Man, Being an Answer to Mr Burke's Attack on the French Revolution* (Dublin 1791). Those who embraced his ideals (for which he was imprisoned briefly in Paris) were called Paineites. Paine's doctrine, with its heady rhetoric – 'My country is the world and my religion is to do good' – was seized upon by a people deprived of their rights.

THE RIGHTS OF MAN
Anon.

This song was first printed in Paddy's Resource, *a collection of revolutionary ballads written by United Irish members and sympathizers, published in Belfast in 1795 and re-issued in 1796. An expanded edition was printed in Dublin in 1798 – Drennan's 'Wake of William Orr' and the anonymous song 'Edward' appeared in this later edition. The book was published in Philadelphia in 1796 and New York in 1798. Many United Irish sympathizers emigrated or fled to the newly established United States during the 1790s.*

> I speak in candour, one night in slumber
> My mind did wander near to Athlone,
> The centre station of this Irish nation
> Where a congregation unto me was shown.

Beyond my counting upon a mountain
Near to a fountain that clearly ran,
I feel to tremble, I'll not dissemble
As they assembled for the rights of man.

All clad in green there I thought I seen
A virtuous Queen that was grave and old,
Saying Children dear, now do not fear
But come and hear what I will unfold.
This fertile country, near seven centuries
Since Strongbow's entry upon our land,
Has been kept under with woes un-numbered
And always plundered of the rights of man.

My cause you chided, you so derided
When divided, alas you know.
All in disorder round Erin's border
Strife, grief and murder has left you low.
Let each communion detest disunion,
In love and union join hand in hand.
And believe old Grania that proud Brittania
No more shall rob you of the rights of man.

Then I thought the crowd all spoke so loud
And straightway vowed to take her advice.
They seemed delighted and all united
Not to be frightened but to rejoice.
Her harp so pleasing she played amazing
I still kept gazing but could not understand.
She sang most enchanting and most endearing
In words most cheering to the rights of man.

Throughout the azure sky I then did spy
A man for to fly and for to descend.
And straightway came down upon the ground
Where Erin round had her bosom friends.
His dazzling mitre and cross was brighter
Than stars by night or midday sun.
In accents rare then I do declare
He prayed success for the rights of man.

THE SWINISH MULTITUDE
Anon.

Many of the songs in **Paddy's Resource** *were intended to be sung to well-known airs of the time. 'The Swinish Multitude' is written to the tune of 'The Lass of Richmond Hill'. This song was the most popular work of Leonard McNally (1752-1820), whose dramas and comic operas enjoyed considerable success. He was a member of the United Irishmen from the early 1790s and was friendly with most of its leaders, defending Napper Tandy and Emmet at their respective trials. However, from at least 1794 he was also a paid agent of the government. His treachery was only revealed after his death when his son applied for the annuity paid in recognition of his father's services.*

> Give me the man whose dauntless soul
> Oppression's threat defies,
> And bids, tho' tyrants thunder roll,
> The SUN OF FREEDOM rise;
> Who laughs at all the conjur'd storms,
> State sorc'ry wakes around;
> At pow'r in all his varying forms –
> At title's empty sound.
>
> Give me the soul whose lustrous zeal,
> Diffusing heaven-born lights,
> Instructs a people how to feel,
> And how to gain their rights;
> Who nobly scorning vain applause,
> Or lucre's fraudful plan,
> Purely inlists for freedom's cause –
> The dearest cause of Man.
>
> Hail ye friends united here,
> In virtue's sacred ties!
> May you, like virtue's self keep clear
> Of pensioners and spies,
> May you, By Bastilles ne'er appall'd
> See NATURE'S RIGHTS renew'd
> Nor longer unaveng'd be called
> 'THE SWINISH MULTITUDE.'

Hail to the men where e'er they be,
Whose kindling minds advance
In reason's path, – All hail, ye FREE!
Of Holland, or of France!
She comes for ALL! Sweet Freedom comes!
To no one region bound;
The cause of Human Weal assumes,
And claims the globe around.

From vice to vice, while state craft flies,
May we its crimes pursue;
Pierce to the Source from whence they rise,
And hold them up to view.
This be our great, our steadfast task,
Resolv'd our strength to try;
This glory from our hearts we ask –
For this WE DARE to *die*.

THE RISING OF THE MOON
John Keegan Casey ('Leo')

This, one of the rebellion's most evocative ballads, conveys the undercover urgency of revolutionaries preparing to strike. It is therefore included in this section of the anthology.

Casey (1846-70) came from Milltown, Rathconrath, near Mullingar in County Westmeath. He was imprisoned for his Fenianism and he contributed to The Irish People, *the* Boston Pilot *and the* Shamrock. *His other well-known song, the gentle 'Máire, My Girl', is in complete contrast.*

'Oh! then, tell me, Sean O'Farrell, tell me why you hurry so?'
'Hush, mo bhuachaill, hush and listen,' and his cheeks were all a-glow.
'I bear orders from the Captain, get you ready quick and soon,
For the pikes must be together at the rising of the moon.'

'Oh! then tell me, Sean O'Farrell, where the gathering is to be?'
'In the old spot by the river, right well known to you and me.
One word more – for signal token whistle up the marching tune,
With your pike upon your shoulder, by the rising of the moon.'

Out from many a mud-wall cabin eyes were watching thro' the night,
Many a manly breast was throbbing for the blessed warning light,
Murmurs passed along the valley like the banshee's lonely croon,
And a thousand blades were flashing at the rising of the moon.

There beside the singing river that dark mass of men was seen,
Far above the shining weapons hung their own beloved green.
'Death to every foe and traitor! Forward! Strike the marching tune,
And, hurrah, my boys for freedom! 'tis the rising of the moon.'

Well they fought for poor old Ireland, and full bitter was their fate –
Oh! what glorious pride and sorrow fills the name of Ninety-Eight –
Yet, thank God, e'en still are beating hearts in manhoods burning noon
Who would follow in their footsteps at the rising of the moon!

UNITED CALL

*During the lead-up to the rebellion, the United Irishmen distributed a Proclamation.
It was written by John Sheares and read:*

Irishmen! your country is free, and you are about to be avenged. That vile Government
which has so long and so cruelly oppressed you is no more! Some of its most atrocious
monsters have already paid the forfeit of their lives, and the rest are in our hands. The
national flag – the sacred green – is at this moment flying over the ruins of despotism;
and that capital which, a few hours past, had witnessed the debauchery, the plots and
crimes of your tyrants, is now the citadel of triumphant patriotism and virtue! Arise,
the united sons of Ireland: arise, like a great and powerful people, determined to live
free, or die! Arm yourselves by every means in your power, and rush like lions on your
foes. Consider, that for every enemy you disarm, you arm a friend, and thus become
doubly powerful. In the cause of liberty, inaction is cowardice, and the coward shall
forfeit the property he has not the courage to protect. Let his arms be seized, and
transferred to those gallant spirits who want and will use them. Yes, Irishmen! we swear
by the Eternal Justice, in whose cause we fight, that the brave patriot who survives the
present glorious struggle, and the family of him who has fallen, or shall fall hereafter in
it, shall receive from the hands of a grateful nation an ample recompense out of that
property which the crimes of our enemies have forfeited into our hands, and his name
shall be inscribed on the great national record of Irish revolution, as a glorious example
to posterity; but we likewise swear to punish robbers with death and infamy. We also
swear, that we will never sheath the sword until every being in the country is restored
to those equal rights which the God of nature has given to all men – until an order of

things shall be established in which no superiority shall be acknowledged among the citizens of *Erin* but that of virtue and talent.

Rouse all the energies of your souls; heed not the glare of a hired soldiery or aristocratic yeomanry; they cannot stand the vigorous shock of freemen; their trappings and arms shall soon be yours, and the detested Government of England, to which we vow eternal hatred, shall learn that the treasures it exhausts on its accoutered [*sic*] slaves, for the purpose of butchering Irishmen, shall but farther enable us to turn their swords on its devoted head.

Many of the military feel the love of liberty glow within their breasts, and have already joined the national standard. Receive, with open arms, such as shall follow so glorious an example; they can render signal service to the cause of freedom, and shall be rewarded according to their deserts. But, for the wretch who turns his sword against his native country, let the national vengeance be visited on him – let him find no quarter. Attack them, by day and by night, in every direction. Avail yourselves of the natural advantages of your country, which are innumerable, and with which you are better acquainted than they are. When you cannot attack them in fair force, constantly harass their rear and flanks, cut off their visions and magazines, and prevent them, as much as possible, from uniting their forces. Let whatever moment you cannot devote to fighting for your country be passed in learning how to fight for it, or preparing the means of war; for war, war alone, must occupy every mind and every hand in Ireland, until its soil be purged of all its enemies.

Vengeance! Irishmen! vengeance on your oppressors! Remember what thousands of your dearest friends have perished by their merciless orders! Remember their burnings, their rackings, their torturings, their military massacres, and their legal murders – remember Orr!

THE BOLD BELFAST SHOEMAKER
Anon.

The influence of French and American republicanism, religious discrimination and agrarian unrest affected a population that was growing rapidly. Young men joined secret societies and heard about the probability of a French invasion. Some 'listed in the train', but later deserted.

Come all you true born Irishmen, where-ever you may be
I hope you'll pay attention and listen unto me.
I am a bold shoemaker, from Belfast Town I came
And to my great misfortune I listed in the train.

I had a fair young sweetheart, Jane Wilson was her name,
She said it grieved her to the heart to see me in the train.

She told me if I would desert to come and let her know,
She would dress me up in her own clothes that I might go to and fro.

We marched to Chapelizod like heroes stout and bold,
I'd be no more a slave to them, my officer I told,
For to work upon a Sunday with me did not agree
That was the very time, brave boys, I took my liberty.

When encamped at Tipperary, we soon got his command
For me and for my comrade bold, one night on guard to stand.
The night it was both wet and cold and so we did agree
And on that very night, brave boys, I took my liberty.

The night that I deserted I had no place to stay,
I went into a meadow and lay down in the hay.
It was not long that I lay there until I rose again,
And looking all around me I espied six of the train.

We had a bloody battle but soon I beat them all
And soon the dastard cowards for mercy loud did call.
Saying spare our lives brave Irewin and we will pray for thee,
By all that's fair we will declare for you and liberty.

As for George Clarke of Carrick, I own he's very mean,
For the sake of forty shillings he had me took again
They locked me in a strong room my sorrows to deplore,
With four on every window and six on every door.

I being close confined then I soon looked all around
I leaped out of the window and knocked four of them down,
The light horse and the train, my boys, they soon did follow me
But I kept my road before them and preserved my liberty.

I next joined Father Murphy as you will quickly hear
And many a battle did I fight with his brave Shelmaliers.
With four hundred of his croppy boys we beat great Lord Mountjoy
And at the battle of New Ross we made eight thousand fly.

I am a bold shoemaker and Irewin is my name
I could beat as many Orangemen as listed in a train;
I could beat as many Orangemen as could stand in a row
I would make them fly before me like an arrow from a bow.

Of Organizations

Volunteer companies were established in Belfast in February 1778. By December, they numbered 40,000. Lord Charlemont commanded the Northern Volunteers and the Duke of Leinster headed those in and around Dublin. Napper Tandy was a member of the Dublin Corps of Volunteers. In November 1779 a large body paraded in Dublin calling for free trade and in July of the following year Lord Charlemont and Henry Grattan reviewed them before they enacted a mock battle.

THE DUNGANNON CONVENTION
Thomas Davis

At Dungannon, County Tyrone, on 15 February 1782, 242 delegates from 148 Volunteer corps resolved that the 'claims of any other than the King, Lords and Commons of Ireland to make laws to bind this kingdom is unconstitutional'. A resolution drafted by Henry Grattan began, 'As men and as Irishmen, as Christians and as Protestants, we rejoice in the relaxation of the Penal Laws against our Roman Catholic fellow-subjects.'

Thomas Davis (1814-45) was a founder of The Nation *in 1842. Regarded as Ireland's national poet in his time, he led the Young Ireland movement that his work inspired. His most famous ballads are 'A Nation Once Again' and 'The West's Asleep'.*

The Church of Dungannon is full to the door,
And sabre and spur clash at times on the floor,
While helmet and shako are ranged all along,
Yet no book of devotion is seen in the throng.
In the front of the altar no minister stands,
But the crimson-clad chief of the warrior bands;
And though solemn the looks and the voices around,
You'd listen in vain for a litany's sound.
Say! what do they hear in the temple of prayer?
Oh! why in the fold has the lion his lair?

Sad, wounded and wan was the face of our isle
By English oppression and falsehood and guile,
Yet when to invade it a foreign fleet steered

To guard it for England the North volunteered.
From the citizen-soldiers the foe fled aghast –
Still they stood to their guns when the danger had past,
For the voice of America came o'er the wave
Crying – Woe to the tyrant, and hope to the slave!
Indignation and shame through their regiments speed,
They have arms in their hands, and what more do they need?

O'er the green hills of Ulster their banners are spread,
The cities of Leinster resound to their tread,
The valleys of Munster with ardour are stirred,
And the plains of wild Connaught their bugles have heard.
A Protestant front rank and Catholic rere –
For – forbidden the arms of freemen to bear –
Yet foemen and friend are full sure, if need be,
The slave for his country will stand by the free.
By green flags supported, the Orange flags wave,
And the soldier half turns to unfetter the slave!

More honoured that Church of Dungannon is now
Than when at its altar Communicants bow;
More welcome to Heaven than anthem or prayer
Are the rights and the thoughts of the warriors there.
In the name of all Ireland the delegates swore:
'We've suffered too long and we'll suffer no more –
Unconquered by force, we were vanquished by fraud,
And now, in God's temple, we vow unto God,
That never again shall the Englishman bind
His chains on our limbs, or his laws on our mind.'

The Church of Dungannon is empty once more –
No plumes on the altar, no clash on the floor,
But the councils of England are fluttered to see,
In the cause of their country, the Irish agree;
So they give as a boon what they dare not withhold,
And Ireland, a nation, leaps up as of old.
With a name, and a trade, and a flag of her own,
And an army to fight for the people and throng.
But woe worth the day if, to falsehood or fears,
She surrender the guns of her brave Volunteers.

In March 1782 at the Rotunda, Dublin, 150,000 Volunteers convened to claim Parliamentary reform, while Napper Tandy led artillery and bedecked horse past Parliament House. The guns bore scrolls that read 'O Lord, open Thou our lips, and our mouths shall show forth Thy praise'. By 1784 Catholics were allowed join and Belfast Protestants actually collected for Catholic church-building.

Other forces arose, including the agrarian Protestant Peep-o'-Day Boys (1784) and 'Rightboys' in Munster and Leinster (1785). Initially in Armagh, later all over Ulster, peasant Ulster Catholics formed a defence organization (September 1785). It was the equivalent to the Peep-o'-Day Boys. Later, midland Catholic peasants took on the name Defenders, as they perpetrated actions against clergy and tithe proctors.

In March 1787 the Tumultuous Risings Act (The Whiteboy Act) introduced provisions of the British Riot Act to Ireland. It was directed against people who administered or accepted illegal oaths or who hampered in any way the collection of tithes. The Volunteer movement waned and its support had eevaporated by the end of 1790.

On 1 April 1791, in Belfast, Samuel McTier and others decided to form an association that would unite all Irishmen 'to pledge themselves to our country'. In October of the same year the Society of United Irishmenwas formally founded. Initially, its members were mainly Ulster Presbyterians and liberal Protestants seeking Parliamentary reform and the removal of religious grievance.

EARLY FRUSTRATIONS

The difficulties experienced in setting up any organization are evident in memoranda and entries in Wolfe Tone's diary.

1791

July 14th. I sent down to Belfast, resolutions suited to this day, and reduced to three heads. 1st, That English influence in Ireland was the great grievance of the country. 2nd, That the most effectual way to oppose it was by a reform in Parliament. 3rd, That no reform could be just or efficacious which did not include the Catholics, which last opinion, however, in concession to prejudices, was rather insinuated than asserted.

I am, this day, July 17, 1791 [*sic*], informed that the last question was lost. If so, my present impression is to become a red-hot Catholic; seeing that in the party, apparently, and perhaps really, most anxious for reform, it is rather a monopoly than an extension of liberty, which is their object, contrary to all justice and expediency.

October 11th. Arrived at Belfast late, and was introduced to Digges, but no material conversation. Bonfires, illuminations, firing twenty-one guns, Volunteers, &c.

October 12th. Introduced to McTier and Sinclair. A meeting between, McTier, Macabe, and me. Mode of doing business by a Secret Committee, who are not known or suspected of co-operating, but who, in fact, direct the movements of Belfast. Much conversation about the Catholics, and their committee, &c., of which they know wonderfully little at *Blefescu* [Belfast]. Settled to dine with the Secret Committee at Drew's, on Saturday, when the resolutions, &c., of the United Irish will be submitted. Sent them off, and sat down to new model the former copy. Very curious to see how the thermometer of Blefescu has risen, as to politics. Passages in the first copy, which were three months ago esteemed too hazardous to propose, are now found too tame. Those taken out, and replaced by other and better ones. Sinclair came in; read and approved the resolutions, as new modelled. Russell gave him a mighty pretty history of the Roman Catholic Committee, and his own negotiations. Christened Russell *P.P. Clerk of this Parish*. Sinclair asked us to dine and meet Digges, which we acceded to with great affability. Went to Sinclair, and dined. A great deal of general politics and wine. Paine's book, the Koran of Blefescu. History of the Down and Antrim elections. The Reeve of the shire a semi-Whig. P.P. very drunk. Home; bed.

October 13th. Much good jesting in bed, at the expense of P.P. Laughed myself into good humour. Rose. Breakfast. Dr McDonnell. Much conversation regarding Digges. Went to meet Neilson; read over the resolutions with him, which he approved.

DECLARATION AND RESOLUTIONS OF THE
SOCIETY OF UNITED IRISHMEN OF BELFAST

In the present era of reform, when unjust governments are falling in every quarter of Europe; when religious persecution is compelled to abjure her tyranny over conscience; when the rights of man are ascertained in theory, and that theory substantiated by practice; when antiquity can no longer defend absurd and oppressive forms, against the common sense and common interests of mankind; when all government is acknowledged to originate from the people and to be so far only obligatory as it protects their rights and promotes their welfare: We think it our duty, as Irishmen, to come forward, and state what we feel to be our heavy grievance, and what we know to be its effectual remedy. WE HAVE NO NATIONAL GOVERNMENT; we are ruled by Englishmen, and the servants of Englishmen, whose object is the interest of another country, whose instrument is corruption, and whose strength is the weakness of Ireland; and these men have the whole of the power and patronage of the country, as means to seduce and to subdue the honesty and the spirit of her representatives in the legislature. Such an extrinsic power, acting with uniform force in a direction too frequently opposite to the true line of our obvious interest, can be resisted with effect solely by *unanimity, decision, and spirit in the people*; qualities which may be exerted most legally, constitutionally, and efficaciously, by that great measure essential to the prosperity and freedom of Ireland, AN EQUAL REPRESENTATION OF ALL THE PEOPLE IN PARLIAMENT. We do not here mention as grievances, the rejection of a place-bill, of a pension-bill, of a responsibility-bill, the sale of Peerages in one House, the corruption publicly avowed in the other, nor the notorious infamy of borough traffic between both; not that we are insensible of their enormity, but that we consider them as but symptoms of that mortal disease which corrodes the vitals of our Constitution, and leaves to the people, in their own Government, but the shadow of a name.

Impressed with these sentiments, we have agreed to form an association, to be called 'THE SOCIETY OF UNITED IRISHMEN:' And we do pledge ourselves to our country, and mutually to each other, that we will steadily support, and endeavor, by all due means, to carry into effect, the following resolutions:

> *First, Resolved*, That the weight of English influence in the Government of this country is so great, as to require a cordial union of ALL THE PEOPLE OF IRELAND, to maintain that balance which is essential to the preservation of our liberties, and the extension of our commerce.
>
> *Second,* That the sole constitutional mode by which this influence can be opposed, is by a complete and radical reform of the representation of the people in Parliament.
>
> *Third,* That no reform is practicable, efficacious, or just, which shall not include Irishmen of every *religious* persuasion.

Satisfied, as we are, that the intestine divisions among Irishmen have too often given encouragement and impunity to profligate, audacious, and corrupt Administrations, in measures which, but for these divisions, they durst not have attempted; we submit our resolutions to the nation, as the basis of our political faith.

We have now gone to what we conceive to be the remedy. With a Parliament thus reformed, every thing is easy; without it, nothing can be done: and we do call on and most earnestly exhort our countrymen in general to follow our example, and to form similar societies in every quarter of the kingdom, for the promotion of constitutional knowledge, the abolition of bigotry in religion and politics, and the equal distribution of the rights of man through all sects and denominations of Irishmen. The people, when thus collected, will feel their own weight, and secure that power which theory has already admitted as their portion, and to which, if they be not aroused by their present provocations to vindicate it, they deserve to forfeit their pretensions FOR EVER.

MINUTE

A 1792 entry in the Proceedings of the Society of United Irishmen of Dublin*:*

It was not till very lately that the part of the nation which is truly colonial, reflected that though their ancestors had been victorious, they themselves were now included in the general subjection; subduing only to be subdued, and trampled upon by Britain as a servile dependency. When therefore the Protestants began to suffer what the Catholics had suffered; when from serving as the instruments they were made themselves the objects of foreign domination, then they became conscious they had a country – Ireland. They resisted British dominion, renounced colonial subserviency and … asserted the exclusive jurisdiction of this Island.

THE LIBERTY TREE
Anon.

Taking example from the French Revolution, a custom among United Irishmen of planting a 'Liberty Tree' began.

It was the year of '93,
The French did plant an olive tree
The symbol of great liberty
And the people danced around it.
'Oh was not I telling you,'
The French declared courageously,
'That Equality, Freedom and Fraternity
Would be the cry of every nation.'

In '94 a new campaign,
The tools of darkness did maintain
Gall's brave sons did form a league
And their foes they were dumb-founded.
They gave to Flanders liberty
And all its people they set free
The Dutch and Austrians home did flee
And the Dukes they were confounded.

Behold may all of Human-kind,
Emancipated with the French combine
May laurels green all on them shine
And their sons and daughters long wear them.
May every tyrant shake with dread
And tremble for their guilty head
May the Fleur-de-Lis in dust be laid
And they no longer wear them.

For Church and State in close embrace
Is the burden of the Human Race
And people tell you to your face
That long you will repent it.
For Kings in power and preaching drones
Are the cause of all your heavy groans
Down from your pulpits, down from your thrones
You will tumble unlamented.

'Oh was not I telling you,'
The French declared courageously,
'That Equality, Freedom and Fraternity
Would be the cry of every nation.'

THE TREE OF LIBERTY

Anon

*Out of chronological order , it is worth giving the Orange Order's riposte here. It refers
to the Sheares Brothers, of whose execution we will learn later.*
    J.B. Esq. of Lodge No. 471 included the poem in A Collection of Loyal Songs.

Sons of Hibernia, attend to my song,
Of a tree call'd th'Orange, it's beauteous and strong;
'Twas planted by William, immortal is he!
May all Orange brothers live loyal and free.
    Derry down, down, traitors bow down.

Around this fair trunk we like ivy will cling,
And fight for our honour, our country, and king;
In the shade of this Orange none e'er shall recline
Who with murd'rous Frenchmen have dar'd to combine.
    Derry down, down, Frenchmen bow down.

Hordes of barbarians, Lord Ned in the van,
This tree to destroy laid an infamous plan;
Their schemes prov'd abortive, tho' written in blood,
Nor their pikes, nor their scythes could pierce Orange wood.
    Derry down, down, rebels bow down.

While our brave Irish tars protect us by sea,
From false perjured traitors this island we'll free;
Priest [Murphy's] war-vestment they'll find of no use,
Wherever we meet them they're sure to get goose.
    Derry down, down, priestcraft bow down.

Hundreds they've burn'd of each sex, young and old,
From Heaven the order – by priests they were told;
No longer we'll trust them, no more to betray,
But chase from our bosoms those vipers away.
    Derry down, down, serpents bow down.

Rouse then, my brothers, and heed not their swearing,
Absolv'd they have been for deeds past all bearing;
Mercy's misplac'd, when to murderers granted,
For our lands and our lives those wretches long panted.
 Derry down, down, reptiles bow down.

Then charge high your glasses, and drink our Great Cause,
Our blest Constitution, our King, and our Laws;
May all lurking traitors, wherever they be
Make the exit of Sheares, and Erin be free.
 Derry down, down, traitors bow down.

ORANGE ORDER

After a fight between Protestant Peep-o'-Day Boys and Catholic Defenders at The Diamond, Loughgall, County Armagh, in September 1795, an Orange Society was formed. Its members perpetrated atrocities against Catholics, driving many of them out of Ulster. James Sloan of Loughgall became the first Grand Master of the Orange Order that emerged later, while the first Loyal Orange Lodge was founded in Dyan, County Tyrone. The Orange Order's strength quickly leaped to an estimated 100,000. Its oath ran as follows:

I, A.B., do solemnly and sincerely, in the presence of God, profess, testify, and declare that I do believe that in the Sacrament of the Lord's Supper there is not any transubstantiation of the elements of bread and wine into the body and blood of Christ, at or after the consecration thereof by any person whatsoever; and that the invocation or adoration of the Virgin Mary, or any other saint, and the sacrifice of the Mass, as they are now used in the Church of Rome, are superstitious and idolatrous. And I do solemnly in the presence of God profess, testify, and declare that I make this declaration and every part thereof in the plain and ordinary sense of the words read unto me as they are commonly understood by the English Protestants without any evasion, equivocation, or mental reservation whatsoever, and without any dispensation already granted me for this purpose by the Pope or any other authority or person whatsoever, or without any hope of any such dispensation from any person or authority whatsoever, or without thinking that I am or can be acquitted before God and man, or absolved of this declaration, or any part thereof, although the Pope or any other person or persons, or power whatsoever, should dispense with or annul the same, or declare that it was null and void from the beginning.

THE LOYAL TOAST

Sir Jonah Barrington (1760-1834) was a Judge to the Admiralty in 1798. His
books, Personal Sketches of His Own Times *and* The Rise and Fall of the
Irish Nation, *illuminate the period. He appeared to oppose the Act of Union, and so*
enjoyed the confidence of prominent United Irishmen. Some, however, suspected him
of informing and subsequent self-advancement gives credence to the theory.

Barrington's wife, the inquisitive daughter of a silk merchant, dressed in her
father's finest materials and sat in her St Stephen's Green window where she could see
Lady Clonmell in her Harcourt Street home. Lord Clonmell complained and Sir Jonah
had the window blocked up. Commentators have suggested that his deference to Clon-
mell supported the theory of his being less than patriotic.

The glorious, pious and immortal memory of the great and good King William – not
forgetting Oliver Cromwell, who assisted in redeeming us from Popery, slavery, arbitrary power, brass money and wooden shoes.

May we never want a Williamite to kick the **** of a Jacobite! and a **** for the
Bishop of Cork! And he that won't drink this, whether he be priest, bishop, deacon,
bellows-blower, grave-digger, or any other of the fraternity of the clergy; may a north
wind blow him to the south; a west wind blow him to the east! May he have a dark
night – a lee shore – a rank storm – and a leaky vessel, to carry him over the river Styx!
May the dog Cerebus make a meal of his rump, and Pluto a snuff-box of his skull; and
may the devil jump down his throat with a red-hot harrow, with every pin to tear a gut,
and blow him with a clean carcass to hell! Amen!

Sir Jonah considered the toast a mere 'excuse for getting loyally drunk as often as pos-
sible'. He added a footnote:

Could his majesty, King William, learn in the other world that he has been the cause of
more broken heads and drunken men, since his departure, than all his predecessors, he
must be the proudest ghost and most conceited skeleton that ever entered the gardens
of Elysium.

Another popular version of the toast goes:

Here's to good King William III, of pious, glorious and immortal memory, who saved
us from slaves and slavery, knaves and knavery, rogues and roguery – brass money and
wooden shoes. And all who deny this toast: may they be slammed, crammed and
jammed into the great muzzle of the gun of Athlone, and blown on the hob of hell,
where he'll be kept roasting for all eternity, the devil basting him with melted bishops
and his imps pelting him with priests. And may the gun fired into the Pope's belly, and
the Pope into the devil's belly and the devil into hell and the door locked tight and the
key safe forever in an Orangeman's pocket.

LETTER FROM A SOLDIER

At the 'Battle of the Diamond' in 1795 a group of Protestants known as The Wreckers came from Portadown and Rich Hill to Loughgall. There were skirmishes and house-burnings for two days. The Wreckers were leaving on Monday 21 September when a party of Defenders from Cavan, Tyrone and Monaghan arrived in the village and broke the windows of a Protestant home. An eye-witness described the scene that followed.

Down swept the Protestant Boys from the hill, shooting as they came, and with their swords and bayonets they spread the wildest confusion, and made terrible slaughter among the papists on whose side men, women and children were now huddled up. All that followed was a havoc – a cold-blooded and brutal massacre ... Everyone fled, and you could see men dragging their wives and brothers, pulling their wounded sisters after them, leaving their fathers dead on the ground.

Years later, on 19 October 1839, The Globe *newspaper published a letter with a Newmarket address.*

Sir,

As a cornet in the 24th Light Dragoons, then commanded by the late Lord Wm. Bentinck, I accompanied the regiment to Ireland in 1795. We disembarked at Dublin, and proceeded to Clonmel, from whence, in the autumn of that year, a squadron was suddenly ordered in consequence of the disturbed state of the country, to proceed to Armagh. To this squadron I was attached. Very shortly after our arrival the Caithness Highlanders, commanded by Sir Thomas, then Major, Molyneux, relieved a regiment of Irish militia stationed at Armagh. The County of Armagh was then in a very disturbed state, arising from the feuds between the Protestant and Catholic population, unhappily too much encouraged by the dominant party; but of these religious dissensions the Orange Societies, fostered and encouraged by the father of the present Colonel Verner, had their origin. The avowed object of the Protestant party was to drive the Catholics out of the country.

In the course of the following year the whole regiment took up its quarters at Armagh and the neighbourhood. It so happened that I commanded a detachment of the regiment at Loughall, in the very centre of that part of the County of Armagh where the disturbance most prevailed, and not very far distant from the spot where the Battle of the Diamond took place. There I remained several months, and during that period I had witnessed the excesses committed by the Orange party, who now began to form themselves into lodges, and the dreadful persecutions to which the Catholic inhabitants were subjected. Night after night I have seen the sackings and burnings of the dwellings of these poor people. And notwithstanding the active exertions of the Sovereign of Armagh, under whose orders the military frequently scoured the country, our movements were so closely watched that these depredations were continued almost with impunity. When we arrived at a burning dwelling the perpetrators had fled across the country, and their course could only be traced by the fires they left in their progress.

Many of the Orangemen, however, notwithstanding the secrecy with which they conducted their proceedings, were discovered on private information, and brought to trial. But most of them, through the influence of their party, escaped, either altogether or with slight punishment.

In one case, a most atrocious one, a man had been sentenced to death; this man's sentence was respited, and I well remember the whole country round being illuminated with bonfires in manifestation of the joy of the Orangemen on that occasion. The result was an increased measure of persecution; many poor families were driven from their homes, their dwellings burnt, and themselves obliged to take shelter among their Catholic brethren in Connaught. These outrages were not unfrequently accompanied with bloodshed.

I may mention one of these dreadful scenes, of which I was myself an eye-witness, during our nightly patrol. We had already reached a heap of ruins, when a shot was heard, apparently about a quarter of a mile from the fire. On proceeding to the spot we discovered a dying man, whom the miscreants had shot in his house in their retreat from the fire. They had fired through the window in to the room where the man was sitting with his family. The poor fellow died a few minutes after our arrival.

It is impossible for me to describe, at this distance of time, the horrors and atrocities I witnessed during that period, which Major Molyneux describes as being without disturbance. Indeed, such was the state of the County of Armagh, that our regiment was quartered in the different mansions of the gentry of the county.

Mr O'Sullivan states that the Battle of the Diamond broke the neck of the Irish rebellion. It so happened that I was quartered at Market-hill, the house of Lord Gosford, when the rebellion of 1798 broke out, and I can positively assert, and I appeal to the history of those times, that the Catholics had no share in the disturbances of that period, at least in the North of Ireland.

The rebellion, it is well known, was brought out by the United Irishmen, who were none of them Catholics, and not one of the leaders who were convicted and executed in the Counties of Down and Antrim were of that creed. On the contrary, when the troops assembled at Castledawson, under General Knox, a most active magistrate, a resident in that town, Mr Shiel, who with his sons were in a corps of yeomanry, and took a most decided part in the suppression of the rebellion, were Roman Catholics.

'AN OLD OFFICER OF CAVALRY'

THE ORANGE YEOMANRY OF '98

Anon.

The History Of Orangeism *by M.P. (Dublin & Glasgow 1882) tells of the origin and rise of the Orange Order. In one section, it comments on poems and songs sung at Orange meetings 'after the mysteries of the lodge have been disclosed'. Having offered the following sample — written after the rebellion — M.P. adds, 'Little wonder that Orange outrages follow fast upon Orange Lodge meetings, where such blasphemous productions, rendered more exciting by deep potations, are permitted to arouse the religious frenzy of ignorant fanatics.' Ulster yeomanry units were often recruited from Orange Lodges.*

I am an humble Orangeman —
My father he was one;
The mantle which the sire once wore
Has fallen to the son:
He ranked with those who quelled their foes —
The foes of Church and State —
The gallant Orange yeomanry
Who fought in Ninety-eight!

The light which led their spirits on
O'er battle-field did shine,
Each breast was Freedom's temple pure,
Each heart was Freedom's shrine;
As sinks the day in glorious ray,
Some sunk — and bright their fate,
The gallant Orange yeomanry
Who fought in Ninety-eight!

Behold the Orange peasant, or
The Orange artizan;
Go view his home, observe his ways;
You'll find it is his plan,
Through woe or weal, with godly zeal,
True men to imitate —
The gallant Orange yeomanry
Who fought in Ninety-eight!

To guard the faith which Luther preached
The rights which William won,
The Orangeman relies upon
His Bible and his gun;
He prays for peace, yet war will face,
Should rebels congregate;
Like the brave Orange yeomanry
Who fought in Ninety-eight!

'Who fears to speak of '98?'
This was the silly note
Of one who was afraid to put
His name to what he wrote;
He was afraid – they're all afraid –
They know we'd gag their prate,
As did the Orange yeomanry
Who fought in Ninety-eight!

In peace, like watchful silent stars,
Can Orangemen remain;
In war, their energies are like
The surges of the main;
And each true-hearted Orangeman
Would smile, though death await,
As did the Orange yeomanry
Who fought in Ninety-eight!

🐜 🐜 🐜

Of Personalities

Lord Edward Fitzgerald (1763-98) was the fifth son of the Duke of Leinster and great-great grandson of Charles II. He was one of twenty-one children born to an emotional mother, who was daughter of the Duke of Richmond. Edward joined the United Irishmen and went to France with Arthur O'Connor to try to organize French assistance for a revolution. His wife's ancestry proved a stumbling-block, but he returned and headed a military committee of the United Irishmen. He denounced martial law and

prepared for rebellion with or without French assistance. He escaped a celebrated raid on Oliver Bond's house and went on the run. An informer
told of his Thomas Street, Dublin, hide-out and he was seized there on 19
May 1798. He killed a member of the raiding party but was himself
wounded seriously. He died on 4 June, in Newgate Prison.

HAPPY IN KILDARE

*On the east side of the market square in Kildare town stands Kildare Castle, beside
which Lord Edward Fitzgerald and his wife Pamela lived. Their house was called
Leinster Lodge. Fitzgerald once wrote to his mother about the place. The note suggests
that he was a keen gardener:*

My little place is much improved by the few things I have done and by my planting. By
the bye, I doubt if I told you of my flower garden; I got a great deal from Frescati. I
have been in Kildare since Pam's lying-in and it looks delightful, though all the leaves
were off the trees, but so comfortable and snug. I think I shall pass a delightful winter
there. I have got two fine clamps of turf which look so comfortable and pretty. I have
paled my little flower garden before my hall door with a lath paling like the cottage and
stuck it full of roses, sweet briar, honeysuckle and Spanish broom. I have got all my
beds ready for my flowers so you may guess how I long to be down to plant them.

The little fellow will be a great addition to the party. I think when I am down there
with Pam and child, of a blustering evening, with a good turf fire and a pleasant book,
coming in after seeing my poultry up, my garden settled, flower-beds and plants covered for fear of frost, the place looking comfortable and taken care of, I shall be as
happy as possible; and since I am, I shall regret nothing but not being near my dearest
mother, and her not being one of our party. It is indeed a drawback and a great one,
our not being more together. Dear Malvern, how pleasant we were then: you can't
think how this time of year puts me in mind of it.

Your affectionate son,

E.F.

APPREHENDED IN ULSTER

*Charles Hamilton Teeling (1778-1850) was a Lisburn journalist. He was a member
of the United Irishmen and the Defenders, and brother of Bartholomew, who helped to
negotiate the French invasion and was aide-de-camp to Humbert at Killala. He wrote
a personal narrative of the 1798 rebellion. In an early section he describes being
arrested in Ulster, referring to Camden, Castlereagh and Cornwallis. Lord Camden*

was Viceroy of Ireland from 1795 to 1798. He led a corrupt cabinet including his nephew Robert Stewart Castlereagh, the second Viscount Castlereagh, and was related through marriage to Lord Edward Fitzgerald. Appointed Acting Chief Secretary of Ireland in March 1798, his post became permanent the following November.

Lord Cornwallis replaced Camden as Viceroy in mid-June1798. He was sent to Ireland expressly to win the war against the rebels and impose a settlement that ensured unity with England.

It was in the autumn of the year 1796 that government commenced active operations against the United Irish Societies by the arrest of those men who were either considered the decided partisans of the cause, or suspected of being favourable to the system of union. The principal performer in this scene was, of all men, the last who could have been supposed ambitious of exhibiting in such a character. A man whose influence and example had so powerful an effect in rallying the youth of his native province, that all seemed proud to emulate the virtues which had elevated him to a distinguished situation, through the confidence and partiality of his countrymen. Strange, indeed, that Lord Castlereagh should have been the selected tool of the Camden administration, to drag the companions of his youth, and the early associates of his political fame from the peaceful bosom of their families to the horrors of an Irish Bastile [*sic*]. Ireland witnessed his delinquency with sorrow, but she had not anticipated the extent of the evils which awaited her, in the dismemberment of her power and the extinction of her independence by a legislative union with Britain.

I was myself the first victim to the political delinquency of Lord Castlereagh. On the 16th of September, 1796, while yet in my eighteenth year, I was arrested by him on a charge of high treason. The manner of my arrest was as novel as mysterious, and the hand which executed it the last from which I could have suspected an act of unkindness. Lord Castlereagh was the personal friend of my father, who admired him as the early advocate of civil and religious liberty. He was a member of the illustrious band of Irish Volunteers; and his name to this hour stands recorded amongst the most conspicuous characters who formed the first great political association in Ulster for that redress of grievances which the united exertions of the people only could obtain.

When, in the year 1790, the representation for Down was contested, and the independence of that great and populous county threatened through the powerful influence of the Downshire family and a combination of local interests hostile to the rights of the people, Lord Castlereagh, then the Honourable Robert Stewart, was selected by his countrymen for his talents and his patriotism; and after the most obstinate political contest ever witnessed in Ireland, he was triumphantly returned to Parliament, supported not only by the suffrages but by the pecuniary contributions of the friends of civil and religious liberty. On this memorable occasion Lord Castlereagh publicly subscribed to a test, which, in expressing the sense of his constituents, marked out the line of his parliamentary duty, pledging himself, in language the most unequivocal, to the unceasing pursuit of parliamentary reform. The penal laws at this period operated against my father's personal exercise of the elective franchise, but neither his fortune nor his best exertions were unemployed in the service of his friend. What then must have been my astonishment when I found myself a prisoner in the hands of the man whom I had been early taught to regard as a model of patriotism!

The evening preceding my arrest had been passed in one of those gay and cheerful assemblies for which at that period the north of Ireland was distinguished, and in which Lord Castlereagh and other members of his family not unfrequently mingled. The recollection of those early scenes is still fresh in my remembrance, and the delightful entertainment they afforded was a true criterion of the polished manners and the social feeling of the inhabitants of my native town. Accompanying my father on the following morning on a short excursion on horseback, we were met by Lord Castlereagh, who accosted us with his usual courtesy and politeness. We had proceeded up the street together, when having reached the house of his noble relative, the Marquis of Hertford, we were about to take leave of his lordship – 'I regret', said he, addressing my father, 'that your son cannot accompany you'; conducting me at the same moment through the outer gate, which, to my inexpressible astonishment, was instantly closed, and I found myself surrounded by a military guard. I expostulated, and in no very measured language, against what I considered a foul and treacherous proceeding, and with warmth I demanded that the gate should be reopened, and my father admitted. This, after some deliberation, was assented to. My father entered; he looked first on me, then sternly on Castlereagh, and with a firm and determined composure inquired the cause of my arrest. 'High treason!' replied his lordship. Our interview was short; my father was not permitted to remain. It may well be conceived at this moment what were his emotions: he bade me adieu with a proud but a tender feeling; and whilst my hand, locked in his, felt the fond pressure of paternal love, his eye darted a look of defiance, and soul swelled indignant with conscious superiority over the apostate patriot and insidious friend.

My father pursued his intended route, too sorrowful to return to his family, and too proud to betray the feelings which agitated his heart. It may appear somewhat strange that a man who bore the liveliest attachment to his domestic circle, and who was to me not only the affectionate parent but also the companion and friend, should in a moment like the present, the most painful perhaps he had yet encountered, proceed on his business with so much apparent composure. But he was a man of no ordinary cast: to the liveliest sensibility were associated the firmest characteristics of mind; his intellectual powers were strong, and the gifts of nature had been improved by an education of the most liberal stamp. Affluent in circumstances, and connected by the most respectable links to society, he was possessed of much popularity, and retained the confidence and esteem of his countrymen through a long and an honourable life. But his pride was innate, and subsequent persecution and misfortune could never bend it.

My horse was led home by a faithful domestic, but to that home I never returned: nor was a numerous, and till then a happy family ever again congregated within its walls.

THE WAKE OF WILLIAM ORR

William Drennan

William Orr (1766-97) was a wealthy Presbyterian farmer and yeoman from Farran-
shane, County Antrim, who spoke out against assassinations. He was a member of the
United Irishmen and became the first person to be tried and convicted under the
Insurrection Act of 1797. The charge was the administration of an illegal oath to
United Irishmen. There were allegations concerning jury-members in Orr's trial being
given drink, and about the foreman stating that a verdict could not be reached.
Although thought to be innocent, he was hanged in Carrickfergus on 14 October
1797. Because his execution aroused indignation, the call 'Remember Orr' was a
common one in rousing rebels to action during 1798.

William Drennan (1754-1820) was born in Belfast, educated in Scotland and
practised medicine in Belfast, Newry and Dublin. He was a member of the United
Irishmen and wrote their original prospectus. He was acquitted on a charge of sedition
in June 1794 and then discontinued active membership.

There our murdered brother lies;
Wake him not with woman's cries;
Mourn the way that manhood ought –
Sit in silent trance of thought.

Write his merits on your mind;
Morals pure and manners kind;
In his head, as on a hill,
Virtue placed her citadel.

Why cut off in palmy youth?
Truth he spoke, and acted truth.
'Countrymen, UNITE,' he cried,
And died for what our Saviour died.

God of peace and God of love!
Let it not Thy vengeance move –
Let it not Thy lightnings draw –
A nation guillotined by law.

Hapless Nation, rent and torn,
Thou wert early taught to mourn;

Warfare for six hundred years!
Epoch marked with blood and tears!

Hunted thro' thy native grounds,
Or flung reward to human hounds,
Each one pulled and tore his share,
Heedless of thy deep despair.

Hapless nation! hapless Land!
Heap of uncementing sand!
Crumbled by a foreign weight:
And, by worse, domestic hate.

God of mercy! God of peace!
Make this mad confusion cease;
O'er the mental chaos move,
Through it SPEAK the light of love.

Monstrous and unhappy sight!
Brothers' blood will not unite;
Holy oil and holy water
Mix, and fill the world with slaughter.

Who is she with aspect wild?
The widowed mother with her child –
Child new stirring in the womb
Husband waiting for the tomb!

Angel of this sacred place,
Calm her soul and whisper peace –
Cord, or axe, or guillotine,
Make the sentence – not the sin.

Here we watch our brother's sleep:
Watch with us, but do not weep:
Watch with us thro' dead of night
But expect the morning light.

THE DYING DECLARATION OF WILLIAM ORR

From *The Press* of 17 October 1797

The following is the DYING DECLARATION of Mr Orr as it came to us:

My Friends and Countrymen,

In the thirty-first year of my life, I have been sentenced to die upon the gallows and this sentence has been in pursuance of a verdict of twelve men, who should have been indifferently and impartially chosen; but how far they have been so, I leave the the country from which they have been chosen, to determine; and how far they have discharged their duty, I leave to their God and to themselves. – They have, in pronouncing their verdict, thought proper to recommend me as an object of humane mercy; in return, I pray to God, if they have erred, to have mercy upon them. The Judge, who condemned me, humanely shed tears in uttering my sentence; but whether he did wisely, in so highly commending the wretched informer who swore away my life, I leave to his own cool reflection, solemnly assuring him and all the world, with my dying breath, that the informer was forsworn. The law under which I suffer, is surely a severe one; may the makers and promoters of it, be justified in the integrity of their motives and the purity of their own lives – by that law, I am stamped a felon, but my heart disdains the imputation. My comfortable lot and industrous course of life, best refute the charge of being an adventurer for plunder: but if to have loved my country, to have known its wrongs, to have felt the injuries of the persecuted Catholics, and to have united with them and all other religious persuasions, in the most orderly and least sanguinary means of procuring redress: – If those be felonies, I am a felon, but not otherwise. Had my counsel (for whose honourable exertions I am indebted) prevailed in their motion to have me tried for High-treason, rather than under the *Insurrection Law*, I should have been intitled then to a full defence, and my actions and intentions should have been better vindicated; but that was refused, and I must now submit to what has passed.

Lastly, a false and ungenerous publication having appeared in a newspaper stating, certain alledged confessions of guilt on my part, and thus striking at my reputation, which is dearer to me than life, I take this solemn method of contradicting that calumny: I was applied to by the High-Sheriff, and the Rev William Bristow, Sovereign of Belfast, to make a confession of guilt, who used entreaties to that effect; this I peremptorily refused; did I think myself guilty, I should be free to confess it, but, on the contrary, I glory in my innocence.

I trust, that all my virtuous countrymen will bear me in their kind remembrance, and continue true and faithful to each other, as I have been to all of them. With this last wish of my heart, not doubting of the success of the cause for which I suffer, and hoping for God's merciful forgiveness of such offences as my frail nature may have at any time betrayed me into, I die in peace and charity with all mankind.

WILLIAM ORR

Carrickfergus Gaol, October 5, 1797

O'CONNOR FALY'S RECOLLECTIONS

'The Pike Head' is the title of the opening chapter of Ninety-Eight: Being the Recollections of Cormac Cahir O'Connor Faly *(late Colonel in the French Service) of that awful period. Faly's grandson, Patrick C. Faly, collected and edited the material and A.D. McCormick illustrated it. Published in 1897 by Downey & Co., 12 York Street, Covent Garden, London, the opening section of the book describes the atmosphere of the period immediately preceding the rebellion. In the Dublin into which Faly arrived in 1797,*

The beggars (who were numerous) were curiously talkative and familiar, sometimes even eloquent and witty, as were also their indistinctly separable congeners the vendors of newspapers, ballads, accounts of executions, and oranges. While more profusely polite (as well as more wildly abusive should occasion serve) than those of Edinburgh, the lower classes here did not seem to me to have that servile instinct towards rank and money which I had observed to prevail in Britain. If they got money out of you, they in the pleasantest way in the world left you under the impression that yours was the privilege to give, and theirs the right to accept. They had the airs of unfortunate gentlemen dispossessed of their estates, of wandering dethroned princes whose land had been taken from them, regal in squalor, dignified in dirt. I mentioned this to my father, who said, 'And so they are! And what am I?'

The town seemed to be just crawling with soldiers. I saw some of the great people driving up to the Parliament House in College Green, ministers and such-like, protected by dragoons – and they needed it. The people would have had their blood else.

Beside the dragoons and the guards and sentries, there were a great many evident soldiers in citizens' clothes, who, I was informed, were employed under Major Sirr.

The coach driver who bore Faly to his parents' home near Sligo told stories as they travelled. At Lutrellstown, near Lucan, he mentioned

the inhuman tyrant 'Satanides' as the commander in chief [Carhampton] was nicknamed by some who appreciated his talents and character. A dread reputation of a quasi-supernatural kind clung to this remarkable man, whose delight in wickedness and power to devise and execute it seemed characteristic of a spiteful fiend rather than a mere sinful human being, and strange and horrible tales of doings beyond the ordinary run of outrage and vice said to occur within the concealing wood of Lutrellstown ...

In a Mullingar inn, Cormac Faly met the fair Mary Doyle. They did not know that a scoundrel named Reynolds would keep the yeomen informed of their movements. Mary Doyle accompanied the party when they moved northwards. At a later stop, the Faly coachman introduced them to someone:

There came down the mountain to us a strange and terrible old man, with wild pale blue eyes and a long matted beard, dressed in rags, half naked, like King Lear in the storm. Indeed, I have heard it suggested by learned men that King Lear was originally an Irishman, and that his true name was Leary, and it occurred to me that this might be one of the family. Mary Doyle said 'That is Connel-an-Bard. He is strange in his head, and his mind is asleep since fifty years ago, when he went with his four sons to Scotland to fight in the rising of 1745. His sons were all killed, and he alone came back, and found his house burnt.' The old man held up his arms to heaven and sang in Irish to an air that was alternatively triumphant and plaintive:

> Welcome the war-ships across the grey water
> Bringing Righ Tiarlach and wild geese from France!
> The grey raven sharpens the strong beak for slaughter,
> In the gold of the morning the white sails advance.
> Caoine! for dauntless young heroes shall fall!
> Caoine! ye widows of Saxon and Gall!
> Lead and we'll follow for ever and ever,
> Hands that smite heavily, hearts that are true.
> Lead and we'll follow for ever and ever,
> Sláinte-geal Tíarlach! Righ Tíarlach abú!
> Ubabú! Connel abú!

When Faly reached his destination at Kildrinan on the west coast, he discovered that the local yeoman captain was a kinsman. When this fellow made advances to Mary Doyle, Faly intervened and struck him. Mary Doyle, in gratitude, advised him to go on the run. She brought him to a hide-out where he met a distinguished individual of the period:

We entered a large chamber with a low arched roof which had evidently been part of the crypt at one time. A lamp hung from one of the arches, and under it was a table at which three men were sitting and studying some papers. The table was oblong, of common planks painted brownish red and supported by trestles. On one side, facing us as we came in, sat a man, large boned and powerful-looking, with grizzled hair cut quite short into the nape of his neck, with an expression of stern determination mingled with a certain flavouring of innocent vanity, which was a curious combination. He would not see sixty years again, I thought. At one end, on his right, sat a man of thirty or more, of medium size, dark-complexioned, with intelligent eyes, a moustache, and a general appearance both military and foreign. At the opposite end sat a man of fair complexion and hair whose face I could not well see. An empty chair on the remaining side denoted that our friend Denis Maguire had been sitting there.

Denis repeated my story to the elderly man, whom he addressed as General. That gentleman looked at me fixedly, and then said, –

'He is a tall fellow, and educated, you say?'

'He is, and comes of a good old stock.' Here he gave some explanations of my family history which I will omit.

'Is he to be trusted, do you think?'

'Oh, devil doubt him! His father was with me in America in '76 and '77. Besides, he's got the right side of Miss Mary Doyle, and it takes an honest boy to do that, not to speak of defeating the armed forces of the Crown in a pitched – or pitch-forked battle in Mullarkey's shebeen.'

'Sir', said I to the man they addressed as General, 'I don't know you, but I trust you, and I am in danger of my life. If you don't believe that I am an honest friend of Ireland, there is nothing to prevent your shooting me where I stand. No one will be the wiser, and then maybe you'll feel safe.'

'Young gentleman', said the General, 'don't be so infernally tragic. We have important interests in our hands, and have to be perpetually on our guard. It is not only you or only me that this is a matter of life and death to. Are you willing to take the oath to the Irish Republic?'

'I am.'

'Then by G— I trust you, and you're heartily welcome to our rather *triste* headquarters. Maybe next time I come it will be General Carhampton's turn to hide in holes in the ground and mine to be making a tour of inspection of the forces. What did Colonel D'Arcy say your name was?'

'Cormac Cahir O'Connor Faly of Faly and Kildrinan.'

'*In posse*. We will put you, and your good father, in esse one of these days.'

He wrote down my name, and continued,

'Do you understand French?'

'After a fashion.'

'That's a good thing. Ever been drilled, by moonlight or otherwise?'

'Mr Faly has lived until lately *in partibus infidelium*,' interposed D'Arcy, 'for reasons which are no fault of his, and therefore had no opportunity of cultivating those manly exercises.'

'Well, well, there's the makings of a fine captain of a company in him. You'll live to wear a green coat with gold lace to it yet, Mr Faly.'

'That's a beautiful coat you wore of your own, General, the day you received the barony Executive Committees here,' said Mary.

'The uniform of a major in the service of the French Republic, One and Indivisible,' remarked the General with extreme complacency, 'which I have the honour to be entitled to wear, though imposing to the eye, and dear to the heart of a true lover of liberty, as I have humbly asserted myself to be –'

'You were mighty humble, General dear, I remember', said D'Arcy, 'when you commanded a brigade of artillery in Dublin in '83 and had 'Free Trade or —' inscribed on the breaches of the guns.'

'I trust,' continued the General, again mounted on his oratorical hobby, 'that however humble and unconsidered as an individual' (he looked, as people often do who speak in this way, as if he thought himself much the reverse), 'I may always continue to take a just pride in my country's service, and the uniform which it is my privilege to wear. Young lady, there is in my portmanteau here the uniform of a General of the Irish Republic, which surpasses that even of a French major, and will in days to come, I hope, be seen leading the brave men of Connaught to victory.'

I afterwards had occasion to learn that this strange man, for all his dandyism and childish attachment to laced uniforms, was a capable and determined leader and a man of indomitable spirit and patriotism. He continued, in a less exalted tone, –

'And what is your calling or business, Mr Faly?'

'I have been studying medicine.'

'*Tres bien*. We shall want it, including surgery. Now, listen! Will you, Cormac Cahir O'Connor Faly, *ci-devant* Prince of Leinster and Lord knows what else, swear to be faithful and bear true allegiance to the Irish Republic, now virtually established, and defend it and the principles of liberty and equality by force of arms when called upon by your legitimate superior officers at any time, and never inform or give evidence against any member of it, or of any patriotic society or organization?'

'Indeed I will, and be proud to do it.'

'Spoken like your father's son!' said D'Arcy.

'You take this oath of your own free will and inclination?'

'I do.' In any case it was too late to hesitate, and the proposal exactly jumped with my temper and inclinations.

'I'll take that oath and keep it, General. Make your mind easy about that.'

'That's a gallant fellow', said the General, holding out his hand, which I grasped.

'I'd better be going now', said Miss Doyle, 'or Mr Faly will be getting anxious about his son.'

'Faith, his anxiety won't be much lessened by what you have to tell him, Mary, *agradh*. Is Lord Carhampton come yet?' asked D'Arcy.

'Not when we left. He'll arrive this afternoon. God save you kindly, Cormac, and thank you for all you've done to-day.'

'Thank *you*, Mary dear, for saving my life, to be of more use, I hope, to the country and to you.' And we clasped hands, and I thought the expression of her eyes was kind, and a thought anxious.

'Good-bye to you, General, and gentlemen.'

'Good-bye. *Au revoir, citoyenne*,' said the General, adding, 'and I wish I was a younger man, like your recruit here, my dear.' And the gentlemen all rose and bowed, as she went out by the wattle and gorse door, which D'Arcy held open for her.

'Now, Mr Faly, as we have trusted you so far, we will do so completely. Our friend Colonel D'Arcy you know this' (indicating the fine intelligent-looking dark young man) 'is Colonel Hervey Montmorency Morres, formerly of the Austrian service, now in our own, and this is Mr Counsellor John Corrigan, of Dublin, who represents the Executive Directory established in that city in *Brumaire* last. Finally, I am James Napper Tandy, as this country will find out.'

Napper Tandy escaped to France. An ill-equipped peasantry, aroused by passionate words and promises from him and others, rebelled.

THE WEARING OF THE GREEN
Anon.

Dion Boucicault (1820-90) used this ballad in his Arrah-na-Pogue, *a melodrama of the Fenian rising of 1865. For that reason, some consider him to be its composer. He may well have composed it from the second version below. It appears here because of its reference to Tandy.*

I

Oh then Paddy dear, and did you hear the news that's goin' around?
The shamrock is forbid by law to grow on Irish ground!
Saint Patrick's Day no more we'll keep, his colour can't be seen,
For there's a cruel law against the Wearin' of the Green.
I met with Napper Tandy, and he took me by the hand,
Sayin',' How is poor old Ireland, and what way does she stand?'
She's as poor, distressful country that ever you have seen,
'Cause they're hanging men and women for the Wearin' of the Green.

So now, if the colour we must wear is England's cruel red
Let it remind us of the blood that Irishmen have shed;
Go, pull the shamrock from your hat, and cast it on the sod,
But never fear, 'twill take root there, though underfoot it's trod.
When laws can stop the blades of grass from blowin' as they grow,
And when the summer leaves dare not their hue and colour show,
Then I will change the colour that I wear in my caubeen;
But till that day, please God, I'll stay with the Wearin' of the Green.

II

I met with Napper Tandy, and he took me by the hand,
Sayin, 'How is old Ireland, and how does she stand?'
She's the most distressful country that ever yet was seen,
They are hanging men and women there for the wearing of the green.
My father loved you tenderly, he lies within your breast,
While I, that would have died for you, must never so be blest;
For laws, their cruel laws, have said that seas should roll between
Old Ireland and her faithful sons who love to wear the green.
O wearing of the green, O wearing of the green,
My native land, I cannot stand, for wearing of the green.

I care not for the Thistle, and I care not for the Rose;
When bleak winds round us whistle, neither down nor crimson shows,
But like hope to him that's friendless, when no joy around is seen,
O'er our graves with love that's endless blooms our own immortal green.

O wearing of the green, O wearing of the green,
My native land, I cannot stand, for wearing of the green.

KATHLEEN MAVOURNEEN

*Hugh Tallant, 'Rebel to King George the Third', kept a record of the rebellion of
1798. In 1898 Randal McDonnell edited it and published it as* Kathleen Mavourneen – A Memory of the Great Rebellion. *An early excerpt gives a human
impression of Tone, Fitzgerald and Town-Major Henry Charles Sirr.*

That I came again to the coffee-house in High Street, and that I came very soon, can be
easily guessed by those who have been placed in a like situation.

But if anyone should be greatly inclined to blame me for my conduct in carrying
on so close an acquaintance with one beneath me in rank, and of a different faith, let
me remind them of my lonely situation and of my girl herself I can truly say, that if
purity of thought and loveliness of person are the marks of good birth and breeding,
then she was fit to rank with the finest lady in the land.

So these happy days passed by, and friendship was changing rapidly I think to
something deeper.

I loved to watch the way her eyes lit up when I appeared and made my weak excuse
about stepping in by accident, though both of us were well assured that I had come
direct, on purpose to see her only and to listen to her talk. Oh, foolish, happy, well-
remembered days, how often has the memory of them cheered and refreshed my
heavy-laden spirit, and helped to bring me safely home through times of dull despair.

It was some three weeks after my arrival in the city that one evening, when I was in
the coffee-room, a gentleman of some thirty years of age, and very handsome in
appearance, stepped in for some refreshment. I remember very foolishly feeling jealous
of his familiar method of addressing Kathleen, and I grew quite angry at the loud care-
less way he asked her who the new customer might be.

But, indeed, I might have spared myself such unnecessary pangs had I understood
his character as I understand it now. When he entered the room, and took a seat beside
the fire, I had made up my mind to preserve a cold and distant manner, and to render
conversation almost impossible.

But, I found my resolutions failing, and my fit of sulks soon vanished under the
charms of his conversation. In some ten minutes time he knew as much about me as my
mother did, and I knew nought of him, except that his name was Tone, and that the
present state of government in Ireland was a thing too disgraceful to be spoken of. And

from his method of talking very little of himself, and a great deal about me, I discovered wherein the true art of conversation consists. Which is to find out what your companion's interests are, and so sympathetically to discuss them, as to render him sufficiently pleased to inquire after yours. Not like the majority of talkers whose streams of weary egotism wash all sympathy away, and rudeness is found to be the only efficient dam to stop the current of their selfish thoughts. We met many times after this, he keeping the conversation always on general topics, and carefully avoiding all matters political.

One day, however, I asked him straight out what he thought of the state of the country, and what he would suggest as a cure. He made no answer, but rose up, and entering the shop, told Kathleen to tap at the door if any stranger came in, and returning, he carefully closed the door. Then seating himself on a chair by the opposite side of the fire, he made answer to my question.

'To understand the state of Ireland,' said he, 'and to be in a position to suggest a cure, you must understand what the conduct of England has been to this country for the last few hundred years.' And then he talked to me like a father, as the saying is, with an earnestness that sometimes frightened me, like a man with a boiler inside him, and not very far off from an explosion.

'Since 1172,' he went on, 'when the Norman invasion first took place, has this island ever had any real peace or has it ever been justly governed by England? No; I tell you a thousand times no. When the Norman settlement on the east coast was established, and the invaders were commencing to mingle with the native race, and becoming, as the old historians have it, "more Irish than the Irish themselves", then the noble English race across the water, fearful that such an union might result in the formation of a great Irish nation, passed a lot of barbarous laws to check this union, and by means of these laws was fostered that race-hatred which is as strong today as ever.

'This I call the first period of injustice. The second period began under the Tudors when the policy of the Government was to treat the natives so badly, that they were forced of necessity into rebellion. The wars which followed were simply wars of extermination – the attempt of the English people to blot out from the earth all traces of the Irish race. If they failed, it was not owing to want of encouragement from home. Read, for example, about the wars of Elizabeth's reign, and you may well wonder with me if they mean it satirically when they speak of that bad woman as "good Queen Bess". Their object was, of course, to free the land from the "Irish barbarians" and appropriate it for themselves!

'Read what the author of the *Faerie Queene* has said about this period, and wonder how a man who wrote such poetry could coolly participate in the barbarous cruelties which were perpetrated on the native race. They succeeded in confiscating the land beyond their expectations, and so proved themselves then as now the greatest and most successful race of robbers in the world.' And here he swore a great oath which I leave out.

'This concludes my second period,' he continued, 'the third period commences when Oliver Cromwell came over with the love of God in his heart, and left a blessing in the mouths of the people around Drogheda and Wexford.

'He was a great man for praying and for prayerful excuses for his conduct, but when he came at last to face his God I think those two performances in Ireland must have hung very heavily on his soul.

'This concludes my third period.

'The fourth period commences when King James, being unable to obtain support in England, came over to settle his troubles here. God knows this poor land had been distracted enough, and was now enjoying a sort of peace, when the news arrived that William, that man of pious and immortal memory, had landed at Carrickfergus to assist in tearing open all the ancient wounds once more. Why should I weary you with the history of those days. You know the sort of glory that King James was covered with at the battle of the Boyne. You know how the war concluded with Limerick's famous treaty which, had it been honourably observed by England, would have given this poor land the peace it sighed for.

'But why speak about it and the Penal Laws which followed; you, as a Catholic, understand them far too well.

'This concludes my fourth period.

'The fifth period begins when the House of Hanover occupied the throne.

'When the Catholics were completely crushed and disorganized by the Penal Laws, and could, therefore, afford but little sport, the English people turned their thoughts to endeavouring to crush all the resources of this country.

'On every trade which flourished in Ireland heavy laws were laid which crushed any attempt to rival England, and brought this country to the very verge of ruin. You know how men like Swift, and Molyneux, and Lucas, exposed the shameful conduct of the sister country, and how she only withdrew those laws when terrified into submission by Henry Grattan and the Volunteers of '82.

'And now I enter upon the last period which commences in our own day. You know how the Catholics are crying out for Emancipation from the Penal Laws, and for the full franchise; and you know that their claims are true and just.

'Do you believe that the English Government will grant all they demand? I tell you, never. Do you know that even now Mr Pitt has set his heart upon the idea of an Union, which simply means the shattering of the Irish Constitution? And my own belief is that we never can have any rest or justice until this country's free from English interference, and a nation once again. This is the only cure. So that is all I know about the matter, and that is why I love the English race,' cried he, with another great oath in conclusion.

'Oh, hush,' cried I, holding up my finger and trying to look shocked at the expression; for I had always been well brought up at home, having been taught that those who used such expressions as 'damn' were themselves in danger of future condemnation.

'I know,' said he laughing, 'it's a sad failing. Now would you ever dream that I once taught in a Sunday class at Townsend Street, and in my College days had great thoughts about Holy Orders.'

I think he must have been laughing at me all the time, but, indeed, this habit of his would always have been a great bar to his advancement, had he failed in entering his profession and been taken with a calling for the Church.

Still he never swore as many others did, putting in oaths at every second word (which spoils the good effect, I think, and only wearies) but introduced them at important points of the narrative to show his great sincerity of conviction. And I could never bring myself to feel vexed at his profanity, for his oaths so seemed to relieve his pent-up feelings, that after two or three of an explosion, his conversation would flow on with a renewed freshness.

Well, as you can easily imagine, I pondered all these facts of history in my heart, and I remember the morning as well as if it were only yesterday, when that great longing took possession of my soul to set to work to right my country's wrongs, and make the poor down-trodden people free.

On the very afternoon of that day, as the Fates would have it, I fell in with Mr. Tone as he was coming down Eccles Street, on his way to the Courts. For, as you all know, he was by profession a barrister, though I doubt if he was ever much of a success.

If brains and an admirable manner were the only requirements, he might have risen to a post of honour and have been a star of exceeding splendour; but I find that in this, as in the other professions, fat influence often helps the lean fraud up the ladder, and fools are pitchforked into high positions where wise and worthy people ought to be.

I walked a good part of the distance with him, and told him all my hopes and dreams.

I remember how the handsome face lit up, and how he paused for a moment and clasped my hand. 'Mr Tallant,' he cried out, 'oh, for a few more hearts like yours to help me, and I might hope to see the old flag flying once again, and blot out all the tears and discords of six hundred years of woe.'

We parted at Rutland Square, but not before I made him promise to let me have a share in his ambitions. For at that time, though he was outwardly working on constitutional lines, as Secretary to the Catholic Committee, he was at heart a complete rebel, and had already, I believe, matured his plans for the great rebellion, and a complete separation from the sister country.

The day after the above meeting, I was standing in the coffee-shop, talking to Kathleen Tyrrell, when Lord Edward Fitzgerald drove past, in an open carriage, towards Thomas Street, and with the lovely Pamela by his side. This was my first glimpse of him, and you may feel sure, I was properly interested, for at that time it was well known that his heart was with the people, though few, I imagine, had even a faint idea that he was actually then engaged in plotting open rebellion.

When Kathleen caught sight of him, her spirit rose, and I well remember how she pointed after him, and cried out to me, 'There goes the noblest heart in Ireland. What place could a man, with his rank and position, not attain to under this corrupt Government if he wished. But no, like the Old Geraldines he comes from, he keeps his honour pure, all undaunted takes his place beneath the Flag of Freedom.'

I was so carried away by her enthusiasm, that I took small notice of the figure which had darkened the door, and waving my hat above my head, we both cried out together, 'Lord Edward, God bless him!'

Suddenly a harsh voice sounded in my ears, 'A dangerous name to call a blessing on, young man, in these unsettled days,' and turning round, I beheld a sinister-looking man leaning against the door of the shop, dressed in the uniform of a British major.

As he crossed the shop and entered the coffee room, I turned round fiercely to answer him, when Kathleen held up her finger in an agony of supplication. 'Keep quiet, for God's sake, keep quiet,' she whispered, 'it's Sirr – Major Sirr from the Castle.' And at the name of that man, although he had not yet reached the full stretch of his reputation, my heart turned to lead inside me, while a chill fell upon me like the fear of death.

EDWARD

Anon. (air composed by William Shields)

Lord Edward Fitzgerald's betrayal and arrest in 1798 were tragedies for the United Irishmen. Captain Ryan was an unarmed member of the arrest party. He came to Major Swan's assistance and grappled with Fitzgerald who stabbed him up to fourteen times until his bowels hung out. Ryan died on 30 May after great suffering, and Lord Edward died of his wounds on 4 June. The poem spares no gory detail. Shields composed the tune for an opera, Rosina. *The lyrics appeared in* Paddy's Resource.

> What plaintive sounds strike on my ear!
> They're Erin's deep-ton'd piteous groans,
> Her harp, attun'd to sorrow drear,
> In broken numbers joins her moans.
> In doleful groups around her stand
> Her manly sons (her greatest pride),
> In mourning deep, for by the hand
> Of ruthless villains Edward died.
>
> Th'assassin horde had him beset,
> As slumbering on a bed he lay,
> Arise, my Lord, Swan cries, up get,
> My prisoner you I make this day.
> Unaw'd our gallant chief up steps,
> And in his vengeful hand he takes
> His dagger keen – quite hard it gripes,
> Then to the savage crew he speaks.
>
> 'Come on who dare – your courage shew,
> 'Gainst Erin's steady children's chief,
> Your burthen'd soul at single blow
> I'll from your body soon relieve.'

Fear-stricken at his manly form,
The blood-stain'd tribe, save Swan, back drew;
Who from our chieftain's potent arm
Receiv'd a stroke that made him rue.

Aloud he shriek'd, then Ryan came
Unto his aid with trembling steps;
Mean caitiff Ryan, lost to shame,
With deeds most foul was full your cup.
Like vivid lightning at him flew,
With well-aim'd point, our hero sweet,
The dastard's blood he forthwith drew,
And left his bowels at his feet.

So wide the gash, so great the gore,
That tumbling out his entrails came:
Poor grov'ling wretch! you'll never more
Attempt to blast unsullied fame;

A baser death should you await,
The hangman's rope – not Edward's hand,
The gallows-tree should be your fate,
Your life deserv'd a shameful end.

Next came on Sirr, half dead with fear,
Deep stain'd with crimes his guilty mind,
He shook all through, by Edward scared,
Like aspen leaf before the wind;
With coward step he advanc'd slow,
Dreading to feel our Edward's might,
Tho' eager for to strike a blow,
Yet fearful to appear in sight.

Assassin-like, he took his stand
Behind the door – and there he stood,
With pistol charg'd in either hand,
So great his thirst for Edward's blood;
Upon his brows stood imp of hell,
Within his heart a devil foul,
Dire murder dire, and slaughter fell,
Had full possession of his soul.

His bosom friend suggested then
A bloody deed – a devil's act –
An hell-fram'd thought ... *Arise Ye Men,*
Revenge, revenge the horrid fact.
Sound, sound aloud the trump of war,
Proclaim that Edward's blood is spill'd!
By traitor's hand, by coward Sirr,
Revenge! Revenge! for Edward's kill'd.

    🐜   🐜   🐜

Of Bantry Bay

An Irish rebellion might have succeeded with Wolfe Tone's proposed invasion of 1796. The French plan was to join with Irish rebels in ejecting the poorly armed British and establishing an Irish republic. A French fleet sailed for Ireland, carrying 14,000 men. Its ships became separated and only fifteen, bearing 6400 men including Wolfe Tone, arrived in Bantry Bay on 21 December. A calm sea made conditions for landing perfect. No landing took place, however, as the frigate bearing General Hoche was among those that had lost touch with the convoy, and the French decided to await its arrival. Next day snow and sleet began to fall and 'a Protestant wind' separated the vessels. By Christmas Eve a raging storm blew. The fleet raised anchor and returned to France.

THE SEAN-BHEAN BHOCHT
Anon.

Anglicized, it is spelt 'The Shan Van Vocht'. 'The 'Poor Old Woman' is Ireland unfree,
unfortunate, hoping for a French invasion.

Oh! the French are on the sea, says the Sean-bhean Bhocht;
The French are on the sea, says the Sean-bhean Bhocht;
Oh! the French are in the Bay, they'll be here without delay,
And the Orange will decay, says the Sean-bhean Bhocht,
And the Orange will decay, says the Sean-bhean Bhocht.

And where will they have their camps? says the Sean-bhean Bhocht;
Where will they have their camps? says the Sean-bhean Bhocht.
On the Curragh of Kildare, the boys they will be there
With their pikes in good repair, says the Sean-bhean Bhocht;
And Lord Edward will be there, says the Sean-bhean Bhocht.

Then what will the yeomen do? says the Sean-bhean Bhocht;
What will the yeomen do? says the Sean-bhean Bhocht.
What should the yeomen do but throw off the red and blue
And swear that they'll be true to the Sean-bhean Bhocht,
And swear that they'll be true to the Sean-bhean Bhocht.

And what colour will they wear? says the Sean-bhean Bhocht;
What colour will they wear? says the Sean-bhean Bhocht.
What colour should be seen where our fathers' homes have been
But our own immortal green? says the Sean-bhean Bhocht,
But our own immortal green? says the Sean-bhean Bhocht.

And will Ireland then be free? says the Sean-bhean Bhocht,
Will Ireland then be free? says the Sean-bhean Bhocht.
Yes, Ireland shall be free from the centre to the sea;
Then hurrah for liberty! says the Sean-bhean Bhocht,
Then hurrah for liberty! says the Sean-bhean Bhocht.

NEWS OF THE FRENCH

An extract from Teeling's History of the Irish Rebellion of 1798 *describes react-ion among United Irishmen prisoners in Kilmainham Jail to news of the aborted invasion at Bantry Bay.*

It was at the still hour of night, in the depth of the wintry storm, when the old year had nearly run its course, and the approach of the new was anticipated with alternate hopes and fears, when every moment increased suspense, and every footstep caught the lis-tening ear, that the long vaulted passages announced the approach of feet, which pro-claimed the arrival of the most unlooked for but welcome of friends.

The moment was to us one of the deepest interest. The country was agitated; the government was alarmed; all the disposable military force was in motion, for a hostile squadron hovered on the peaceful shores of the south, and the capacious bay of Bantry was crowded with foreign masts. Never had Ireland experienced an hour of greater excitement – never was her population more agitated with alternate hopes and fears.

The prisons were crowded with the most popular characters of the day; and, as the troops were passing that in which we were confined, some detachments halted, and cheered us on their march to the south. The anxiety of the people increased as alarm for our safety or hopes for our liberation prevailed. The sanguinary measures of the administration had alienated the great majority of the nation, and the minority possessed neither the influence nor the power to contend with the approaching storm. Everything without the Cabinet bespoke the alarm that prevailed within, for government had neither the wisdom to conciliate the people, nor the talent to direct the disposable force, with which the were ill prepared to encounter a bold and adventurous foe. Hurry, confusion, and disorder marked the advance of the army; all was terror, doubt and dismay; troops disaffected, horses wanting, the munitions of war badly supplied, and even the bullet was unfitted to the calibre of the cannon which a defective commissariat had supplied. The general's culinary apparatus only was complete; and, while the troops had to contend with the severity of the winter's storm, the mountain's torrent, roads broken up by the floods or rendered impassible from the depth of the drifted snow, peril and dismay in the front, hunger and privation in the rear, everything that could gratify the palate, even to the satiety of taste, was profusely provided for the general's table. And, thus prepared, the unwieldy Dalrymple faced to the south, to meet the invincible Hoche, the victor of La Vendée, followed by the bravest troops the republic of France could boast. But the elements protected the empire for Britain, and the country was preserved from the havoc of war. Hoche was separated from his troops by the winter's storm; and the army having no instructions to land in his absence, the expedition returned to the ports of France.

This was a most interesting period for Ireland – a single breeze might have rendered it the most eventful. The solicitude of the country watched for the safety of the prisoners, who, being considered as national hostages, were in a two-fold degree the objects of concern, both to the government and the people, but with feelings the most opposite in nature.

The people, sensitively alive to the situation of those confined, had concerted measures for the liberation of a selected few, and the necessary means were provided for conveying us to a post of safety. The presence of friends, endeared to us by the double bond of country and personal esteem – the solemn hour of their visit – the apparent mystery which hung around it, the excitation of the moment, and the importance of the subject when disclosed; how they arrived; by what means they found entrance, – all afforded matter for deep conjecture. Whether the confidence of the prison authorities was secured, their hopes encouraged, or their fears allayed, is not the object of present inquiry. No suspicion was breathed, no alarm evinced. The rank of the visitors formed a guarantee of security, for their names were associated with the most influential in the land. The object of their visit was fully attained; those to whom it was necessary to communicate were appraised of all that was interesting to learn; and the actors in this important scene returned uninjured, uninterrupted, and unsuspected to this hour. They had executed a commission, which, at that particular moment, none but themselves were competent to perform; and as it was attended with a risk, in which discovery must have involved both life and fortune, the generous act has left a grateful impression on the hearts of those who yet survive, which no change of country or clime can ever efface.

While the French fleet remained on the coast, the alarm on one hand was more than counterbalanced by the hopes entertained on the other; and the following simple occurrence is in some measure illustrative of the general panic that pervaded every department in any degree connected with the government.

For some days an intense frost had prevailed, and the snow had fallen in deep and heavy drifts, but the atmosphere had become more mild, and an imperceptible thaw had already commenced. The snow with which the lofty parapets of the prison had been surcharged, and nearly bending under the weight, now came tumbling in heavy masses, with tremendous crash, on the smooth and deep-flagged passages below, and re-echoing from the vaulted walls in the interior of the prison, resembled the noise of a distant but approaching cannonade. It was near the hour of midnight – all were aroused – the alarm excited was almost beyond the bounds of belief. The prison authorities were palsied with terror. The sentries paced their solitary rounds, in vain looking for relief, and expecting momentary destruction; the prisoners alone were unmoved, for the imagined cannon of the foe menaced no ill to the captive in the cell. At this period of unprecedented alarm, no idea of resistance was entertained for a moment to the emancipation of all within. We were addressed by the prison authorities, with every expression of confidence and kindness. They were unmeasured in their professions of respect – they deplored the privations we had encountered – they shifted the blame from themselves to a higher quarter, and implored the protection of the prisoners of state. A little time, however, disclosed the cause of the alarm; terror subsided – confidence was resumed, and the sentry again proclaimed 'All's well.'

WEEP! GALLIA WEEP!

From The Press, *a Dublin newspaper controlled by the United Irishman Arthur O'Connor. The poem is a eulogy to General Lazare Hoche, who had just won fame by defending Quiberon, on the coast of Brittany, from French Royalists in English pay, when Tone requested him as leader of the first 1796 expedition to Ireland.*

> Weep! Gallia weep! in sorrow droop thy head,
> Thy Hoche, thy hero, and thy friend is dead;
> That man so truly great in freedom's cause,
> That brave defender of his country's laws;
> Who, from her fields the Pitt-leagued tyrants chased,
> And all the hordes of slaves that laid them waste;
> Made the crown'd robbers of his native soil,
> Shake on their blood-stain'd thrones and quit their spoil.

Now pale and breathless, lo! the hero lies,
As envious fate had call'd him to the skies,
But still unconquered, tho' resigned his breath,
He springs immortal from the arms of death;
O! friend of man, upon thy honoured bier,
The good and brave shall drop a grateful tear;
Bright fame, thy virtues from oblivion save,
And snatch thy honours from the silent grave,
From age to age thy glorious deeds impart,
And make thy monument each Patriot's heart.

GENERAL WONDER IN OUR LAND
Anon.

A song expressive of general relief felt by loyalists at the failure of the French expedition.

General wonder in our land,
And general consternation;
General gale on Bantry strand,
For general preservation.

General rich he shook with awe
At general insurrection;
General poor his sword did draw,
With general disaffection.

General blood was just at hand,
As General Hoche appeared;
General woe fled through our land,
As general want was feared.

General gale our fears dispersed,
He conquered general dread;
General joy each heart has swelled,
As General Hoche has fled.

General love no blood has shed,
He left us general ease,
General horror he has fled,
Let God get general praise.

To that great General of the skies,
That sent us general gale,
With general love our voices rise
In one great general peal.

   🐜   🐜   🐜

Of Oaths

Reports on forms of oath taken during the rebellion varied, depending on the leanings of the narrator. Inauthentic versions were often circulated to arouse indignation or passions. Members of the United Army were alleged to have taken various forms of oath in a most public and solemn manner, as service in the movement progressed.

TAKING THE OATH

The loyalist writer S.L. Corrigan recorded numerous cases of United Irish intimidation:

Michael Hogan of Newport, swore, before William Anderson, a magistrate, on 12th March, 1798, that, on the first of said month, he was invited by Daniel Ready into his house to drink, and, in the course of conversation, he offered him fifty guineas if he would murder Robert Lloyd and Francis Quinn, Esqrs; and informed him that, in the course of a few nights, the United men would put Mr Waller of Castlewaller, and Mr Anderson of Foxhall, to death; and he showed him the plan of a pike, according to which he was to get fifty made by a blacksmith.

    Oliver Brown of Boolaree, swore an information, before George Bennett, Esq., on the 18th April, 1798, that, on the night of 1st March, a number of people, about four hundred, assembled on the hill of Tullagh, where they formed themselves into ranks under officers and sergeants; that James Keary and Daniel Colliston acted as officers, and that the said party marched three abreast into the village of Templetoohy.

    John Maher of Ballingarry, swore, before William Despard, Esq., on the 8th May, 1798, that, on the night of the 29th April, Denis Maher of Grashagh gave him a written paper containing a kind of catechism or constitution of the United Irishmen, and swore him the oath of secrecy, and to be true to the said constitution until they met again, which, he told him, would be the Sunday after, at Kilbechan chapel; and informant declared that he took said oath through fear of the said Denis Maher and the party that attended him.

OATHS OF THE UNITED IRISHMEN

A Test Oath for the United Irish Society, agreed in Dublin in November 1791, omitted two anti-English sections passed in Belfast during the previous month. It read:

I, A.B., in the presence of God, do pledge myself to my country that I will use all my abilities and influence in the attainment of an adequate and impartial representation of the Irish nation in Parliament, and as a means of absolute and immediate necessity in the attainment of this chief good of Ireland, I will endeavour, as much as lies in my ability, to forward a brotherhood of affection, an identity of interests, a communion of rights, and a union of power among Irishmen of all religious persuasions, without which every reform in Parliament must be partial, not national, inadequate to the wants, delusive to the wishes, and insufficient for the freedom and happiness of this country.

So help me God.

In 1795 the test oath took cognizance of the nature of the Society that had evolved:

I, A.B., do voluntarily declare, that I will persevere in endeavouring to form a brotherhood of affection among Irishmen of every religious persuasion; and that I will also persevere in my endeavours to obtain an equal, full, and adequate representation of all the people of Ireland. I do further declare, that neither hopes, fears, rewards or punishments, shall ever induce me, directly or indirectly, to inform on, or give evidence against, any member or members of this or similar societies, for any act or expression of theirs, done or made collectively or individually, in or out of this society, in pursuance of the spirit of this obligation.

So help me God.

PRIVATE'S OATH

I, A.B., do solemnly and sincerely swear, and take God and his only Son our Lord Jesus Christ to witness, that I will at all times be obedient to the commands of my officers; that I am ready to lay down my life for the good of my country; that I have an aversion to plunder, and to the spilling of innocent blood; that I will fight courageously in the field, and give mercy where it can be given; that I will avoid drunkenness, as tending to disorder and ruin; that I will endeavour to make as many friends and as few enemies as possible; that above all, I detest cowardice, and that I will look upon him as an enemy, who will stand back in the time of battle.

So help me God.

OFFICER'S OATH

In the awful presence of God, who knows the hearts and thoughts of all men, and calling my country to witness, I, A.B., officer in the ———, do solemnly swear, that I do not consider my life my own when my country demands it; that I consider the present moment calls for a proof of the sincerity of that sentiment, and I am ready and desirous to stand the test, and do aver, that I am determined to die or lead to victory; and that all my actions shall be directed to the prosperity of the common cause, uninfluenced by any inferior motive: and I further declare my utter aversion to all alarmists, union-breakers, and cowards, and my respect and obedience to the commands of my superior officers.

So help me God.

THE BLACK TESTS

Loyalists claimed that two other oaths were hidden from the disaffected Protestants and Presbyterians within the United Irishmen. They were called the Black Tests:

I, A.B. do solemnly swear, by our Lord Jesus Christ, who suffered for us on the cross, and by the Blessed Virgin Mary, that I will burn, destroy, and murder all heretics, up to my knees in blood.

So help me God.

The second was added to the Private's test if he was a Roman Catholic, and read as follows:

Every loyal Irish Protestant heretic I shall murder, and this I swear.

The first letter of each word of the second oath, when put together, forms the word ELIPHISMATIS. This was the password of all who had taken the black test. Some sources suggest that it was given only to a few, who constituted a sort of 'special branch' within the rebel army for committing atrocities.

WEXFORD OATHS

On learning of the arming of rebels, Lord Mount Norris and some colleagues visited Catholic churches after Masses during January 1798 and forced men to take this oath:

I do hereby declare upon the Holy Evangelists, and as I hope to be saved through the merits of my blessed Lord and Saviour, Jesus Christ, that I will be true and faithful to his Majesty King George the Third, and to the succession of his family to the throne; that I will support and maintain the Constitution, as by law established; that I am not a United Irishman, and that I never will take the United Irishman's oath; that I am bound, by every obligation, human and divine, to give every information in my power to prevent tumult and disorder; that I will neither aid nor assist the enemies of my King or my country, and that I will give up all sorts of arms in my possession: all the above I voluntarily swear –

So help me God and Redeemer!

After this incident, some loyalist Catholics met in Ballycanew parish and voluntarily signed a declaration oath which they forwarded through Mount Norris to the Lord Lieutenant, Camden. Father Michael Murphy from Ballycanew countersigned.

May it please your Excellency,
We, the Roman Catholic inhabitants of the parish of Ballycanow [*sic*], this day assembled in the chapel, holding in abhorrence the barbarous outrages lately committed, and seditious conspiracies now existing in this kingdom, by traitors and rebels, styling themselves United Irishmen, think it incumbent on us, thus publicly, to avow and declare our unalterable attachment and loyalty to our most revered Sovereign King George III, and our determined resolution to support and maintain his rights and our happy Constitution. And we do further pledge ourselves to co-operate with our Protestant brethren of this kingdom, in opposing, to the utmost of our power, any foreign or domestic enemy, who may dare to invade his Majesty's dominions, or disturb the peace or tranquillity of this country.

THE BIRDS DID WHISTLE AND DID SWEETLY SING

❧ 1797-98 ❧

Of Informing

The most despised informer of the rebellion was Thomas Reynolds (1771-1836) of Kilkea Castle, Kildare, a man married to a sister of Wolfe Tone's wife. The son of a Dublin textile merchant, he was educated in Liège. After inheriting his father's considerable business, he was swindled by an associate of the firm and became bankrupt. He joined the United Irishmen but became frightened when he learned the plans for a rebellion. Through an intermediary named Cope, the Under-Secretary, Edward Cooke, was offering large sums of money for information. Reynolds informed Dublin Castle of the meeting of the Leinster Directory of the United Irishmen on 12 March 1798 at the home of Oliver Bond. For this, he received a lump sum of £5000, an annual pension of £1000 and employment with the British service abroad.

AN INFORMER'S OUTLINE

The note by which Thomas Reynolds informed on the Leinster Directory, when edited for punctuation, spelling and abbreviations, read:

There is a room on the first flight, at the head of the stairs, in which the company dined last Monday. The other flight leads up to the drawing room and other parts of the upper rooms in the house.

The meeting will certainly be on Monday morning. Not known for certain till 12 o'clock on the Sunday, the hour – but thinks it will be 10.

The parties for an immediate rising are violent and are to bring their papers demonstrating their force. They assert, and say will prove, that 2700 soldiers in the barrack, and the majority of Lehaunstown Camp are at their side, and will immediately join a rising and desire but 20 minutes notice to seize the camp and march off to Dublin.

If the meeting takes effect on Monday and the parties taken, it is supposed there will be county meetings all over the Kingdom immediately held. If information can be obtained where the meetings are held in the different places, all the principal persons concerned in the respective counties, it is probable, will attend. Will obtain what information and communicate it.

THE SHAM SQUIRE

Francis Higgins is the pantomime villain of the period, whose passing of information led to the arrest of Lord Edward Fitzgerald. His story is told by W.J. Fitzpatrick (1830-95) in The Sham Squire and the Informers of '98 *(Dublin 1866), a bestseller of the time,* Ireland before the Union *(1880) and* Secret Service under Pitt *(1892), from which the following account derives.*

Thomas Reynolds, through a merchant called Cope, allegedly informed on Lord Edward Fitzgerald. Another shady character lurks in that episode, however. Mr Francis Higgins, 72 St Stephen's Green, Dublin was a shoe-black and later the proprietor of a basement huckster shop close to Green Street courthouse. Higgins used a slight casual encounter with the Earl of Clonmell, John Scott, to advance himself. Scott was Chief Justice of the King's bench, who as Attorney General was dismissed for claiming that England had no authority to bind Ireland by Acts of Parliament. Higgins, heavily involved in the betrayal of Lord Edward Fitzgerald, had no such noble inclinations.

His parents, Patrick and Mary, were from Downpatrick, Co. Down. They moved to Dublin where Francis was born in a cellar and reared a Catholic. His father became an attorney's clerk and Francis earned money tending to the needs of patrons of Fishamble Street music-hall by ferrying porter in pewter tankards from a nearby inn. The red-headed lad also swept paths outside shops and after a spell shoe-shining and huckstering himself, became an attorney's clerk for the firm of Bourne, St Patrick's Close. There he forged documents to establish himself as a man of property, and a relative of Lord Clonmell. He became a Protestant, too, and all to impress a lady of means. There are several accounts of Higgins changing his religion one way or another, in order to benefit financially, and of his befriending servants of judges and riding in their carriages to compound his image. In a bill published in the *Freeman's Journal* of 21 October 1766, a Grand Jury described Higgins as:

> a person of evil name, fame, and dishonest conversation, and a common deceiver and cheat ... not minding to gain his livelihood by truth and honest labour, but devising to cheat, cozen and defraud William Archer of his moneys, fortune, and substance, for support of the profligate life of him, the said Francis Higgins, and

with intent to obtain Mary Anne Archer in marriage, and to aggrieve, impoverish and ruin her, and with intent to impoverish the said William Archer, his wife, and all his family, by wicked, false and deceitful pretences … The said F. Higgins, by the same wicked pretences, procured Mary Anne Archer to be given in marriage to him, to the great damage of the said William Archer, to the great discomfort, prejudice, injury, and disquiet of mind of the said Mary Anne and the rest of the family, to the evil example of all others and against the peace of our said Lord the King, his crown and dignity.

Evidence told how the couple married and moved to Lucan. Mary Anne found Higgins undesirable and ran home. Higgins chased her and caught up on her as she entered her own house. There was a violent struggle with her mother who tried to prevent him from entering. Mrs Archer was injured. Higging was imprisoned in Cutpurse Row but when the case was heard and he was found guilty, he got off with a year in jail and a nickname, for Judge Robinson referred to him as a 'Sham Squire'.

Mary Anne gave birth but gave the infant into the care of a friend with the warning that Higgins was never to know its whereabouts. When she died of a broken heart, Higgins tried to discover his offspring but failed. He married a female worker in the prison (whose father had been Daniel O'Connell's gaoler), proving again that in spite of a hump and gross appearance, this strange mixture of coarseness and humanity had a way with the ladies. After his release he became a hosier at The Wholesale and Retail Connemara Sock and Stocking Warehouse, Smock Alley and was President of the Guild of Hosiers by 1775. Ambitious in the extreme, Higgins used every deceit possible to gain access to the Dublin social circle. The Lord Clonmell connection again helped when, around 1781, he became an attorney-at-law, with an address at Ross Lane. Most of his cases were at the court presided over by Scott.

Lord Carhampton, Governor and Custos Rotulorum of Dublin, who patronized Higgins, ill-treated a young whore in a house run by a Mrs Llewellyn. The madam was tried for complicity and sentenced to death. Francis Higgins, it was said, influenced its being quashed. Dublin's humorists were quickly on target as they penned a parody of the popular 'The Night before Larry Was Stretched', satirizing an accomplice of Llewellyn's also on trial:

> Oh the night ere Edgeworth was tried
> The council all met in despair
> The pressmen were there, and besides
> A good doctor, a lord and a mayor.
> Justice Sham, then, a silence proclaimed,
> The bullies, they all of them harkened,
> Poor Edgeworth, sez he, will be framed,
> His daylights might even be darkened
> Unless we can lend him a hand.

The power of the press was apparent to Higgins so he lent money to the proprietor of the influential *Freeman's Journal*, but right away took steps to indict him for non-payment of the debt. Incredibly, he appears to have acquired ownership of the publication for a quarter of its value on foot of this ploy.

Now the Sham Squire really swaggered. He wore a three-cocked hat fringed with the down of a swan, bright yellow vest and breeches, a green, swallow-tailed jacket, violet gloves and tassled boots. He carried a long, gold-knobbed staff. His indoor wear was augmented by diamond brooches and rings. For patronizing the quality and the powerful in his newspaper he received numerous favours. For a while he acted as coroner for Dublin city and as County Sheriff, in which capacity he tried certain obscure cases with all the haughty grandeur of a high-court judge. For his ill-treatment of Catholic defendants and corrupt practices he gained a new nickname: Signor Shamando.

When the Marquis of Buckingham assumed the vice-regality of Ireland, it was feared that, because of unpopularity won when he was here as Lord Temple, he would receive no welcome. Francis Higgins saw an opportunity to curry favour. He hired a mob, fitted them with silken ropes and harness, and had them drag the dignitary's carriage to Dublin Castle. Continuing his attempts to please the establishment, Higgins changed the thrust of the *Freeman's Journal* to being its staunch supporter. Shamando moved to a fashionable Hugenot house at 72 St Stephen's Green, where he dined with judges and entertained the leading socialites of Dublin. He also became involved in running a secret gambling-house of low repute in Crane Lane, a stone's throw from Dublin Castle and the office of the Board of Police. Dublin balladeers noticed and Higgins found himself in their song-sheets:

> Alas! All gone! may every virtue weep,
> Shamando lives and Justice lies asleep.
> How shall I wake her? Will not all the cries
> Of midnight revels, that ascend the skies,
> The sounding of dice-box, and the shrieking whore
> The groans of all the destituted poor
> Undone and plundered by this outcast man,
> Will not these wake her?

At this stage Higgins was overweight and pockmarked, a disgusting sight, lampooned in the public prints but welcomed for his wit at table. He now had a country seat at Kilmacud and women procured for him by a flashman. Instead of paying them, however, he forced them to pay him, threatening to drag them to his court charged with prostitution. In his gambling-house he employed men to cheat patrons and to foment trouble, then recommend their master as solicitor to the wrongdoers. The *Dublin Evening Post* described it as:

> a notorious school of nocturnal study in the doctrine of chances; a school which
> affords to men of the town an ample source of ways and means in the pluckings of
> those unfledged green-horns who can be inveigled into the trap; which furnishes to

the deluded apprentice a ready mart for the acquisition of experience, and the disposal of any loose cash that can be purloined from his master's till; which affords to the working artisan a weekly asylum for the reception of that stipend which honest industry should allot to the purchase of food for a wife and children; and which affords to the spendthrift shopkeeper a ready transfer office to make over the property of his creditors to the plunder of knaves and sharpers.

John Magee, editor of the *Dublin Evening Post,* was relentless in his criticism of Higgins. Often, he included Lord Clonmell in his diatribe so Higgins drew Scott's attention to this and they connived to have Magee charged. Clonmell himself heard the four fiats, each marked with £7800 (an enormous figure at the time), at the suit of Higgins and others, including Richard Daly of Crowe Street Theatre, a duellist who had also killed a marker with a billiard-ball. An anecdote tells how Magee, during the hearing, referred to Higgins as the Sham Squire. Lord Clonmell rebuked him, saying he would not allow any nicknames in his court. Magee retorted, 'Very well, John Scott!' When Magee was acquitted, the conspirators sought, unsuccessfully, to have him certified insane.

Now Higgins had his own elegant coach, with yellow trim and coat of arms emblazoned on its brown panels. He scoffed at denouncement from the pulpit, in spite of which he attended regularly at St Audeon's church. Sometimes he even dispensed charity as he drove away. He presided at times with John Toler (who would become Lord Norbury) but also occupied the Lord Mayor's bench on occasions. His wealth from extortion, gambling-house and newspaper was boosted by gratuities from the government earned by informing.

On the bridge over the Liffey at Leixlip at twilight one day in 1798, a young yeoman questioned a peasant in a frieze coat and corduroy knee-breeches, driving a few sheep. Sentinel Nicholas Dempsey waved on the disguised Lord Edward Fitzgerald, United Irish leader who supported revolution without waiting for French assistance. He went into hiding in Dublin and continued with his preparations for insurrection. From one house to another he moved to avoid capture. On 15 May 1798 Dublin Castle issued the following Proclamation:

> The Lord Lieutenant and Privy Council of Ireland have issued a proclamation declaring that they have received information upon oath, that Lord Edward Fitzgerald has been guilty of High Treason, and offer a reward of £1,000 sterling, to any person who shall discover, apprehend, or commit him to prison.

On 17 May Major Sirr was notified of Fitzgerald's whereabouts by the Under Secretary. Three days later an account of Fitzgerald's capture was published by the Castle. It described how the house of the feather merchant in Thomas Street was raided by the notorious Major Sirr and his men, and how Fitzgerald was wounded, captured and sent to Newgate prison after putting up a spirited resistance. He died there on 4 June from his wounds.

Many years afterwards a second-hand bookdealer in Henry Street bought some discarded documents and publications from an official of Dublin Castle. A record of secret service monies expended during 1798 revealed the entry: 'June 20th, F.H. Discovery of L.E.F., £1000.' Irishmen argued the probability of its alluding to Higgins. Others, mainly Thomas Reynolds, had been suspected of informing and Higgins certainly did not convey the information direct, they avowed. It became one of the great talking-points of the period. Everyone knew that Higgins plied information to keep the establishment on his side. But was he guilty in this instance?

The correspondence of Lord Cornwallis, Lord Lieutenant and Commander-in-Chief, eventually threw some light on the case. First of all it revealed that Cornwallis received notification from the Under-Secretary that Higgins, among others, was entitled to share the secret-service allotment of £1500 per annum. But the most damning entry recommended Higgins for a pension of £300. The proprietor of the *Freeman's Journal* said the Under Secretary, 'was the person who procured for me all the intelligence respecting Lord Edward Fitzgerald, and got ——— to set him, and has given me much information …' The part played by Francis Higgins was made clear but the mystery of the unnamed individual remained. It was generally accepted that an associate of Higgins's named Magan, who had helped him organize a reception for Lord Buckingham and remained a drinking and dining partner, was the man in question.

A person's last will and testament often reveals characteristics not apparent during life. Higgins's was no exception. He left £1000 to a female friend, £100 to his housekeeper, £50 to an asylum for ruined merchants, £100 to the Lying-In Hospital provided a bed was named in his honour. He left £20 to the Blue Coat Hospital, £400 to a Colonel O'Kelly, £100 to Fr O'Leary and many smaller bequests. The Sham Squire wanted no sham tomb; it was to be a slab, well secured with brickwork, stone and lime, in Kilbarrack cemetery.

Francis Higgins died on 19 January 1802. Dubliners would say, thirty-seven years later, that the 'Big Wind' was as bad as the night the Sham Squire died. His Kilbarrack tomb was fashioned in 1804. A list of his larger bequests was carved upon it and the epitaph 'Sacred to the Memory of Francis Higgins.' It did not always receive due respect: one of Dublin's aldermen, it was said, never passed the graveyard without dismounting from his horse, going to the tomb and screaming insults at the Sham Squire. Another 'old gentleman of eccentric disposition, who lived at Howth, was in the habit, on his way to Dublin, of halting at Kilbarrack and dancing Jig Polthogue on the flat tombstone'. In *The Irish Magazine* of October 1810 Watty Cox implied that Higgins realized that 'religion was a good disposable article in skilful hands'; he instanced a protegé called Conway, Higgins's succesor as editor of the *Freeman's Journal*, who, he claimed, called to the Squire's tomb 'and after reading with impassioned energy the eulogium it bore, burst into tears, and declared upon his honour, the composition was unequalled in the history of sepulchral literature'. Later, a sledge-hammer was used to smash part of the imposing slab and although a reward was offered for information on the perpetrators, none was forthcoming. Even when his escapades were almost forgotton, a roughly hewn inscription appeared, below a diagram of a gallows and a pike:

> Here lies the monster
> Higgins,
> Lord Edward Fitzgerald's informer.

🐦 🐦 🐦

Of Proclamations

Lieutenant-General Gerard Lake originally commanded the northern portion of the country and partially succeeded in disarming Ulster in 1797. He disagreed with General Sir Ralph Abercromby's ideas on reform and replaced him in an acting capacity as Commander in Chief in March 1798. An ally of Camden's, Lake pursued a heavy-handed policy towards dissenters. He imposed a curfew on Dublin and himself took command when the army pushed on to Wexford, defeating the rebels at Vinegar Hill. He indulged in severe reprisals, so Cornwallis despatched him to Mayo. He suffered defeat at Castlebar but pursued the Franco-Irish force and defeated them at Ballinamuck, County Longford.

GENERAL LAKE'S PROCLAMATION

Belfast, March 13, 1797

Whereas the daring and horrid outrages in many parts of this province, evidently perpetrated with a view to supersede the laws and the administration of justice by an organized system of murder and robbery, have increased to such an alarming degree, as from their atrocity and extent to bid defiance to the civil power, and to endanger the lives and properties of his Majesty's faithful subjects; and whereas, the better to effect their traitorous purposes, several persons who have been enrolled under the authority of his Majesty's commission, and others, have been forcibly and traitorously deprived of their arms; it [has] therefore become indispensably necessary for the safety and protection of the well-disposed to interpose the King's troops under my command: and I do hereby give notice that I have received authority and directions to act in such manner as the public safety may require. I do therefore hereby enjoin and require all persons in this district (peace officers and those serving in a military capacity excepted), forthwith to bring in and surrender up all arms and ammunition which they may have in their possession to the officer commanding the King's troops in their neighbourhood.

I trust that an immediate compliance with this order may render any act of mine to enforce it unnecessary.

Let the people seriously reflect, before it is too late, on the ruin into which they are rushing; let them reflect upon their present prosperity, and the miseries in which they will inevitably be involved by persisting in acts of positive rebellion; let them instantly, by surrendering up their arms, and by restoring those traitorously taken from the King's forces, rescue themselves from the severity of military authority. Let all the loyal and well-intentioned act together with energy and spirit in enforcing subordination to the laws, and restoring tranquillity in their respective neighbourhoods, and they may be assured of protection and support from me.

And I do hereby invite all persons who are enabled to give information touching arms or ammunition which may be concealed, immediately to communicate the same to the several officers commanding his Majesty's forces in their respective districts; and, for their encouragement and reward, I do hereby promise and engage that strict and inviolate secresy [sic] shall be observed with respect to all persons who shall make such communication, and that every person who shall make it shall receive a reward the full value of all such arms and ammunition as shall be seized in consequence thereof.

G. Lake, Lieutenant-General

Commanding the Northern District.

🐜   🐜   🐜

Of Kildare

After minor skirmishes around Dublin, rebels struck their first significant blow at Prosperous, County Kildare, on the night of 23-4 May 1798. A cotton mill in the village had failed during the previous decade, leaving a high rate of unemployed young men. About forty members of the North Cork Militia under Captain Swayne and a Lieutenant and twenty Ancient British cavalrymen (Welsh Fencibles stationed in Ireland) occupied one permanent and one temporary barracks. Swayne enlisted the aid of the clergy and an influential local doctor, Esmonde, in trying to persuade the local United Irishmen to hand in arms. This failed, so Swayne began a series of brutal raids for arms. In the process he also seized farm stock and destroyed property. This alienated Esmonde, although he continued to enjoy Swayne's hospitality. The doctor was like many men of status at the time: leaders of the yeomen by day and leaders of the United Irishmen by night. He dined and drank with Swayne on 23 May and Swayne was probably less than sober when he retired to bed in the barracks.

At about two o'clock in the morning of 24 May, the rebels, including Esmonde, under Captain Andrew O'Farrell of Blackhall, Clane, attacked and killed two sentries and gained access to the sleeping quarters of the barracks. They numbered 500, according to one contemporary account. They killed Swayne in his bed, took out his body and burned it in a barrel of tar before being surprised by other soldiers who awoke and routed them. Two or three of the rebels were killed, but their comrades surrounded the barracks and set it alight with straw and whin bushes. A local woman, Ruth Hackett, caried furze bushes for the fire from the bog nearby. The rebels agreed to the garrison's appeal for the safe release of wives and children. Then the soldiers all moved upstairs but the flames reached them and they threw themselves out the window, many landing on the spears of the rebels' pikes. A fierce fight developed, and most of the garrison lost their lives. A rebel prisoner being held in custody was rescued.

Yeomanry reprisals followed. These included the burning of Staplestown church, across the bog from Prosperous.

THE SONG OF PROSPEROUS
Anon.

During the hours following the battle of Prosperous, rebel attacks on Clane, Ballymore-Eustace and Naas took place. This ballad recalls most of the actions that occurred in County Kildare.

On the twenty-fourth of May, at the dawning of the day,
Our boys went under arms Prosperous to invade;
With hand and heart we marched under Captain Farrell's orders,
It's in the town we halted and set it in a blaze.

There were red-hot balls a-flying, the groans of soldiers dying,
Flames in the air were flying, and Swayne expiring there.
To retreat our Colonel gave orders, but we never faltered,
Until killed, wounded, and slaughtered, we won the battle there.

Next morning Naas was tattered, and all our brethren slaughtered.
Many a valiant hero lay bleeding on the green,
Our Colonel he forsook us, and cursed Griffith took him,
He immediately was detected and ordered into jail.

Phil Mite the informer cruel, he robbed us of our jewel,
May the heavens vengeance on him pour down,
God and his holy angels may for ever hate him,
May he be afflicted with the heavenly frown.

The boys we have forsaken, Kilcock town have taken,
Leixlip, Johnstown, and Maynooth, with all its cavalry,
And home we then returned, Sparkes house we burned,
In recompense for Kennedy that died there on a tree.

Our Captains they combined, and all together joined,
Straight we marched that night in camp on Wileys' Hill,
Disciplined and well armed, but soon we were alarmed,
All by a point of war beat by the Highlandmen.

Three hours we gave battle, where cannon balls did rattle,
Like hail and claps of thunder they flew about our ears;
Our powder and ball did fly tremendous through the sky,
Three hundred of their soldiers we left lying there.

The cowards from us flew, in ambush themselves threw,
The army then all slew when we were fled away;
By the terror of that day, our captains ran away,
To Newtown bog we returned, the informer Gaitly killed.

Colonel Aylmer bold, a valiant heart of gold,
He never was controlled but fought most manfully,
He was general-in-chief, commander over the Irish banner,
Maintaining Erin's rights and sweet liberty.

The bloody adulterous crew, they thought us to subdue,
But well we made them rue the day they did begin
Whipping and destroying; but our brave Irish boys,
Soon they let them know we were United men.

If Ireland had behaved like Wicklow, Wexford, and Kildare,
The green flag would be hoisted through town and country,
To conclude and make an end, heres a health to United men,
Long may they live and reign over bloody tyranny.

RATHANGAN'S EDWARD MOLLOY
John Frazer (Jean de Jean)

Captain Thomas Spencer, land agent to the Duke of Leinster, commanded the single corps of yeomen in Rathangan, County Kildare. Captain Langton and a small force of Cork Militia supported him. On 26 May a young farmer, Captain John Doorley, led an attack on the town and the garrison withdrew to Philipstown, now Daingean, in County Offaly. The Black Horse Regiment, stationed there, accompanied them back to Rathangan. The rebels had erected barricades and put up a determined defence. They repelled the counter-attack. Then the repelled attackers met, by chance, a party of South Cork militia with a cannon and availed of its firepower to dislodge the rebels. Thomas Spencer was a septuagenarian and a kind land agent. Many people from Rathangan and surrounding areas objected strongly to his being piked to death after the rebels' occupation. John Doorley had no part in the deed and condemned it and its perpetrators. Yet his farmhouse surrounded by the Bog of Allen was burned in reprisal. When the King's forces were back in command of Rathangan, they hanged a rebel, Edward Molloy of Mount Prospect. They singled him out because he was a former yeoman. A song in his praise also tells about the battle of Rathangan.

Born soon after the rebellion, Offaly man John Frazer became a cabinet-maker in Dublin. He edited Trades Advocate *and contributed to* The Nation *and other nationalist publications. He used the nom-de-plume Jean de Jean and published a collection of poems under that title.*

> What use in delaying for vengeance to strike?
> Has each bosom a heart, has each shoulder a pike,
> On, on to Rathangan, 'tis full to the gorge
> With the red-handed ruffians of black-hearted George.
>
> Who stabbed with their bayonets, in search of pike-heads,
> The thatch of our cabins, the ticks of our beds?
> Who lashed us like hounds till we reddened our tracks,
> From triangle to threshold with blood from our backs?
> The cruel destroyer 'tis just to destroy
> What says our young captain, brave Edward Molloy?
>
> Six feet to the forehead, with muscle and limb
> To match, had made out his commission for him,
> But a spirit in danger more recklessly brave,
> True men never followed to glory or grave.

Though heart never beat in the breast of a dove
With gentler affection for women to love.
His wisdom withal and his rough honest pride
In the people their tyrants both robbed and belied,
Confirmed to the man, what he won as a boy
An empire of friendship for Edward Molloy.

Then forward he strode to the first in the van,
Laid his arm like a bar on the breast of the man
And cried with an energy deepening his tone
As if a vexed prophet's combined with his own:

'Return I command you, there is not a chance
Of holding Rathangan, unaided by France.
Aye call me a traitor, though traitorous rogue
Is below me as much as the nails in my brogue.
But yet shall not be led our good cause to destroy
And ourselves for a tilly by Edward Molloy.

In hurry is ruin, in prudence is power,
Sure the gains of this day will be lost in an hour,
Though the bosom in hearts and the shoulder in pikes
Outnumbered the barley in grains and in spikes.

For morning or midnight, the battle may come
And Red-coat is ready at tap of a drum,
But frieze-coat is never prepared to break out
Till battle to battle may chorus the shout,
Await but that moment and earth has no joy
Like heading your onslaught for Edward Molloy.'

Alas! for his counsel, their wounds were too fresh
And the goad had been driven too deep in their flesh.
Brave fellows! they measured the pike with the gun,
And Rathangan was theirs ere the set of the sun.

'All lost' he exclaimed, as they rushed to the town,
'Our cause with the day will to darkness go down.'
But he dashed to the front, for his heart would not yield
To his own weighty reasons for quitting the field,

While friends to his country had need to employ
The wisdom or weapon of Edward Molloy.

Woe, woe to the victors, the day light had sunk.
The routed had rallied, the victors were drunk,
Disordered and scattered, but tyrants may thank
Their vanity more than the liquor they drank.

The sleepers were butchered, the stragglers were slain
While searching for weapons to grapple again.
Yet fierce were the flashings of courage that then
Had nothing to fire it but dying like men,
Till wearied and wounded, alone, to employ
A score of Black Horse, stood brave Edward Molloy.

There rose in Rathangan a lamp-post but fail
The powers of my purpose to finish my tale,
The curse of a widow condemned it to rot,
Ere the tears of her orphans were dried on the spot.

Men showed me that post and I wandered until
No marvel seems strange, yet it haunted me still,
For I swore at its foot that my land should be free
Or tyrants should find such a lamp-post for me,
Though I listened in silence and wept when a boy
For the failure and fate of brave Edward Molloy.

VENGEANCE

*On 23 May 1798 a seventeen-year-old Lieutenant William Giffard was travelling on
the mail coach from Limerick to Dublin. His father, Captain John Giffard of the Dublin
City Militia, was a well-known conservative. His uncle was a Limerick man, General
Duff (some reports say this is incorrect, that his father was a popular militia captain, a
friend of Duff's). At Kildare, rebels took Giffard from the coach and piked him. General
Duff moved a column from Limerick to Monasterevan in less than forty-eight hours of
forced marching. He wrote to his Commander-in-Chief, General Lake, saying that he
was about to surround rebel headquarters in Kildare town with seven pieces of artillery,
150 dragoons and 350 infantryman, to make an example of the rebels.*

A short time before the arrival of Duff's troops, a group of rebels assembled at Knockaulin Hill near the Curragh and surrendered their arms. Accounts of terms offered for this action vary. Some say they promised a release of prisoners, including Lord Edward Fitzgerald. Others claim that nothing was offered save a pardon to rebels and permission to return to their homes. Encouraged by the surrender, General Sir Ralph Dundas, from his quarters in Castlemartin near Kildare, wrote on 16 May to the Under -Secretary, Edward Cooke. Sir Ralph was Midland Area Commander. Part of his letter said:

The last four days have furnished me with many very affecting scenes — my house filled with the poor deluded people, giving up their arms, receiving protections, and declaring that moment to be the happiest in their lives. Be assured that the head of the Hydra is off, and the County of Kildare will, for a long time, enjoy profound peace and quiet.

Further flushed with optimism, Dundas issued a proclamation offering a free pardon to any rebel who would, on 29 May, gather at Gibbet Rath, straddling the Dublin-Cork highway near Kildare, and surrender his arms. His humane action did not have the approval of his superiors but since he had promised it, they supported his decision. Over 350 rebels accepted the terms and arrived at the Rath.

An escapee from Gibbet Rath, a man named Harrington, passed on his account of what happened to Colonel Patrick Kelly. Kelly was a United Irishman from Kilcoo, Athy. He was a delegate at a meeting with government representatives, General Dundas and General Lake, that negotiated the agreement to surrender weapons. The meeting, authorized by Lord Camden, took place at Castlemartin House, Kilcullen, on 28 May. Monasterevan yeomen involved in the massacre corroborated Harrington's statement, Kelly claimed.

Without ceremony, Duff commanded the rebels, as he called them, to throw their arms into a heap, and after this had been complied with, he ordered them to kneel at a distance from where the arms were thrown, saying loudly at the moment, to beg the King's pardon for the outrage of having rebelled. This command, so perfidious in its meaning and tendency, was complied with; which being done, a dead silence appeared to prevail among the troops. Major General Sir James Duff instantly thundered out, 'Charge, and spare no rebel!' Havoc, consternation and death now spread themselves on all sides. The horror of the scene was and is indescribable.

The cutting down and slaughtering of this unarmed multitude was but too easily accomplished; the troops consisted entirely of horsemen — the Black Horse, commanded by General Dunn, and the Foxhunters, commanded by Lord Roden, besides Capt. Bagot's yeomen cavalry, were too powerful executioners to be withstood by men who were disarmed and upon their knees. The number of victims who fell beneath these murderers' murdering sword was 325. In one street alone of Kildare town, distant from the scene of slaughter about two English miles, there were reckoned 85 widows the following morning. This carnage outweighs in enormity every act committed on either side, the army or the people, throughout the disasters of '98. The memory of it should never be effaced – it should instruct the warrior to spare, and the vanquished not to confide.

It happened now, unfortunately for the town of Kildare, that the nephew of General Sir James Duff was a passenger in the Limerick coach; and on its arrival in the town the countrymen were scattered over part of it; and their attention was directed to see who might be inside. On discovering this young man, and finding that he was (from his own words) the nephew of a General in the army, these ill-guided men dragged him out of the coach and piked him. This circumstance alone, horrible to relate, and not to be palliated by any act of suffering or punishment inflicted on the perpetrators, might be adduced by some in extenuation of the subsequent crime of the uncle. The dispassionate reader cannot, however, exculpate such a monster (independently of his treachery and Punic faith) for a general butchery and carnage. It was not with him, as a heathen writer advised, 'Parcere subjectis et debellare superbos.' To spare the contrite, and subdue the haughty. The people on the Rath of the Curragh of Kildare should not have been collectively immolated to appease the manes of an individual.

A few of the victims, it was said about five, escaped by running through the ranks as they were charging. A few lay as if dead, and being woefully hacked and mangled, were passed over as some of the heap of slaughtered men. One athletic young fellow ran about a mile and half, when he was pursued by eight yeomen of Bagot's corps; he gained a fallow field just adjoining the Curragh, and having so far escaped his pursuers, he stooped and picked up two stones, which he flung with such vigour against two of them, that he disabled both, and rendered them unable to discharge their pistols. Two more came on, and by a further effort he disabled a third also, with stones which he scrambled up. It was said that two more fired at him without effect, but it was acknowledged by them that he parried the firing with so much alertness as to elude any aim they could take. The last of the yeomen assailants, who is still living in Monasterevan and whom they call Ned Cooper, received a blow of a stone from this intrepid Kildare man, in the hip, and by its effects limps and walks lame to this day. At length a dragoon, being commanded by a sanguinary officer to cut him down, the poor countryman, after all his fatigue and fighting, received a sabre wound on the neck, as he scrambled over a ditch, and fell as dead.

THE BATTLE OF OVIDSTOWN
Anon.

Ovidstown is close to Kilcock, County Kildare. When the rebels captured Maynooth on 14 June 1798, they regrouped behind their defences in the north Kildare areas of Hortland, Newtown and Ovidstown. Some reports suggest that rebels from Meath and

Wexford joined them. The intention was to advance on Dublin while the English were dealing with the troubles in Wexford. Women in the neighbourhood were busy preparing breakfast for up to 5000 rebels under William Aylmer, Hugh Ware and George Luby, when a regiment of Scottish Fencibles surprised them. On 18 June Aylmer called on the main body of his men to fall back on Ovidstown Hill while pikemen carried out a frontal assault on the enemy artillery lines.

Contrary to his orders, the pikemen attempted to encircle their objective but were cut down at a place ever since called 'The Murdering Ditch.' Names of local leaders appear in these verses. Ballinafagh and Donadea are close to Prosperous. Barretstown is near Ballymore-Eustace, and there is a Donore in both counties Kildare and Meath.

> Oh Mary, get my coat of green,
> It's near the break of day,
> On a retreat my name shall be,
> It's not at home I'll stay,
> The ancient race unto disgrace
> Shall ne'er be brought by me,
> Oh, I'm away to Ovidstown to fight for liberty.
>
> With pike so keen, and sash of green,
> That emblem dear to me;
> Oh, I'm away to Ovidstown to fight for liberty.
> Captain Farrell, he has gone,
> He was in Donadea;
> The moon is up and Hanlon's troops
> From home are gone away.
> Before we dull to-morrow's sun
> A glorious sight you'll see,
> On all Dara's plains, we'll break our chains
> And set old Ireland free.
>
> There is Captain Burke from Barrettstown,
> He's gone with his brave band
> Of full three-hundred green clad youths
> He has at his command,
> And Cox's Corps has left Donore;
> I fear that late I'll be,
> To reach the ground where the trumpet sounds
> To set old Ireland free.

Oh Mary, get my coat of green,
It's near our parting time,
On the old hill of Ballinafagh
We will fall into line;
Oh! there's the shout, the boys are out,
Hurrah! ghrádh gheal mo chroídhe,
With that brave band I'll join my hand
And set old Ireland free.

RESILIENCE

A letter, dated 6 June 1798, from an Oliver Barker, Clonard, County Meath, to John Lees, the Secretary of the Irish Post Office, tells of their distress. Unedited, it reads:

Sir

This morn at ½ after two o clock, we attacked a party of the rebels, in a place called Dreead in the County Kildare, with a party of the Limerick militia, the Canal infantry, Balina and Clonard cavalry. They were soon put to flight, and took to a bog, where many of them fell by the infantry. It is incredible, the way they lived. Horses, cows, sheep &c were found after them, with a number of offensive weapons. They stood to receive but one fire from the infantry when they fled in every direction in the bog which prevented the cavalry being of any assistance. They lay under the ditches like pigs, without a tent or any covering. The soldiers from Killcock [*sic*] attacked the rebels at Timahoe (which lay the other side of the bog) at the same time we did. I believe they fled in like manner as with us. I cant tell the number kill'd, but the King's troops burn'd many houses which were deserted by the owners.

    I am Sir
    Your Humble Servt
    Oliver Barker

Of Offaly

Government forces burned the town of Clonbullogue, County Offaly, during the rebellion. Informers helped them in capturing rebels after the battle of Rathangan, executing them and planting their heads upon a bridge near Clonsast. Some still call it the Rebel Bridge.

THE BOYS OF CROGHAN
Anon.

*This Offaly poem tells of four who were transported when a man named Counihan
informed on them. No such men reached Australia alive.*

You loyal-hearted Irishmen I hope you will draw near
And likewise pay attention to these few lines you hear.
It's concerning four young heroes as you all may understand,
For fourteen long years transported far from their native land.

My curse on you, black Counihan, and the same on you a grudge.
We went across the country till we came to Rochfordbridge
And as we were going across that way we met this perjured man
And fourteen years transported was far from our native land.

He went up to the Carrick and there our names gave in
And swore we were the four young heroes broke into his cursed den.
The two Egans, Moore and Hannan, who never were afeared.
It's to a place called Croghan, boys that there were decent reared.

My name is Barty Egan and the same I'll ne'er deny,
It is of no disgrace, me boys, that I must pass you by.
I never was a party man but that you all know well
But it's to the boys of Croghan now I'll bid a long farewell.

Farewell to Derryarken, its lofty shades and trees,
Where in the summer season the honey feeds the bees,
Farewell along I bid adieu, no more on it I'll gaze;
But on thou lofty hill of Croghan, where I spent my youthful days.

Farewell unto my brothers, and all my sisters there.
And all my friends and neighbours who are sorry now for me,
Farewell to tender mother whom I now shall see no more;
I am for fourteen long years transported far from our native shore.

Now to conclude, to make an end. I have no more to say;
But beware of Páidin Counihan, keep far out of his way;
For if you don't you're sure to rue, as you may understand;
For afeared like us he'd have you sent far from your native land.

Of Meath

In mid-May a large force of County Meath rebels controlled the main northern artery to the capital. Their camp was on the Hill of Tara, former seat of the High Kings of Ireland and an excellent defensive position. Their strength was enhanced when they captured arms, equipment and prisoners from a Scotch Fencible Regiment, the Reay Highlanders, and forced its NCOs to train selected rebels in the newly acquired weaponry. General Craig led a force out of Dublin to dislodge the rebels. Despite having artillery, he withdrew hurriedly. Less inept was Captain Blanche, the leader of the Scotch regiment who had avoided capture. He rallied the local yeomanry and, on May 26th, attacked the Hill of Tara.

After softening up the rebel position with cannon, Blanche led a daring charge. Yeoman cavalry support were to have made an encircling movement but they deserted. Despite this, Blanche won an outstanding victory and killed scores of rebels. His achievement re-opened communications between Dublin and the north and finished the rising in Meath.

MICHAEL BOYLAN

Anon.

Michael Boylan is alleged to have fought at Tara. The ballad dwells on the old story of the informer and goes as far as naming him.

Come all you worthy members, your attention now I pray,
It's well you may remember those words I'm going to say,
I'm here in close confinement, no hopes of liberty,
Condemned to die for treason against His Majesty.

In Gullen I was taken, being on the 3rd of June,
To Drogheda a guard conveyed me, where I received my doom,
I was in expectation the speaker would set me free,
Till I received my sentence by Dan Kelly's perjury.

The day my trial came on my verdict first came clear,
Altho' my prosecutors to me they proved severe,
Tom Hanvy acted as a foe, altho' he favoured me that day,
Till in came Daniel Kelly, and swore my life away.

He swore I had ten thousand men all at my own command,
To assist the French invaders as soon as they would land,
He swore I was a collector to support the union's cause,
And the jury cried out, Boylan you must die by martial laws.

When I heard the dismal news it's in my jail I lay,
I scarcely got one moment but one hour to pray,
It's with a feeble trembling heart my book I took in hand,
The tears came trickling from my eyes, quite motionless I did stand.

I met my aged father as from the jail I come,
Crying 'Heaven must I part with you my dear and loving son',
I kindly did salute him but not one word could I say,
I bowed my tender body and then was hurled away.

It's to the town-hall I was brought, the place I was to die,
I being not the least afraid, till the fatal tree I spied,
My sight began to fail me, my book I scarce could read,
To think in my bloom of being cut down, my tender heart to bleed.

Farewell my honoured father, since parted we must be,
Likewise my loving mother, your face I ne'er will see,
Farewell my tender brother, and sisters all adieu,
In the 25th year of my age I take my leave of you.

I own I was united bold and that I ne'er deny,
And often times I [roved] in spite of the yeomanry,
If I would an informer prove I'd gain my liberty,
But before I'd an informer prove I'd die on the gallows tree.

This is my last declaration, I conclude in grief and woe,
It was Dan Kelly's perjury that proved my overthrow,
In the 25th year of my age I die with a heart most free,
Michael Boylan is my name, and all good Christians pray for me.

Of Wicklow

BALTINGLASS PARISH INFORMATION ON MAP

The Rev. Charles Robinson of Knockrigg, Baltinglass, obviously a concerned loyalist, sent a rough map to the government on 7 May 1798. It outlined robberies of arms, maiming of animals and theft of liquor and sheep. It also showed locations of unauthorized tree-felling, no doubt assuming it to be for pike-handle manufacture. In some cases, the map contained illustrations. One, for example, outlined iron gates that were stolen from the High Sheriff, Henry Harrington at Grange Con. An unsigned note accompanied the map. Uncorrected, it reads:

The inclosed paper is a rough scetch of all the townlands in the parish of Baltinglass, and as the County Wicklow upon the late general return of men, arms & subscriptions, made about 2 months since, to furnish Mr. Arthur O'Conner with authoritative credentials, excelled in these points any other county in Ireland in proportion to its extent; and as I have reasons to think the parish of Baltinglass, exceeded any other parish in that county in its number of United men, arms &c it may probably prove a satisfaction by and by to you, in case you should think proper to send any army into that quarter to compel the surrender of arms, to have a draft immediately taken of its extent and a few of the principal inhabitants; particularly such as have already suffered or such as have contributed to this horrible conspiracy & impending rebellion.

YR HUMBLE SARVNT

W. Kildal from Arklow wrote to John Lees, secretary of the Irish Post Office, outlining action against the rebels. He did not know that the rebels were even then rising in Kildare and Meath.

67

Arklow, May the 24th 1798

Dr Sir,

Since my last we are taken men evry day and get infermensions and more piks 2 hundred ball cartridges but not the gons yet but I hope we will soon the gords on the houses continu and live well both men & horshes a mr pery was taken yesterday a united ofeser and is in gorey as the King of united men is taken lord Eeward I trust in God we will soon pull down the Crapys. We put on piched capes on some of them there is a great many of the vilins run a way I remain sir yr most obant

    humble sarvnt

    W. Kildal

DUNLAVIN GREEN

Anon.

On the day Kildal wrote his letter, 24 May, at Dunlavin, County Wicklow, the Wicklow Militia, killed forty prisoners, and at Carnew a week later, a further fifty. Figures vary in some accounts. Yeomen suspected of being sympathetic to the United Irishmen were among the victims. There was never any official confirmation of the atrocities.

In the year of seventeen ninety-eight,
A sorrowful tale the truth unto you I'll relate
Of thirty-six heroes, to the world they were left to be seen,
By false information they were shot on Dunlavin Green.

Bad luck to you, Saunders, their lives you sold away.
You said a parade would be held on that very day.
The drums they did rattle and the fifes they did sweetly play.
Surrounded we were and quietly marched away.

Quite easy they led us as prisoners through the town
To be shot on the plain we then were forced to kneel down.
Such grief and such sorrow in one place it was ne'er before seen
As when the blood ran in streams down the dikes of Dunlavin Green.

There is young Andy Ryan has plenty of cause to complain,
Likewise the two Duffys who were shot down on the plain,
And young Mattie Farrell whose mother distracted will run
For the loss of her own darling boy, her eldest son.

Bad luck to you Saunders, bad luck may you never shun,
That the widow's curse might melt you like snow in the sun.

The cries of those orphans whose murmurs you shall never screen,
For the loss of their own poor fathers who died on the Green.

Some of our boys to the hills they have run away.
More of them have been shot and some have run off to sea.
Michael Dwyer of the mountain has plenty of cause for the spleen
For the loss of his own dear comrades who died on the Green.

WICKLOW LORE

Before her death on 30 April 1935, Mrs O'Toole from Ballinglen, County Wicklow, passed on many stories about 1798. This was recorded by Pádraig Ó Tuathail in July 1934 and published by the Folklore of Ireland Society in Béaloideas IV *(1934), pp. 393-5. Her date for the burning of Boolavogue church is incorrect. (See Chronology, 26-7 May 1798.)*

The swearing in of my grandfather Larry Byrne took place at the wedding of a friend before the rebellion of '98 broke out. Michael Dwyer swore him in, and told him to unite all the boys that might think well of it. He started in at Blackrock and Aughavanagh, Glenmalure and the Seven Churches, and united all the boys that were in '98 from that quarter; and Michael Dwyer on the other hand through Imaal his native place and all round, and again '98 broke out they had every man and boy in the Wicklow Mountains that was worth his salt ready for the fight.

The fourteenth night of May the rebellion broke out in the lower part of Wexford by the chapel in Boolavogue being set on fire. The priest was in bed, and he dreamed the chapel was on fire, and he jumped up, and it was really on fire, past been quenched or put out. Then he got up and dressed himself, and he saddled his horse. He started up through Wexford, and he gathered up three farming men on horse-back, and they came on through the whole County Wexford and gathered up all the help that would join them until they came to Carnew, and they was in Carnew by breakfast time in the morning, and they started from that on through the mountains to Aughavanagh and they was in Aughavanagh by evening time. When they came to Aughavanagh the news spread and the boys came in their dozens and joined them in a large army at Aughavanagh.

Then later on there did a regiment of British soldiers land called the Durham Fencibles, and they was encamped on the lands of Kiladuff joining Ballymanus, and they had a general over them, a General Skerrett, one of the best men that ever landed in Ireland, a noble gentleman, and done the most good for the opposite people – that is the Irish.

And then there did another regiment come over called the Hessians and they were volunteers from England, farmers' sons, big soft fellows well-kept, well dressed and had fine horses, a whole regiment of them; and they went up and down through the country and shot some parties, and said they would go up to Aughavanagh to clean up the rebels that were annoying the Crown. They went on until they came to a level plain about 40 or 50 acres, but it was rocks and bogs a good deal of it, so they eyed out this place and allowed they'd go up there and hunt out the rebels and shoot them down. So Dwyer and the boys were waiting for them – they had got word of them coming on to them, and they were waiting for them; and Dwyer was the cleverest man and there was never a duck hardier on the pond than he. He planted his men at each side of this plain in hiding and told some to go out in front out of gun shot and to tempt the soldiers on; when he'd give the signal they could fire; and he had a sea whistle that could be heard eleven miles away. The soldiers dashed into what seemed to be a level place I told you about, but it was rocks and bogs and sloughs, and the horses stumbled and fell, and they got them up again, and they started on foot, but they wasn't as well up as the mountain fellows. So Dwyer gave the signal for the side parties to pour in on them and to fire on them, and they did so, and they shot them to a man. They went up to Aughavanagh, and they was set upon by the boys at Aughavanagh, the United Irishmen – the 'rebels' as they called them – they set upon them and they was cleaned up to a man – there wasn't as much as one of 'em left to tell the tale. The horses went round the roads and the bogs and the hills, with the bridle reins dragging beside them and the saddles on their backs, but no rider. The people let the horses wander over the hills and never as much as took the reins or saddles off of them, but a big snow the year after killed them all.

So after two or three days the inhabitants became very uneasy to see the dead bodies of the big fat Englishmen lying there and no one to bury them, and they said to each other: 'What are we going to do?' They wouldn't lay hands on them nor they wouldn't bury them. One of them came down to the corps to Kiladuff, and he made it known to the general – General Skerret to see if he would send up his men to bury his brother Englishmen that had been lying on the plains shot for so many days; they would give them some assistance. So they dug a big trench, and they dragged the dead bodies into it with the horses, and covered them up, and then they expected that they would annoy them by night, but they never did. They never saw one of them.

🐜 🐜 🐜

Of Execution

BILLY BYRNE OF BALLYMANUS
Anon.

'Throw a stone in Wicklow and it will hit a Byrne.' So a local saying goes, and the name crops up frequently in the '98 rebellion story. This is a typical ballad, with place-names and family names abounding.

It was in the year of ninety-nine, we had reason to complain
For we lost our brave commander, Billy Byrne was his name.
In Dublin he was taken, and brought to Wicklow jail,
And to our consternation for him they'd take no bail.

And when they had him taken, those traitors they came in,
There was Dixon, Doyle and Davis and likewise Bid Doolin;
They thought it little scruple his precious blood to spill,
Who never robbed nor murdered nor to any man did ill.

And when he was a prisoner they loud against him swore,
That he a captain's title upon Mount Pleasant bore;
Before the King's grand army his men he did review,
And with one piece of cannon he marched on to Carrigrue.

It would melt your heart with pity how these traitors did explain,
How Byrne worked the cannon on Arklow's bloody plain;
They swore he led the pikemen on with hearty right good will,
And on his retreat to Gorey three loyal men did kill.

One of these persecutors, I often heard him tell,
How at his father's table he was always treated well;
And in his brother's kitchen where many did them see,
So the Byrnes were well rewarded for their civility.

They swore he had a thousand men all under his command,
All ready for to join the French as soon as they would land;
They swore he was committed to support the United cause,
The judge he cried out 'Guilty' to be hanged by England's laws.

My curse light on you, Dixon, I ne'er will curse your soul,
Upon the stand at Wicklow you swore without control,
The bearing of false witness you thought it little sin
To deprive the County Wicklow of the flower of its men.

Where are you, Matthew Davis, or why don't you come on,
To prosecute the prisoner who now lies in Rathdrum?
The devil has him fast in chains repenting of his sin,
In lakes of fire and brimstone and sulphur to the chin.

When the devil saw him coming he sang a pleasant song,
Saying 'Welcome, Matthew Davis, what kept you out so long?
Where is that traitor Dixon, to the Crown so loyal and true,
For him I've a warm corner and for cursed Bid Doolin too.'

God rest you, Billy Byrne, may your name for ever shine
Through Wicklow, Wexford and Kildare and all along the line;
May the Lord have mercy on his soul and all such men as he,
Who stood upright for Ireland's right and fought for Liberty.

WALKING GALLOWS

*One character from 1798 deserves special treatment, if only for the dread his name
instilled at the time. There is more oral evidence than documentation on this despised
militiaman, who was greatly feared in Wicklow, Longford and elsewhere before and
during the rebellion. Indeed his conduct and others like him helped to kindle the
flames of that revolution.*

I wrote an essay on Walking Gallows *in* Irish Rogues, Rascals and Scoundrels *(1992), using oral and secondary sources. A consensed version follows.*

> This wretch of whom we have but an imperfect account, was born in Upper
> Newcastle, County Wicklow *c.*1766, bred an apothecary in Dublin ... Beneath
> [his] aspiring genius ... he united the character of a gentleman with those of judge
> and executioner ... (Watty Cox's *The Irish Magazine, or Monthly Asylum for Neglected
> Biography*, January 1810)

Edward Hepenstal, a lieutenant in the 88th Regiment and County Wicklow Militia, is
best remembered by his nickname, Walking Gallows. He was so called because he was
big and strong and often strangled victims in an unusual manner.

The normal method of hanging then was the traditional gallows – a rope slung
from a tree, a bridge, a triangle or a permanent gallows. The process was drawn out,
even to the extent that the victim was given copious drinks of water to refresh him
between sequences. Hepenstal, however, simply placed a noose around rebels' necks
and dragged them along the road after him while they screamed in pain. The hadsome
giant had two medium-sized assistants who strolled along at either side of him. They
would catch young rebels and place the rope around their necks, ready for their master's work. The judge, historian, and Member of Parliament, Sir Jonah Barrington, in
his *Personal Sketches of His Own Times* (1832), claimed to know Hepenstal well. He put
his height at six feet:

> He could lift a ton, but could not leap a rivulet; he looked mild, and his address
> was civil – neither assuming nor at all ferocious ... from his countenance [I]

should never have suspected him of cruelty; but so cold-blooded and so eccentric an executioner of the human race I believe never yet existed, save among the American Indians.

His inducement to the strange barbarity he practised I can scarcely conceive; unless it proceeded from that natural taint of cruelty which so often distinguishes man above all other animals when his power becomes uncontrolled. The propensity was probably strengthened in him from the indemnities of martial law, and by those visions of promotion whereby violent partizans are perpetually urged, and so frequently disappointed.

Leading up to and during the 1798 rebellion, Hepenstal's judgment of rebels was arbitrary. If he disliked their appearance, he took action. Barrington ashamedly admits that this behaviour was the subject of jocularity among legal people:

> What in other times he himself would have died for, as a murderer, was laughed at as the manifestation of loyalty: never yet was martial law so abused, or its enormities so hushed up. Being a military officer, the lieutenant conceived he had a right to do just what he thought proper, and to make the most of his time while martial law was flourishing.

Walking Gallows was not without style. If there was not a rope handy, he used a drum rope or his own silk cravat, which he claimed was softer on the victim's neck. To Kerry House, St Stephen's Green, he appears to have been called as extern hangman once. Perhaps he felt that a job in the city demanded a little extra in the way of novelty so he introduced the 'trotting execution'. He wound his cravat into a rope, expertly slid it over a rebel's neck, and secured it by a double-knot. Hepenstal drew the cravat over his own shoulder while his assistant lifted the victim's heels. With a mighty chuck, the hangman drew the unfortunate's face over his shoulder, cheek-by-jowl with his own, then trotted around the cobbled yard imitating a bucking farm-horse, 'the rebel choking and gulping meanwhile, until he had no further solicitude about sublunary affairs'. A final tug in case the neck was not already broken, and the corpse of another rebel was tossed on the ground for Hepenstal's aide to search for valuables.

Walking Gallows operated in other areas besides Wicklow and Dublin. His regiment was stationed in Strabane for a period and he may have been despatched southward from there. The unit caused more than a stir when they advertised in the *Strabane Journal* of 20 April 1795:

> Wanted for the service of the officers who compose the mess of His Majesty's Wicklow Regiment of Militia, twelve beautiful girls who have not inhabited the town of Strabane since the 5th of April … As wages is by no means the object, it is expected that none will apply who do not produce a certificate signed by eight respectable matrons, of their having their virtue pure and unsullied. No girl will answer above the age of 18, or under that of 14. Application to be made to the regimental matron, Mrs Catherine Smyth, Bowling Green, Strabane. N.B. Growing girls of the age of 13 if approved and highly recommended may possibly be taken.

Hepenstal was based in Edenderry, Co. Offaly, with the Wicklow Militia, and operated in Longford and Westmeath in the summer of 1797. He seemed to carry out his evil practice en route from Wicklow because there is evidence of at least one hanging by him in County Kildare, at Carbury. He encountered a suspicious-looking man there and without any evidence, decided he had to be a rebel plotting the death of the king and so disposed of him.

> In ninety-eight, from Ballinree
> Brave Paddy Farrell rode
> To bear his pike, Ireland to free
> Along the Granard road.
> His mare returned that lonely night;
> Alone her master fell
> Yet dying, left a name still bright
> In Ardagh of St Mel. (*Anon.*)

Pat Farrell of Ballinree was regarded as the biggest man in Longford. After the battle of Ballinamuck Farrell retreated to Granard, whose topography offered excellent defensive features. Hepenstal, however, controlled Granard at the time and locals recorded that he 'jerked more men into eternity' than had met their death by violence in four-score years following. In his *Historical Notes of County Longford* (1886), James P. Farrell states:

> His method of hanging was novel in the extreme. Just let him catch a rebel – the rope was adjusted and slung across his shoulder, a pull and a sudden jerk, and the 'rebel's' days on earth were ended. People will wonder that such a wretch would be allowed to walk on green grass in the nineteenth century.

General Lake was expected in Granard after his successes at Ballinamuck and nearby Ballinalee, while Hepenstal was known to have gone to Cavan to summon troops. Farrell was given the task of defending the Finea entrance to Granard, where Hepenstal would arrive. Battle had been joined when the two giants came face to face. 'Farrell, with one ponderous blow of his broken sword-hilt, put Hepenstal hors de combat, and his ragged mob of yeomen soon after took to flight.' About to pursue, Farrell was halted by news conveyed by a messenger. Lake was indeed leading a large contingent of the enemy and their arrival was imminent. With two daring colleagues, O'Keefe and Denison, Farrell organized the defence of Granard once more. Lake arrived and a vicious battle ensued.

Meanwhile, Hepenstal recovered and brought his Cavan troops back to the fight. Farrell's men were therefore being attacked on two fronts. Knowing the fate meted out to the rebels at Ballinamuck, Farrell realized there was no point in continuing the fight. He pivoted his men to the right and escaped down a narrow lane while Lake's and Hepenstal's men, still advancing, clashed and began fighting each other instead of the Longford-men. Farrell, mounted on a white mare, lost Denison and his men. They were surrounded by Hepenstal and his Finea militia. Farrell discovered this and dashed to Denison's assistance. Hepenstal noticed, took aim and fired. Farrell fell and the fight was over.

In recognition of splendid services rendered to the Crown and to the Constitution, Westmeath's Grand Jury voted a service of plate to the officers of the Wicklow Militia at their midsummer assizes of 1797. In protest, a correspondent to *The Press*, a Dublin newspaper published only during 1797 and 1798, cited the conduct of Edward Hepenstal and berated the Grand Jury for using the money of ratepayers who were powerless to object to the presentation. In north Westmeath at the time a gang of bandits robbed and plundered where and when they could. On a stormy night in June they got drunk on poteen near Killare while awaiting the return of one of their men who was missing. They were worried, fearing he might inform the Athlone yeomanry of their intent, which was the robbing of a coach. They went ahead with the hold-up and their doubts were proved genuine – its passengers, armed yeomen, fired on them. Three of the robbers were killed and the remainder were taken prisoner and brought to Mullingar. Two days later, the ringleader of the gang was brought to Moy-vore and handed over to Lieutenant Hepenstal.

At a place then called Gardenstown, near Moyvore, Edward Carroll, a seventy-year-old blacksmith, lived with his three sons. All four were United Irishmen and they forged pike-heads for the rebels. Information on their activities was passed on and Hepenstal was led to local cemeteries and bogs where the pikes were hidden. Then he arrived at the forge along with the informer and some militiamen. Walking Gallows explained all he knew but promised the old man and his sons protection if they handed over their merchandise quietly. Old Carroll complied but Hepenstal immediately killed him with a sabre. The sons were butchered too and the Carroll household, outoffices and haggard were set ablaze. The wife and child of one of the young Carrolls was in the kitchen at the time, but one of the raiders rescued her. Hepenstal reluctantly let her go, calling her a bitch and warning her that if she ever returned or told of what happened, she too would be killed. Hepenstal threw the murdered bodies on a cart and proceeded to Moyvore village. There he arrested three other men, tied them to the shafts of the cart and travelled three miles to Ballymore.

A certain Mrs McCormick offered James Woods, author of *The Annals of Westmeath* (1907), a grotesque picture of the procession leaving a trail of blood as the dead men's entrails dropped down from the cart and became entangled and wound around its axle and wheel-spokes. Beside the militia guarding the group, a drummer beat and a fifer played 'Croppies Lie Down'. Female relatives of the captured men wailed and screamed and those at the end of the group cursed Walking Gallows aloud. On reaching Ballymore, Hepenstal called on various landlords inviting them to witness some 'pigeon-shooting'. Some accepted but Lord Oxmantown questioned Hepenstal's right to execute the men without a proper trial. With disdain, he told Oxmantown that he was in charge. The arrested men, too, pleaded being the sole support of widowed mothers, but they were manacled and forced to kneel down on the village green. Then Hepenstal ordered the militiamen to shoot.

Terrorized countryfolk would not assist the bereaved in wake and burial prepara-
tion; one neighbour offered a bed to carry the bodies to be buried in Moranstown.
Forty houses in Moyvore were burned in the same incident and before leaving the district, Walking Gallows visited Ballymore fair. A farmer was holding out his hand to have
it slapped in the age-old way of sealing a bargain for stock. Hepenstal almost severed
the arm from the shoulder. A young mason begged for mercy on his knees; Hepenstal
struck him down and left him dying. A priest went to give the last rites and three militiamen 'made a riddle of his body'. Seventeen others were 'cut, maimed and abused
[so] that many of them [were] rendered miserable objects for the remainder of their
lives'.

A great folk-history concerning Walking Gallows grew. His relatives disowned him.
Historians argued the improbability of his deserving such notoriety. In particular, they
doubted his hanging methods. On 8 August 1797, however, Hepenstal himself vouched
for his *modus operandi*. At the trial of a William Kennedy, at Navan, the lieutenant told
how he had tied a rope around the neck of the accused and threw him across his shoulder in order to extract information. Kennedy refused to talk and for once Walking
Gallows submitted him for proper trial – presumably in the hope of eliciting more
information. In the event, Kennedy still refused to inform and was executed. At another trial in Athy, Hepenstal admitted to pricking a prisoner with a bayonet as well as
using his familiar rope treatment.

When Lieutenant Edward Hepenstal died, his brother received a handsome pension from the government. Wicklow folklore alleges that Walking Gallows was shot in
Aughavanagh and placed at the side of the road with a nettle planted in some mud
that had been forced into his mouth. His corpse was left to decompose and receive
the ridicule of passers-by, they say. Soldiers came and attempted to bury Walking
Gallows on the land of a farmer named O'Toole, but he refused permission. Others
followed his example. Eventually he was buried opposite a public house at Raheen.
Markers were placed at the head and foot of the grave to show the size of the executioner and hundreds visited the grave to express derision.

Watty Cox's *The Irish Magazine* (January 1810) disagrees and says Hepenstal died in
his bed at his brother's house in St Andrew's Street in 1804. He had developed 'the
most shocking distemper [and] his body was literally devoured by vermin', the account
said. Francis Higgins, the Sham Squire, recorded in his journal of 18 September 1800:

> Died on Thursday night, of a dropsical complaint, Lieutenant Edward Hepenstal,
> of the 68th Regiment [*sic*], sometime back an officer in the Wicklow militia – a
> gentleman whose intrepidity and spirit during the Rebellion rendered much gener-
> al good, and himself highly obnoxious to traitors.

Higgins followed with a tribute to 'the qualities which endeared Mr Hepenstal to
his family and friends' and gave St Andrew's churchyard as Hepenstal's burial place and
1804 as his year of death. Sir Jonah Barrington commented wryly:

Providence, however, which is said to do 'every thing for the best,' (though some persons who are half starving, and others who think themselves very unfortunate, will not allow it so much credit) determined that Lieutenant H——'s loyalty and merits should meet their full reward in another sphere – where, being quite out of reach of all his enemies, he might enjoy his destiny without envy or interruption. It therefore, very soon after the rebellion had terminated, took the lieutenant into its own especial keeping; and despatched a raging fever to bring him off to the other world, which commission the said fever duly executed after twenty-one day's combustion; – and no doubt his ghost is treated according to its deserts; but nobody having since returned from those regions to inform us what has actually become of the lieutenant, it is still a dead secret, and I fancy very few persons in Ireland have any wish for the opportunity of satisfying their curiosity. People however give a shrewd guess, that it is possible he may be employed somewhere else in the very same way wherein he entertained himself in Ireland; and that after being duly furnished with a tail, horns, and cloven foot, no spirit could do infernal business better than the lieutenant.

A Dr Barrett once suggested that the gravestone of Walking Gallows should bear the epitaph:

> Here lie the bones of Hepenstal
> Judge, jury, gallows, rope and all.

The infamous gentleman's widow married a celebrated Dr Patrick Duignan. Sixty years after his death, Hepenstal's nearest living relative wrote to *The Irish Times* debunking all that had been written about Walking Gallows as fable. Because Sir Jonah Barrington and others had used a mere initial 'Lieutenant H——', it was argued, there was no evidence of its referring Edward Hepenstal. Furthermore, wrote the correspondent,

> The acts … were not committed by Lieut H., whose character was in the first instance traduced for party purposes, and blackened by the exaggeration and additions of the dupes to whom the story was told. He was as wholly incapable of such conduct as his appearance and manners seemed to indicate, and the instances given of his cruelty are as little founded in fact as the popular story (accounting for the time and place of his burial being not generally known) that he had been carried off by a familiar which had attended him during life in the shape of a 'black cow.

William J. Fitzpatrick's account in *The Sham Squire and the Informers of '98* (1866) was disputed so that author replied to The Irish Times reiterating his views and quoting other reliable sources in which Hepenstal's full name had been used. 'The face is not always an index to the mind', he said, in answer to the claim that Hepenstal had benign features, and continued:

Before the sweeping denial can be accepted that Hepenstal's exploits gave him, by general consent, the nickname of 'walking gallows,' it is necessary, not only to erase historic record, but to attempt to silence the irrepressible voice of song. A ballad of the day, professing to come from some ultra-loyalist, concludes:

> Now what evil can befall us,
> Since we have got our walking gallows.

Of Wexford

The rebellion in Wexford was in two phases. After swift growth in the strength of the United Irishmen, and initial setbacks at the outbreak of hostilities, the last days of May and early June saw great advances by the rebels. Late June into July they endured a series of crises. Outrages occurred during the campaign. There were examples of naked sectarian atrocities committed by rebels and loyalists. Accounts of deeds of brave men have survived, while dastardly acts have conveniently been forgotten.

BEFORE THE REBELLION

Chevalier De Latocnaye (Jacques Louis de Bougrenet), born in Brittany in 1767, was an officer in the Royal army, forced to flee after the Revolution in 1792. His Promen-ade d'un Français en l'Irlande *appeared in 1797 and in translation a year later.*

From here I proceeded to Wexford, and without wishing it harm, I may say that it is one of the ugliest and dirtiest towns in the whole of Ireland. The excessive exercise in which I had indulged, and to which I had not been accustomed for a long time, com-pelled me to remain here eight days with a fever; and to make matters worse, the greater number of the letters I had for this town were those of my dead friend, Mr Burton Conyngham. However, I received certain attentions. Wexford is situated on a large bay, which at low tide is almost entirely dry. Six or seven thousand acres of ground could here be reclaimed and there would be an additional advantage of making out of the deepened river an important port. At Wexford I found the longest bridge I had ever seen joining two portions of land. I spent seven minutes walking from one end to the other, and from that I assumed that it is at least one-third of an Irish mile in length. This is a favourite walk with the belles of the neighbourhood. There are chairs on which folk may rest on Sundays, and there is a band which attracts a great many people and makes the promenade agreeable. Fortunes in this neighbourhood appear to be more equally divided than elsewhere; there are not to be found any of those monstrous whales of wealth who devour, for their needs, the produce of a province. On the other hand, there are many people in comfortable circumstances, and none excessively rich. The greater part of the proprietors are descendants of Cromwell's soldiers, but as these were numerous in this part of the country, it was necessary to make their lots smaller in order to give something to everybody.

It was in this neighbourhood that Strongbow disembarked some of his troops to help the King of Leinster, MacDermot, who had been dethroned by his countrymen. We know what was the pretext for the invasion by Henry II, King of England, a little later, and how he compelled the different kings and princes of the island to render homage. Nevertheless, the English had to remain within strictly limited territory for more than three hundred years, and did not make themselves masters of the whole island until the time of Queen Elizabeth. The inhabitants of the Barony of Forth, near Wexford, are the descendants of the first followers of Strongbow. They have never mixed with the Irish, and still speak a singular language, which is more akin to Flemish than to modern English. They are like the Flemish also in manner, and marry among themselves. Their houses are cleaner and more comfortable than those of the other inhabitants, and they are also so much more clean in person that they appear quite as a different race.

In the month of July 1793 the White Boys experienced here a complete defeat, and since that time they have not shown themselves. As a great deal has been said and written about them, I believe it will be of interest if I give a few details about their existence. In every country of the world the peasant pays tithe with reluctance; everywhere it is regarded as an onerous impost, prejudicial to the spread of cultivation, for the labourer is obliged to pay on the product of his industry. In Ireland it seems to me a more vexatious tax than elsewhere, for the great mass of the people being Catholic, it seems to them hard that they should be obliged to maintain a minister who is often the only Protestant in the parish, and who exacts his dues with rigour. Beyond the ordinary tithe he has a right, over nearly the whole of Ireland, to one-tenth of the milk of a cow, one-tenth of the eggs, and one-tenth of the vegetables of the gardens. One can easily understand that these conditions may be very severe when the minister exacts his dues in kind, and especially when it is considered that these poor miserable folk have, as well, to supply a subsistence for their own priests. They have often made complaints and claims in connection with this subject, and to these it was hardly possible to give attention without overturning the whole of the laws of the Establishment, as it is called; that is to say, the Established religion. From complaints and claims the peasants came to threats, and from threats to the execution of the things threatened. They assembled at night in great numbers in certain parts of Ireland, and in order that they might recognize each other safely, they wore their shirts outside their clothes, from whence came of name of White Boys. In this garb they overran the country, breaking the doors and gates of ministers' houses, and if they could catch the cattle they mutilated them by cutting off their tails and ears. All they time they did no other violent act, and a traveller might have gone through the country with perfect security. For different offences of the kind indicated the magistrates of Wexford arrested a score or so of the culprits, and immured them in the town prison. Their comrades demanded their liberation, and were not able to obtain it. They threatened then to come and free them by force, and advanced on the town to the number of two or three thousand. There were at the time no troops in Wexford; all that could be gathered up did not number more than one hundred or one hundred and fifty soldiers, who marched to meet the country folk.

On their way to the town the White Boys arrested an officer who happened to be on the road, and sent a messenger to the Major that this officer would answer with his head for the surety of their comrades in jail. This caused much uneasiness in Wexford, where it was feared that they would carry their threat to execution. The Major in charge imprudently advanced before his soldiers to speak with the White Boys, and after some lively discussions, he received a blow from a scythe which laid him dead. Immediately on seeing this the soldiers fired, and in two or three minutes the whole force of the White Boys was broken up and put to flight, leaving behind them several hundreds dead. A few of the unfortunates who were wounded, fearing the punishment which would follow if they should be taken, dragged themselves as well as they could into the corn-fields and hedges, and there perished miserably.

After this battle nothing has been heard of the rebellious peasants, and the country has been quiet. This revolt appears to me to be in little, a perfect parallel to the Revolution in France in its beginnings. I imagine that if, on the approach of these 3000 men, the Wexford authorities had given up their prisoners – and that might have been expected, since they had only 150 soldiers to oppose the countrymen – the pretensions of the White Boys would have been greatly augmented. They would have proceeded to impose their wishes on the country, and perhaps to put the magistrates in prison, and if only the Government had left them alone for three weeks or a month, or had temporized, or parleyed with them, instead of 3000 they would have numbered 30,000 and in all probability would have destroyed the government from which they had, at the beginning, asked favours.

JOINING THE UNITED IRISHMEN

Miles Byrne's Memoirs (1863) make it plain that some Catholic clergy in County Wexford were against the United Irish movement. Here he is referring to the weeks before 23 May, the day set for the rebellion.

There were very few United Irishmen in my part of the country when I was made one, but before a month had elapsed almost every one had taken the test, by the exertions of

Nick Murphy, Johnny Doyle, Ned Fennell, and myself. The priests did everything in their power to stop the progress of the Association of United Irishmen: particularly poor Father John Redmond, who refused to hear the confession of any one of the United Irish, and turned them away from his knees. He was ill-requited afterwards for his great zeal and devotion of the enemies of his country: for, after the Insurrection was all over, Earl Mountnorris brought him in a prisoner to the British camp at Gorey, with a rope about his neck, hung him up to a tree, and fired a brace of bullets through his body. Lord Mountnorris availed himself of this opportunity to show his 'loyalty,' for he was rather suspected on account of not being at the head of his corps when the Insurrection broke out in his neighbourhood. Both Redmond and the parish priest, Father Frank Cavanagh, were on the best terms with Earl Mountnorris, dining frequently with him at his seat, Camolin Park, which place Father Redmond prevented being plundered during the Insurrection. This was the only part he had taken in the struggle.

SWEET COUNTY WEXFORD
Anon.

A Wexford magistrate, Hunter Gowan of Mount Nebo (now Mount St Benedict), established an unofficial 'Orange Lodge' comprising selected bloodthirsty loyalists. From these he formed his own yeomanry. Former magistrates James Boyd, Archibald Hamilton Jacob and Hawtry White were prominent among them. They arrested and transported blacksmiths, shot rebels, burned churches and indulged in other atrocities.

The notorious Gowan and others are remembered in this ballad, which again employs the simple device of filling stanzas with names of places and people.

> As they from Gorey set out that morning,
> You'd pity the groans and the women's tears;
> But on that day we made them pay,
> When they came in view of our Shelmaliers.
> 'Twas from the watch-house into Ballyellis
> To Pavy's height going towards Carnew,
> It's there we had a great engagement,
> Such other pikemen you never knew.
>
> 'Twas early, early on the next morning,
> To Ballarahan we took our way,
> To meet with Gowan and his cursed yeomen,
> To them it was a woeful day.

Cowardly Gowan when he saw us coming,
Turned round and away from us did run,
Like a hunted fox he crossed over the rocks,
When he saw the flash of a Croppy's gun.

We then shot Chamny and Captain Dixon,
And General Walpole got no time to run,
And long Smyth, the slater – the bloody traitor,
He fell that day by a croppy's gun.
When this engagement was all over,
And our brave boys had no more to do,
We crossed Brideswell going to Camolin,
And camped that night at Carrigrua.

Had we the wisdom to follow after,
And not have tarried in Gorey town,
We'd have saved the lives of many a martyr,
That died in Arklow – God rest their souls.
Success attend the sweet County Wexford,
They are the boys that were ne'er afraid.
Of Ancient Britons nor bragging yeomen,
But on such cowards great slaughter made.

PROCLAMATION OF THE PEOPLE OF THE COUNTY OF WEXFORD

Whereas, it stands manifestly notorious that James Boyd, Hawtry White, Hunter Gowan, and Archibald Hamilton Jacob, late magistrates of this county, have committed the most horrid acts of cruelty, violence, and oppression, against our peaceable and well-affected countrymen: now WE the people, associated and united for the purpose of procuring our just rights, and being determined to protect the persons and properties of those of all religious persuasions who have not oppressed us, and who are willing with heart and hand to join our glorious cause, as well as to shew our marked disapprobation and horror of the crimes of the above delinquents, do call on our countrymen at large, to use every exertion in their power to apprehend the bodies of the aforesaid James Boyd, &c. &c. &c. and to secure and convey them to the gaol of Wexford, to be brought before the Tribunal of the People.

Done at Wexford, this 9th day of June, 1798
GOD SAVE THE PEOPLE

FATHER MURPHY

Anon.

During the night of May 26-7, Crown forces burned the local Catholic church and over twenty residences at Boolavogue, including that of the priest, Father John Murphy (1727-98).

Born at Tincurry, Ferns, County Wexford, this hedge-school-educated clergyman was in his mid-forties in 1798. Of local farming stock, he studied in Seville, Spain. Originally, he professed loyalty to the Crown and he was not a member of the United Irishmen. The arson attack in his parish drove him to becoming leader of the rebellion in Wexford. He conducted a stout defence at Oulart on 27 May 1798 and annihilated Foote's force. He marched to Camolin and Ferns, where his men ransacked the Protestant bishop's house. He captured Enniscorthy and Wexford. Moving north he received a poor response to his call for volunteers. After the final defeat at Vinegar Hill, he escaped. Some say the priest was hanged at Taghmon on 26 June 1798; others, like the song's composer, that 'the yeos, at Tullow, took Father Murphy and burned his body upon the rack'. There is no precise record of his final fate.

> Come all you warriors and renowned nobles,
> Give ear unto my warlike theme,
> And I'll relate how brave Father Murphy
> Lately aroused from his sleepy dream.
> Sure Julius Caesar nor Alexander
> Nor brave King Arthur ever equalled him
> For armies formidable he did oppose them,
> Though with two pikemen he did begin.
>
> The Camolin cavalry he did unhorse them,
> Their first lieutenant he cut him down,
> With broken ranks, and with shattered columns,
> They soon returned to Camolin town,
> On the hill of Oulart he displayed his valour,
> Where a hundred Corkmen lay on the plain
> And at Enniscorthy his sword he wielded
> And I hope to see him once more again,
>
> When Enniscorthy became subject unto us,
> 'Twas next to Wexford we marched our men,

And on the Three Rock we took up our quarters,
Waiting for daylight the town to win.
The loyal townsmen gave their assistance
We'll die or conquer, they all did say,
The yeomen cavalry made no resistance,
For on the pavement their bodies lay,

With drums a-beating the town did echo,
And acclamations came from door to door,
On the Windmill Hill we pitched our tents,
And we drank like heroes, but paid no score.
On Carraig Rua for some time we waited,
And next to Gorey we did repair,
At Tubberneering we thought no harm,
The bloody army, it was waiting there,

The issue of it was a close engagement,
While on the soldiers we played warlike pranks;
Through sheepwalks, hedgerows and shady thickets,
There were mangled bodies and broken ranks,
The shuddering cavalry I can't forget them;
We raised the brushes on their helmets straight
They turned about, and they bade for Dublin.
As if they ran for a ten-pound plate.

Well, some crossed Donnybrook and more through Blackrock
And some up Shankill without wound or flaw
And if Barry Lawless be not a liar
There's more went groaning up Luggelaw.
To the Windmill Hill of Enniscorthy,
The British Fencibles they fled like deer;
But our ranks were tattered, and sorely scattered,
By the loss of Kyan and his Shelmaliers.

The streets of England were left quite naked
Of all its armies, both foot and horse,
The Highlands of Scotland were left unguarded
Likewise the Hessians the seas they crossed.
But if the Frenchmen had reinforced us,

And landed transports in Bagenbun,
Father John Murphy would be their seconder,
And sixteen thousand with him would come.

Success attend you, sweet County Wexford
Threw off the yoke and to battle run;
Let them not think we gave up our arms
For every man has a pike and gun.

BOOLAVOGUE
P.J. McCall

The proper Ordnance Survey spelling for the village about eight miles north-east of Enniscorthy is Boleyvogue. Balladeers will have none of that, however, and with its double 'o' it has become by far the most popular rebellion song.

Patrick Joseph McCall (1861-1918), son of a Dublin publican, contributed ballads, verse and sketches to popular newspapers. Other famous ballads of his, 'Kelly, the Boy from Killane' and 'Henry Joy', appear later in this anthology.

At Boolavogue, as the sun was setting
O'er the bright May meadows of Shelmalier,
A rebel hand set the heather blazing
And brought the neighbours from far and near.
Then Father Murphy, from old Kilcormack,
Spurred up the rocks with a warning cry:
'Arm! Arm!' he cried, 'for I've come to lead you,
For Ireland's freedom we fight or die.'

He led us on 'gainst the coming soldiers,
And the cowardly yeomen we put to flight;
'Twas at the Harrow the boys of Wexford
Showed Bookey's regiment how men could fight.
Look out for hirelings, King George of England,
Search every kingdom where breathes a slave,
For Father Murphy of the County Wexford
Sweeps o'er the land like a mighty wave.

We took Camolin and Enniscorthy,
And at Wexford, storming, drove out our foes;
'Twas at Slieve Coillte our pikes were reeking
With the crimson blood of the beaten yeos.
At Tubberneering and Ballyellis
Full many a Hessian lay in his gore;
Ah, Father Murphy, had aid come over
The green flag floated from shore to shore!

At Vinegar Hill, o'er the pleasant Slaney,
Our heroes vainly stood back to back,
And the yeos at Tullow took Father Murphy
And burned his body upon the rack.
God grant you glory, brave Father Murphy,
And open heaven to all your men;
The cause that called you may call to-morrow
In another fight for the Green again.

KELLY OF KILLANE
P.J. McCall

Beauchamp Bagenal Harvey was a Protestant landlord and magistrate who lived in Bargy Castle, near Bridgetown, County Wexford. He was a somewhat inept leader of the United Irishmen in that county. In his capacity as magistrate, during May 1798 he accepted surrender of arms from rebels and brought them to Wexford. The sheriff ordered his arrest and imprisonment. When the rebels were attacking Wexford, Colonel Maxwell released him and sent him to seek terms. They made him their Commander-in-Chief, an appointment for which he was totally unsuited. An ill-conducted attack on New Ross failed and he returned to Wexford and became President of a Provincial Council to manage the affairs of the county. After the fall of Wexford, he attempted to hide out on the Saltee Islands but was captured and executed. His executioners mounted his head on Wexford Session House and tossed his body into the Slaney.

'Citizen' Furlong, a young gentleman farmer, was Harvey's aide. He bore Harvey's foolish surrender demand to General Johnson, who defended New Ross. Sentries of Johnson's well-placed screen shot him dead, infuriating the rebels.

Bagenal Harvey ordered John Kelly to take 800 men and disperse the New Ross screen that had shot Furlong, but not to enter the town. They wiped out the screen

*and, ignoring Harvey's warning, continued on, entering through Three Bullet Gate
and capturing the barracks and its weapons. Kelly was wounded and his men ran riot
but were soon repelled. New Ross was quickly recaptured by Major-General Johnson.*

What's the news? What's the news? O my bold Shelmalier,
With your long-barrelled gun of the sea?
Say what wind from the sun blows his messenger here
With a hymn of the dawn for the free?
'Goodly news, goodly news, do I bring, Youth of Forth
Goodly news shall you hear, Bargy man!
For the boys march at dawn from the South to the North
Led by Kelly, the Boy from Killane!'

'Tell me who is that giant with gold curling hair —
He who rides at the head of your band?
Seven feet is his height, with some inches to spare,
And he looks like a king in command!'
'Ah, my lads, that's the pride of the bold Shelmaliers,
'Mong our greatest of heroes, a Man!
Fling your beavers aloft and give three ringing cheers
For John Kelly, the Boy from Killane!'

Enniscorthy's in flames, and old Wexford is won,
And to-morrow the Barrow we cross,
On a hill o'er the town we have planted a gun
That will batter the gateways of Ross!
All the Forth men and Bargy men march o'er the heath,
With brave Harvey to lead on the van;
But the foremost of all in the grim Gap of Death
Will be Kelly, the Boy from Killane!

But the gold sun of Freedom grew darkened at Ross,
And it set by the Slaney's red waves;
And poor Wexford, stripped naked, hung high on a cross,
With her heart pierced by traitors and slaves!
Glory O! Glory O! to her brave sons who died
For the cause of long-down-trodden man!
Glory O! to Mount Leinster's own darling and pride —
Dauntless Kelly, the Boy from Killane!

PHYSIQUE

Rev. Patrick F. Kavanagh wrote A Popular History of the Insurrection of 1798: derived from every available Record and Reliable Tradition *(Centenary Edition, Cork 1898). In it he described the Wexford rebels:*

The Wexfordmen who composed this army averaged six feet, lathy and bony, rather long oval features, very good-looking generally, brown-haired, felt flower-pot hats, grey frieze swallow-tailed coats, brown mohair vests, double-breasted; frieze or corduroy knee breeches, blue or green garters, pepper-and-salt stockings, shoes with a buckle on the outside and in front of ankle, brass buttons, that are nearly out of fashion now unless in wild districts. Some of them had trustys, or cotha mores, made of frieze, of a peculiar shape, and white ivory buttons. I saw some of those coats; if they were not very handsome, they were very comfortable. Those poor men carried raw wheat in their pockets as provisions, and it was buried with them in Mountainstown and Raffan, and the following season it grew out of the graves and renewed itself for the second year. I think that this much was never published. It is traditionary, but, I am as sure as I live, 'tis true ...

THE BATTLE OF VINEGAR HILL
Rev. P.F. Kavanagh

If Wexford's rising is the most famous part of the rebellion, Vinegar Hill is its most celebrated battle. There, General Lake beat the rebels, some of whom retreated to Wexford town before dispersing.

Proud marched the British army, in scarlet and in gold,
Their trumpets loudly sounding, their banners all unrolled,
To meet the Wexford pikemen, those gallant men and true
Who fought to raise our darling green above the English blue.

To Vinegar Hill their way they took, these English soldiers all,
Their light foot and their cavalry their grenadiers so tall.
Resolved to make these pikemen bold their rashness sorely rue,
Who dared to raise their darling green against the English blue.

And in the rere of this great host it was a sight to see
The long array of steeds that bore their dread artillery.
Their captains and their colonels with drawn swords led the way,
And many a solemn oath they swore of vengeance on that day.

For they thought of Tuberneering, of Ross and Wexford town,
And in silence vowed they'd perish or pluck the green flag down.
Then a young ensign boldly spoke this, his scornful jest:
I'll laugh to see the rebels run their chief before the rest.

We've but to wave our banners and charge them gallantly
To see the peasant foeman before our onset flee;
'Twere shame, indeed, if untaught churls in coming days should boast
They dared in open battle to face a Royal host.

Then to him said a captain, a grey-haired veteran he,
I've met these men in fight before no braver men there be;
We came upon them suddenly, and we were two to one,
And fought them all the summer day till night was coming on.

No quarter did they crave from us, but fell even where they stood,
Brave men were they and in their veins runs the fierce Norman blood;
And thou mayest see, young ensign, ere closing of the day
How well these gallant Wexfordmen can bear them in the fray.

And soon the English army, twenty thousand strong,
Were marshalled round the Hill renowned in story and in song.
Whereon ten thousand pikemen, the flower of Wexford land,
Had for homes and altars gathered to make their final stand.

And soon the battles thunder broke o'er the echoing plain,
And cannon balls fell thickly and musket balls like rain
Upon the hillside where there stood these peasant patriots true
Who fought to raise their Irish green above the English blue.

Soon many a dauntless Shelmalier lay weltering in his gore,
And many a valiant patriot good had fallen to rise no more;
For thickly flew the cannon balls and musket balls like hail,
Till at the slaughter on the Hill the stoutest heart might quail.

Then many a noble heart grew still and many a brave man died,
While crimson streams of heroes' blood ran down the steep hillside.
Then said a trusted leader, Here no longer shall we bide
And see our friends fall unavenged upon this bare hillside.

But before this day is over another blow we'll strike,
Then up my gallant comrades and charge them with the pike!
Our gunmen now can naught avail since all their powder's gone,
But boys we are not beaten yet though they may be two to one;

And well our marksmen did their work for yonder on the plain
Our enemies are weary with the counting of the slain.
We'll charge once more, my comrades brave, these soldiers of the Crown,
And keep our green flag flying as we march to Wexford town!

Then to their feet the pikemen sprang with fierce loud battle-cry,
Each firmly clutched his trusty pike and raised the point on high
And sudden, on that hillside, a steel-tipped forest grew
While borne aloft, before their ranks, their green flag proudly flew.

As rushing down the hill they came, a swift, resistless tide,
Nor dared King George's veteran troops their onset fierce to bide,
But left a passage open wide before their gallant foe,
As with their green flag flying towards Wexford town they go.

And sure no man in any land e'er waged a braver fight,
Or bore themselves more valiantly in struggling for the Right;
Nor from the English foeman just praise shall we withhold
For Englishmen are stubborn foes and cast in warlike mould;
But pity 'tis that freeborn men should strike fair freedom down
And shed their blood in guilty strife for any King or Crown.

AFTER VINEGAR HILL

Sir Jonah Barrington describes the scene:

Immediately after the capture of Wexford, I traversed that county to see the ruins
which had been occasioned by warfare. Enniscorthy had been twice stormed, and was
dilapidated and nearly burned. New Ross showed melancholy relics of the obstinate
and bloody battle of full ten hours' duration, which had been fought in every street of
it; when Lord Mountjoy fell, at the head of his regiment … his regiment instantly
retreated and the triumphant rebel [who killed him] advanced and took his lordship's
watch out of his pocket … The numerous pits crammed with dead bodies, on Vinegar
Hill, seemed on some spots actually elastic as we stood upon them; whilst the walls of
an old windmill on its summit appeared stained and splashed with the blood and brains

of many victims who had been piked or shot against it by the rebels. The court house of Enniscorthy, wherein our troops had burned alive above eighty of the wounded rebels, and the barns of Scullabogue, where the rebels had retaliated by burning alive above one hundred and twenty Protestants, were terrific ruins! The town of Gorey was utterly destroyed, not a house being left perfect; and the bodies of the killed were lying half covered in sundry ditches in its vicinity.

THE BOYS OF WEXFORD
Robert Dwyer Joyce

This lively march has always been included in the repertoire of Irish army bands. It celebrates the part played by Wexford in the rebellion and names famous actions: New Ross, Tubberneering, Oulart and Vinegar Hill. Lieutenant-Colonel Walpole, a man totally unsuited for command, was a foppish aide to the Viceroy who led reinforcements for General Loftus in Wexford. He and his men were annihilated at Tuberneering on 4 June 1798. Lord Mountjoy's Militia, led by Major Vesey, assisted Major General Henry Johnson's defence of New Ross and the main pass across the Slaney so vital to its holders.

Robert Dwyer Joyce (1830-83) received his early education in a County Limerick hedge school. First a teacher, then a physician, he contributed to nationalist publications. In 1861 he published his Ballads, Romances and Songs.

In comes the captain's daughter, the captain of the yeos,
Saying 'Brave United Irishmen, we'll ne'er again be foes.
A thousand pounds I'll bring if you will fly from home with me,
And dress myself in man's attire and fight for liberty.'

CHORUS
We are the boys of Wexford, who fought with heart and hand
To burst in twain the galling chain and free our native land.

'I want no gold, my maiden fair, to fly from home with thee;
Your shining eyes will be my prize – more dear than gold to me.
I want no gold to nerve my arm to do a true man's part –
To free my land I'd gladly give the red drops from my heart.'
CHORUS

And when we left our cabins, boys, we left with right good will
To see our friends and neighbours that were at Vinegar Hill!

A young man from our Irish ranks a cannon he let go;
He slapped it into Lord Mountjoy – a tyrant he laid low!
CHORUS

We bravely fought and conquered at Ross and Wexford town;
Three Bullet Gate for years to come will speak for our renown;
Through Walpole's horse and Walpole's foot on Tubberneering's day,
Depending on the long, bright pike, we cut our gory way.
CHORUS

And Oulart's name shall be their shame, whose steel we ne'er did fear,
For every man could do his part like Forth and Shelmalier!
And if, for want of leaders, we lost at Vinegar Hill,
We're ready for another fight, and love our country still!
CHORUS

THE WIND THAT SHAKES THE BARLEY
Robert Dwyer Joyce

A young man talks of his love for a woman and for his country. He opts to fight and his woman becomes an innocent victim of violence.

I sat within the valley green;
I sat me with my true love.
My sad heart strove the two between,
The old love and the new love:
The old for her, the new that made
Me think on Ireland dearly
While soft the wind blew down the glen
And shook the golden barley.

'Twas hard the woeful words to frame
To break the ties that bound us,
But harder still to bear the shame
Of foreign chains around us.
And so I said 'The mountain glen
I'll seek at morning early
And join the bold United men,
While soft winds shake the barley.'

While sad I kissed away her tears,
My fond arms round her flinging,
The yeoman's shot burst on our ears
From out the wildwood ringing.
A bullet pierced my true love's side
In life's young spring so early,
And on my breast in blood she died
While soft winds shook the barley.

But blood for blood without remorse
I took at Oulart Hollow,
And laid my true love's clay cold corpse
Where I full soon may follow,
As round her grave I wander drear,
Noon, night and morning early,
With breaking heart when e'er I hear
The wind that shakes the barley.

THE CROPPY BOY
Anon.

Participants in the French Revolution had their hair cropped close to the head. The United Irishmen adopted the practice and became known as Croppies. This is one of two well-known ballads concerning anonymous Wexford rebels. Lord Cornwall is an abbreviation, referring to Marquis Charles Cornwallis, who fought in the American war and succeeded Camden as Viceroy in Ireland in May 1798. He became Commander-in-Chief by replacing Lake (who was acting in the appointment) in June. He was sent to Ireland for the express purposes of winning the war against the rebels and imposing a settlement that ensured unity with England.

The section headings in this anthology are taken from the first ballad.

It was early, early, all in the spring,
The birds did whistle and did sweetly sing,
Changing their notes from tree to tree,
And the song they sang was 'Old Ireland Free'.

It was early, early all in the night,
The yeoman cavalry gave me a fright;

The yeoman cavalry was my downfall,
And I was taken by the Lord Cornwall.

'Twas in the guard-house where I was laid
And in the parlour where I was tried;
My sentence passed and my courage low,
When to Duncannon I was forced to go.

As I was passing by my father's door,
My brother William stood there at the door;
My aged father stood at the door,
And my tender mother her hair she tore.

As I was walking up Wexford Street
My own first cousin I chanced to meet;
My own first cousin did me betray,
And for one bare guinea swore my life away.

My sister Mary heard the express,
She ran upstairs in her morning-dress –
Five hundred guineas I will lay me down,
To see my brother safe in Wexford Town.

As I was walking up Wexford Hill,
Who would blame me if I did cry my fill?
I looked behind and I looked before,
But my tender mother I shall ne'er see more.

As I was mounted on the platform high,
My aged father was standing by;
My aged father did me deny,
And the name he gave me was the Croppy Boy.

'Twas in Duncannon that this young man died,
And in Duncannon too his body lies;
All you good Christians that do pass by
Just drop a tear for the Croppy Boy.

SCULLABOGUE MASSACRE

Excuses have been given: reports of slaughter at New Ross and the like. They could never have condoned what happened. It is just that the account of the rebels' most heinous crime should come from a loyalist. S.L. Corrigan describes the massacre of mostly Protestant 'loyalist' prisoners in a barn at Scullabogue, County Wexford:

On the morning of the action at Ross, between the hours of five and six o'clock, one of the rebels that had fled from the battle came galloping to Scullabogue House, where three hundred insurgents were guarding the poor Protestants who had been made prisoners. When he came within hearing, he shouted, 'destroy the prisoners! Destroy the prisoners! our friends are cut off at Ross!' John Murphy, who was captain of the rebel guard, told him, that it should not be done without written orders from the general. About an hour after, another messenger arrived, proclaiming, 'our friends are all destroyed, murder all the prisoners!' Murphy made him the same answer. About ten o'clock, a third express came running on foot, crying 'the priest has sent orders to put all the prisoners to death.'

Immediately the rebel guards stripped off their coats, and prepared for murdering the prisoners, as deliberately as if going to their daily employment. After saying their usual prayers, crossing and blessing themselves, they formed two divisions; one party to massacre those in the dwelling-house, the other, all that were confined in the barn. The first party hauled out thirty-seven from the dwelling-house, and were employed shooting them, while the other division surrounded the barn in the most outrageous manner, placed ladders against the walls to stand on, and set it on fire in every direction. The unfortunate Protestants within, entreated, with the most lamentable cries, for mercy, and pressing forward to the back door, caught hold of it, endeavouring to force their way out. The rebels, however, crowding to that quarter, cut and mangled their hands in such a dreadful manner, that for some time they were prevented. At length the weight of the people behind, pressing upon their mangled friends in the front, made the door give way; but the merciless rebels, as the poor Protestants rushed out, thrust them in again with their pikes, while others were busy in tying bundles of straw, and forcing them into the barn to increase the fire and the pains of those innocent sufferers. During the horrid scene, some of the rebels were loading and firing in upon them, while others were wantonly piercing their burning bodies through with their pikes. This was a mercy, though not intended as such, as it put a speedy period to their miseries; or, if it was so intended, it only confirms the language of Scripture, that 'the tender mercies of the wicked are cruel'.

There was a woman in the barn, who had been wife to one of the North Cork Militia, who was killed at Oulard [*sic*] Hill; finding no way to escape the flames, she thought, if possible, to save her child. She accordingly wrapped her cloak about the infant, and threw it out of the barn; but one of the sanguinary pike-men thrust his weapon through the helpless babe, and, giving a great shout, cried 'd—n you, you little heretic, get in there!' and instantly flung it into the fire. Another child, about two years old (whose parents had been either shot or burned), crept unperceived under the corner of the door, and lay outside the house, close to the wall: when the confusion had in some degree abated, the child was discovered; and a rebel thrusting it through, it gave a violent shriek, and expired in dreadful convulsions. After they had finished their bloody business at the barn, they hastened to the dwelling-house, to make the tragedy more complete. Dead bodies were already strewed round the lawn before the hall-door; others were on their knees crying for mercy, but in vain; humanity had fled the place, and mercy was not known. Of two hundred and twenty-four prisoners, thirty-seven were shot, one hundred and eight-four burned to death, and only three, viz – Richard Grandy, Loftus Frizzel, and — Lett, were suffered to live. Among those unhappy victims, were twenty women and children. These facts have been sworn to.

Bagnal Harvey, though deluded by absurd political speculations, expressed the greatest horror at the inhuman massacre, for which he was deposed, and the cruel savage, Father Philip Roche, was elected in his stead; Father Edward Roche, who had commanded at Wexford, being made Commander-in-Chief. The former denounced the very Protestants who served in the rebel ranks; on which, Bagnal Harvey expressed, that he had seen too late that it was a religious war, and wished to make his escape.

THE CROPPY BOY
Carroll Malone

There is sharp imagery in this popular ballad. The inclination to receive the sacrament of confession before going into battle was always strong among rebel Irishmen. The incident outlined occurred after the battle of New Ross and before Wexford. In Ulysses, *Joyce recalls Lord Edward Fitzgerald's arrest, the Sham Squire and Robert Emmet before alluding to Ben Dollard's 'masterly rendition' of the famous ballad.*

Carroll Malone is the pseudonym of William McBurney (1844-92). He came from County Down but emigrated to America at an early age. A journalist, he used Carroll Malone for much of his work, including his contributions to The Nation.

'Good men and true in this house who dwell,
To a stranger buachaill I pray you tell,
Is the priest at home or may he be seen?
I would speak a word with Father Green.'

'The priest's at home, boy, and may be seen;
'Tis easy speaking with Father Green;
But you must wait till I go and see
If the holy father alone may be.'

The youth has entered an empty hall
What a lonely sound makes his light footfall,
The gloomy chamber is still and bare,
With a vested priest in its only chair.

The youth has knelt to tell his sins.
'In Nomine Dei,' the youth begins;
At 'Mea culpa' he beats his breast,
And in broken murmurs he speaks the rest.

'At the siege of Ross did my father fall,
And at Gorey my loving brothers all,
I alone am left of my name and race,
I will go to Wexford and take their place.

'I cursed three times since last Easter Day –
At Mass-time once I went to play;
When passing the churchyard one day in haste,
I forgot to pray for my mother's rest.

'I bear no hate against living thing.
But I love my country above my King.
Now, Father, bless me and let me go
To die if God has ordained it so.'

The priest said naught, but a rustling noise
Made the youth look up in wild surprise:
The robes were off, and in scarlet there
Sat a yeoman captain with fiery glare.

With fiery glare and with fury hoarse,
Instead of a blessing he breathed a curse:
''Twas a good thought, boy, to come here and shrive,
For one short hour is your time to live.

'Upon yon river three tenders float,
The priest's in one – if he isn't shot –
We hold this house for our Lord the King,
And, Amen, say I, may all traitors swing!'

At Geneva Barracks that young man died,
And at Passage they had his body laid.
Good people, who live in peace and joy,
Breathe a prayer, shed a tear for the Croppy Boy.

BUACHAILLÍ LOCH GARMAIN
Mícheál Óg Ó Longáin

Mícheál Óg Ó Longáin (1766-1837) was born in Carrignavar, County Cork. The Ó Longáins were a hereditary learned family, originally from County Limerick, who had been reduced to living as small farmers and labourers following the destruction of the Gaelic order in the seventeenth century. Many, including Mícheál Óg, continued the family tradition as bards and scribes. He is unique in that while coming from the heart of the Munster Jacobite tradition he became an active United Irishman, very aware of the new Republican France. His poems 'Buachaillí Loch Garman' and Maidin Luan Chincíse' berate the people of Munster for failing to support the rising and are the only known responses to the rising in the Irish language. This one is written as if a Leinster rebel were delivering it. The original manuscript is in the Library of the Royal Irish Academy, Dublin. An explanation accompanies it: 'Mar cuard drong o fearaib Eireann ar Cnoc an Binegire i Laignib san mbliadain 1798, i n-doic go n-eireocad an Mumain agus an curd eile d'Eirinn do congnam leo' (Because a group of the men of Ireland gathered on Vinegar Hill in Leinster in the year 1798, hoping that Munster and the rest of Ireland would rise to help them).

Beir litir uainn do 'n Mhumhain leat,
A rúin dhil 's a stóir,
A's aithris-se tré rún dóibh
Go bhfuil an cúrsa na gcomhair:
Innis gur mó ainnir mhilis mhúinte
Agus leanbh fireann fionn, leis,
A's fear breagh cliste cumtha
Do fúigead or feód

A's fiafraigh créad ná h-éirghid
A's teidheacht linn sa ghleó,
I n-arm ghreanta ghreadhnach
Bheadh faghartha go leór

Cé táimíd-ne brúite millte
'S go leór dár namhaid 'nar dtimcheall
Innis go bhfuil na Laighnigh
Ag adhaint na teine leó.

Do ghluais ó chóige Chonnacht chúinn
Tuille 'gus deich mile laoch
A's adtuaidh ó chuantaibh Uladh iar sin
An oiread eile i bhfíoc 's i bhfaobhar.
Ní bhfuaramair fuaradh ar bith achu
Go rugamar bualadh a's fiche ortha
A's ba traugh mar bhídís cuirp againn
A's fuíl i nde readh lae.

A's cá bhfuil congnamh Muimhneach
Nó'n fíor go mairid beó
I n-arm lonnrach líomhtha
Ná tíd linn 'san ngleó?
A ndeacair-phudhair do dhíoghailt
As Galla-búir dó dhíbhirt
A's fearann dúthchais díleas
Ár sinnsear go deó.

Um Inid 'na dhiaidi sin 'san mbliadiain 1799, is eadh éirig Conntaé an Chláir, acht níorbh é am é acht i dtosach an t-samhrardh roimhe sin, aimsir Chnuic an Vinchair. Bhí a rian air: do buailead a gceann fúta gan mhoill. Dia linn!

Adhmhuighim gur neamh-shlachtmhar atáid na ranna beaga sin déanta, agus dá bhrí sin iarruim agus aitchím sibh-se, a lucht déanta na nduan ndeas, gan mh'imdheargadh tré gach locht nó toibhéim do-chítear libh ionnta, do bhrí go bhfuilim ró-bhuartha anois, agus go bhfuil deifir mhór orm; acct bhíodh a fhios agaibh go raibh aigne mhaith leó.

Bhur searbhóntaoi bocht bith-díleas go bás
Mícheál Ó Longáin

Loosely translated, the poem and prose read:

Bear a letter from us to Munster with you,
Dear trusted friend and relate to them,
Secretly, that a course lies ahead;
Tell that many a sweet mannered young woman

And fair male child also
And a fine, clever man has been left to wither.

And ask why they will not rise
And come with us into battle
In splendid bright arms?
Where mettle is plentiful.
Even though we are bruised and impaired
With hosts of the enemy around us,
Announce that the Leinstermen
Are kindling the fire with us.

From the province of Connaught against us
Marched up to ten thousand warriors;
And after that, from the north, out of the harbours of Ulster
As many more with ferocity and with bitterness.
We received no respite from them
Until we had beaten them once and twenty times more
And it was tragic, at the end of every day,
To see bodies and blood all around us.

And where is the Munstermen's help
Or are they alive at all
In splendid, bright arms alongside us
They come not to fight with us?
Their grievous wrongs to right
And foreign boors to drive
From the sweet, true native land
Of our forefathers forever.

On the Whit Sunday after that, in the year 1799, County Clare rose, but that was not the time, but the beginning of the previous summer, the time of Vinegar Hill. The inevitable happened: they were immediately suppressed, God be with us!

I own that these verses are untidy, and therefore I beg and beseech you, the people who make fine poems, not to chastise me for every weakness and fault you notice in them, because I am in deep stress at this time and because I am in a great hurry, but let you all know that I had a good intention.

Your poor servant, ever-faithful until death,
Mícheál Ó Longain

PERSONAL DISTRESS!

Mount Norris, whom we met earlier, again wrote to Lieutenant Smith at Camp Ferns. At this stage, the rebellion in Wexford was over. Mount Norris's was not.

Dublin, August 7, 1798.

Dear Sir,
I am glad to find that the 4th Battalion of the Flank Companies, has been replaced by so respectable a Regiment as that of Dublin. I have not been well for some days, owing to change of air and mode of living. This circumstance, which affects my Bowels, and some Business of Importance still detains me here. Besides, I am labouring the Point of Compensation for my suffering Brothers, as otherwise how can things go on? As to Duty, I am sorry it falls so hard upon you, but, when I go down, I will take my Share *with my brave fellow Soldiers*. We cannot expect to be paid by our King and Country, without earning our Pay. There is not anything new in Town.

    Yours faithfully,
    Mt. Norris.

Of the North

The United Irishmen had a strong base in Ulster. On 6 June 1798 they rose in rebellion. The main actions of the campaign were at Antrim town and at Ballynahinch. The town of Antrim commanded the Derry-Belfast route. Henry Joy McCracken's first attack on it took place on 7 June and was successful. He rallied his men at Donegore Hill, but received less support than he had anticipated from Antrim Catholics.

The rebels attacked, simultaneously, Randalstown, Ballymena and Larne. Samuel Orr, brother of William, captured the market-house in Randalstown and burned it. He treated captured yeomen humanely. But some of his men came across dragoons retreating from the town and thought they were pursuing them. They scattered. Others followed and this panic spread to McCracken's force in Antrim town.

The collapse of Randalstown meant that heavy reinforcements could arrive without obstruction from Belfast under Colonels Claveringa and Durham. The force included artillery, and a half-hour howitzer barrage forced all but a few of McCracken's men to retreat from the town. This small group became known as the 'Spartan Band'.

Ballynahinch lies in a valley between Montalto Heights to the south and Windmill Hill to the north. General Munroe occupied the town for the rebels, taking Saintfield. He later moved to Montalto and Windmill Hill. Munroe was overconfident and scorned a sensible suggestion to attack Nugent by night before he got a chance to organize a set-piece assault. Furthermore, a religious divide became apparent in his force, some accusing him of wanting to establish a Presbyterian state. Instead, Munroe made a stand and prepared to take on an inevitable attack.

Nugent moved in reinforcements and positioned units to cut off retreat routes. He then drove the rebels from Windmill Hill and began a heavy bombardment of the town and Montalto Heights. This, coupled with a worsening morale problem, caused the rebels to flee.

BELFAST BEFORE THE REBELLION

Chevalier De Latocnaye describes Belfast and its environs in 1796-7:

I was received with much kindness by Mr Birch, whom I had seen on my first arrival, and I proceeded again to Belfast, where I arrived in time for the celebration of the King's birthday, and heard the volleys fired by the garrison in honour of His Majesty. The people of this town, who were represented some time ago as about to rise, appeared now in a sort of stupor hardly distinguishable from fear. In the evening the town was illuminated, and the soldiers ran through the streets armed with sticks, breaking the windows of those who had not lit up their homes, and of a great number also who had done so. They went into all sorts of holes and corners breaking back-windows and the fanlights of doors. They seized their officers and bore them, in turn, on their shoulders through the streets. The yells, coming from the soldiers, and the huzzas were simply terrible. Three weeks earlier it was the people who assembled tumultuously and made a racket. If I may say it, I think a crowd of soldiers and a crowd of people differ very little in point of the danger to be expected; in the former case, however, if the officers have their soldiers well in hand there is less danger, as by the terror they inspire they are able to prevent the excess to which the populace might give way.

I imagine that the people of Belfast will not for long forget the terror in which I found them. General Lake, however, walked the streets the whole night and arrested some soldiers who were becoming unruly; he dispersed the crowd, too, as soon as the time fixed for the illuminations was past. The tow was so agreeable and entertaining to the soldiers that they would have been very glad to begin it again; a report was, indeed, circulated that there would be a second illumination next day. In every country soldiers are delighted with the chance of making a rumpus, than slashing and cutting they like nothing better, and it required all the activity of General Lake to keep them within bounds.

The next day, desiring to see the Sovereign, as the first Magistrate or Mayor is here called, his house was pointed out to me by a poor woman who was near the door. 'There it is,' said she, 'but he is not in, and I am waiting,' she added, 'to make him pay for my broken panes.'

On the same day a man with whom I dined, and who was in a state of alarm, said to me: 'France is in great trouble, Italy is ravaged, a revolution is coming in Spain, Germany is ruined, Switzerland is about to declare war, Holland no longer exists; here we are breaking our windows, and we shall finish, perhaps, with slaughter; – where is peace to be found?' 'Faith,' said I, 'I know one sovereign who has not been troubled, and to whom anyone can go very quickly.' 'And who is he? tell me, Sir.' 'The big Devil in hell,' I answered.

The troubles, however, having made Belfast a somewhat disagreeable resting-place, I provided myself with passports and started out. I was much surprised to see that the soldiers had taken the trouble to break windows as far as two or three miles from the town. I travelled by coach, thinking it not desirable to risk myself on foot, on the road, after what I had seen. I passed successively through Lisburn, Hillsborough, and Dromore; the two first-named are situated in beautiful and perfectly-cultivated country. Hillsborough, where is the castle of the Marquis of Downshire, is on a height dominating a most fertile and rich country. It was at Lisburn that the French refugees first established the linen manufacture which has become the principal industry in Ireland, especially in the north. The three towns were full of soldiers and volunteers. Although I regretted that I could not stop in them a little while, the thought that my stay here might be very far from agreeable, made me push on to a place which I thought might be more settled, or, at any rate, to the place of residence of someone to whom I had a letter of recommendation. Influenced in this way, I came to Banbridge, and was there received at the house of Mr Ross Thomson.

This country is entirely occupied in the manufacture of linen, but the late troubles have made trade to languish. The mills, however, are still going, and it is hoped that a year of peace will restore order and prosperity. Military law was rigorously enforced here on the inhabitants; they were not permitted to have lights on in their houses after nine o'clock, and any person found in the streets after that hour was in danger of being arrested. A fair was held during the time I stayed in this little town, and it passed over quite peacefully; the soldiers promenaded through the market-place and obliged women who wore anything green, ribbon or otherwise, to take it off. Had one-fourth of the precaution taken here been observed in France, there would certainly have been no Revolution. I was much struck here by the thought of the different results which different characters in government may produce. It is remarkable how in France a weak government and foolish ministers have led a people entirely Royalist to slay a King they loved, and whose good qualities they respected, and to destroy a flourishing monarchy for whose prosperity they had been enthusiastic; while here, surrounded by enemies, a vigorous government in Ireland has been able to repress, and hold in the path of duty, a people discontented and seduced by the success of the French innovations.

The boldness of the United Irishmen increased each day as long as the Government did not interfere; many who had joined them had done so out of fear, and there were with them a number of weak, undecided people ready to range themselves on the winning side, and so on the Government's determination to act vigorously, it was only necessary to let the soldiers appear upon the scene, and the difficulties disappeared.

The poor peasant on this occasion, as in so many others, was the dupe of rogues, who put him in the front, and were very careful themselves to stay behind the curtain. The troops went through the country, burning the houses of those who were suspected of having taken the 'Union' oath, or of having arms, and on many occasions they acted with great severity.

On the way to Armagh I passed through a superb country; there is a charming valley, and well-wooded, near Tandragee. Between this town and Armagh I met a company of Orangemen, as they are called, wearing orange cockades, and some of them having ties of the same colour. The peasantry seemed very much afraid of them. I went into one or two cabins to rest myself, and was offered, certainly, hospitality in the ordinary way, but it did not seem to be with the same air as before, and at last, near the town, a good woman said to me, 'You seem to have come from far, my dear Sir, I hope that your umbrella or the string of it will not bring you into trouble.' I laughed at the good woman's fears, but, on reflection, I felt that since she had remarked that my umbrella was greenish, and the cord of a bright green, soldiers might make the same observation, and that in any case it would be very disagreeable to have any trouble over such a silly thing, and I cut the green cord off my umbrella.

THE MAN FROM GOD KNOWS WHERE
Florence Wilson

The Cork-born United Irishman Thomas Russell (1767-1803) was known as 'The Man from God Knows Where'. A close friend of Wolfe Tone's, he befriended Neilson and McCracken while stationed in Belfast with the British army in the early 1790s. This is the longest in the canon of rebellion poems; the 'Dangerous Dan McGrew' of Irish recitations. In And as I Rode by Granard Moat *(1996), Benedict Kiely describes his apprehension as he faced the formidable task of reciting it by heart at Omagh Town Hall. 'Shivering in the wings I stood, as a doctor from Derry sang in a fine soprano about the merry, merry pipes of Pan. To this day that song frightens me. I hated Pan, whoever he was.'*

> Into our townlan', on a night of snow,
> Rode a man from God-knows-where;
> None of us bade him stay or go,
> Nor deemed him friend, nor damned him foe.
> But we stabled his big roan mare;
> For in our townlan' we're a decent folk,
> And if he didn't speak, why none of us spoke,
> And we sat till the fire burned low.
>
> We're a civil sort in our wee place,
> So we made the circle wide

Round Andy Lemon's cheerful blaze,
And wished the man his length of days
And a good end to his ride.
He smiled in under his slouchy hat –
Says he: 'There's a bit of a joke in that,
For we both ride different ways.'

The whiles we smoked we watched him stare
From his seat fornenst the glow.
I nudged Joe Moore: 'You wouldn't dare
To ask him, who he's for meeting there,
And how far he has got to go.'
And Joe wouldn't dare, nor Wully Scott,
And he took no drink – neither cold nor hot –
This man from God-knows-where.

It was closin' time, an' late forbye,
When us ones braved the air –
I never saw worse (may I live or die)
Than the sleet that night, an' I says, says I:
'You'll find he's for stopping there.'
But at screek o' day, through the gable pane,
I watched him spur in the peltin' rain,
And I juked from his rovin' eye.

Two winters more, then the Trouble Year,
When the best that man can feel
Was the pike he kapt in hidin' near,
Till the blood o' hate and the blood o' fear
Would be redder nor rust on the steel.
Us ones quet from mindin' the farms,
Let them take what we gave wi' the weight o' our arms,
From Saintfield to Kilkeel.

In the time o' the Hurry, we had no lead –
We all of us fought with the rest –
And if e'er a one shook like a tremblin' reed
None of us gave neither hint nor heed.
Nor ever even'd we'd guessed.

We men of the North had a word to say,
An' we said it then, in our own dour way,
An' we spoke as we thought was best.

All Ulster over, the weemen cried
For the stan'in' crops on the lan' –
Many's the sweetheart an' many's the bride
Would liefer ha' gone till where He died,
And ha' mourned her lone by her man.
But us ones weathered the thick of it,
And we used to dander along and sit,
In Andy's, side by side.

What with discourse goin' to and fro,
The night would be wearin' thin,
Yet never so late when we rose to go
But someone would say: 'Do ye min' thon snow,
An' the man who came wanderin' in?'
And we be to fall to the talk again,
If by any chance he was One o' Them –
The man who went like the Win'.

Well 'twas gettin' on past the heat o' the year
When I rode to Newtown Fair;
I sold as I could (the dealers were near –
Only three pounds eight for the Innish steer,
An' nothin' at all for the mare!)
I met M'Kee in the throng o' the street,
Says he: 'The grass has grown under our feet
Since they hanged young Warwick here.'

And he told me that Boney had promised help
To a man in Dublin town.
Says he: 'If you've laid the pike on the shelf,
Ye'd better go home hot-fut by yourself,
An' once more take it down.'
So by Comber road I trotted the grey
And never cut corn until Killyleagh
Stood plain on the risin' groun'.

For a wheen o' days we sat waitin' the word
To rise and go at it like men.
But no French ships sailed into Cloughey Bay,
And we heard the black news on a harvest day
That the cause was lost again;
And Joey and me, and Wully boy Scott,
We agreed to ourselves we'd as lief as not
Ha' been found in the thick o' the slain.

By Downpatrick Gaol I was bound to fare
On a day I'll remember, feth,
For when I came to the prison square
The people were waitin' in hundreds there,
An' you wouldn't hear stir nor breath!
For the sodgers were standing, grim an' tall,
Round a scaffold built there fornenst the wall,
An' a man stepped out for death!

I was brave an' near to the edge of the throng,
Yet I knowed the face again.
An' I knowed the set, an' I knowed the walk
An' the sound of his strange up-country talk,
For he spoke out right an' plain.
Then he bowed his head to the swinging rope,
Whiles I said, 'Please God' to his dying hope,
And 'Amen' to his dying prayer,
That the Wrong would cease and the Right prevail
For the man that they hanged at Downpatrick gaol
Was the Man from GOD-KNOWS-WHERE!

A SONG OF THE NORTH
Brian na mBanban

The main players in the County Antrim fight find mention in this song. Brian na mBanban was a pseudonym used by Brian O'Higgins of Carrigaholt, County Clare. He was deported, interned in 1918 and elected to the Dáil in the same year. In 1932 he edited the first Wolfe Tone Annual *and subsequently published it under his own name. 'Brian O'Higgins Christmas cards' were popular reproductions of his verse.*

I sing a song of the Northern Land,
Where the young Republic was bred and born;
Where men of all creed joined hand in hand
To meet the Sassanach might with scorn;
Where heroes fought and where martyrs died
For Ireland's honour and Ireland's weal;
Where faith is stronger than England's pride,
And love more lasting than English steel!

Antrim and Down and Donegal;
Cavan, Fermanagh and green Tyrone;
Derry, Monaghan, Armagh – we love them all
For the tales they tell us of days long flown;
For the songs they sing us of Ninety-Eight;
Of Orr, McCracken, and brave Munroe;
Of Hope, and Russell, and Betsy Grey;
And a thousand others who faced the foe!

From proud Cave Hill up to Breffni's vales,
From the eastern billows to Inishowen,
The breezes are telling a hundred tales
Of the ones who battled to hold their own;
Of boys like Neilson, the young and brave;
Of maids, and mothers, and manly men,
Of priest and parson who gladly gave
Their lives, that the land might be free again!

Men of the North! no shame is yours;
You are still unbeaten by greed and hate;
The hope of the centuries aye endures,
And the faith that was flaming in Ninety-Eight.
The day is dawning when Northern men
Shall sweep the foemen from sea to sea;
And songs of joy will be sung again
At Northern firesides – in Ireland free!

DONEGORE HILL
James Orr

After the battle of Antrim, rebels fled to Donegore Hill. James Orr (1770-1816), the 'Bard of Ballycarry', was a rhyming weaver or 'weaver poet' from Broad Island, County Antrim. He fought with the United Irishmen at Antrim, after which he emigrated to America. He contributed to The Northern Star *and published* Poems on Various Subjects *in 1804.*

> The dew draps wet the fiels o' braird
> That soon the war-horse thartured;
> An' falds were opnd by monie a herd
> Wha lang ere night lay tortured;
> Whan chiels wha grudged to be sae taxed,
> An' tythed by rack-rend blauthry,
> Turned out *en masse* as soon as axed
> An unco throuither squathry,
>   Were we that day.
>
> While close leagued crappies raised the hoards
> O' pikes, pike shafts, forks, fire-locks,
> Some melted lead – some sawed deal boards,
> Some hade, like hens, in byre neuks:
> Wives baked bannocks for their men,
> Wi' tears instead of water;
> And lasses made cockades of green
> For lads wha used to flatter
>   Their prise ilk day.
>
> A brave man firmly leaving hame
> I aye was proud to think on;
> The wife obeying son of shame
> Wi' kindlin' e'e I blink on;
> 'Peace, peace be wi' you! ah, return!
> Ere lang, and lea the daft anes' –
> 'Please Gude (quo' he) before the morn
> In spite of a our chieftains
>   An' guards this day.'

But when the pokes of provender
Were slung on ilka shoulder,
Hags wha to henpeck did'na spare
Loot out the yells the louder –
Had they, whan blood about their heart
Cauld fear make cake and crudle,
Ta'en twa rash gills frae Herdman's quart,
'Twad rouse the calm slow puddle
    I' their veins that day.

Now leaders laith to lea the rigs
Whase leash they feared was broken,
An' privates cursin' purse-proud prigs
Wha brought 'em balls to slacken.
Repentant Painites at their prayers,
An' dastards crousely craikin',
Move on, heroic to the wars
They meant na to partake in
    By night or day.

Some fastin', yet now starve to eat
The piece that butter yellowed;
An' some in flocks, drank out cream crocks
That wives but little valued.
Some lettin' on their burn to mak
The rearguard, goadin', hastened;
Some hunkrin' at a lee dyke back
Boost haughel on, ere fastened
    Their breeks that day.

The truly brave as journeyin' on
They pass by weans an' mithers,
Think on red fiels whare soon may groan
The husbands an' the fathers:
They think how soon the bonnie things
May lose the youths they're true to;
And see the rabble (strife aye brings)
Ravage their homes, while new to
    Sic scenes that day.

When to the top of Donegore
Braid-islan's corps cam postin',
The red-wud, warpin, wild uproar
Was like a bee scap castin';
For ... — ... took ragweed farms
(Fears e'e has still the jaundice),
For Nugent's red coats, bright in arms,
An' rush! the pale-faced randies
    Took leg that day.

The camp's brak up, ower braes and bogs,
The patriots seek their sections;
Arms, ammunition, bread bags, brogues
Lie strewed in all directions.
And some, alas, wha feared to face
Auld fogies, or e'en women,
They swore in pride, tho' yet untried
They yet wad trounce the yeomen
    Some other day.

Come back ye dastards? – can ye ought
Expect at your returnin'
But wives and weans stript, cattle houghed,
An' cots an' claughins burnin',
Na, haste ye hame! ye ken ye'll scape,
That martial law ye're clear O;
The nine-tailed cat or choakin' rape
Is mostly for the hero
    On sic a day.

Saint Paul, I ween, doth counsel weel,
An' somewhere Pope the same in,
That 'first of a', folk should themsel
Impartially examine';
If that's na done, whate'er the loon
May swear to, never swithrin',
In every pinch, he'll basely flinch,
'Guid bye to ye my brethren'
    He'll cry that day.

The ill-starred wights what stayed behind
Were moved by mony a passion;
By dread to stay, by shame to rin,
By scorn and consternation.
Wi' spite they curse, wi' grief they pray,
Now start, now pause – more pity,
''Tis mad to go, 'tis death to stay' –
An unco doleful ditty
    On sic a day.

What joy at home our entrance gave,
'Guid God! is't you? fair fa' ye!
'Twas right, tho' fools may say not brave
To rin before they saw ye!'
'Aye, wife, 'tis true without dispute,
But lest sunts fail in Zion,
I'll have to swear they forced me out;
Better they swing than I on
    Some hangin' day.

My song is done, an' to be free,
Full sair I ween they smarted,
Wha wad hae bell'd the cat awee
Had they no' been deserted;
They lacked the drill, and in my min',
Where it came not before mon,
In tryin' times, maist folk, you'll fin',
Will act like Donegore men
    On any day.

HENRY JOY
P.J.McCall

Henry Joy McCracken was born a Presbyterian in Belfast in 1767. A cotton factory manager, he was a founder-member of the city's branch of the United Irishmen. McCracken became a member of the Ulster Directory. He preached political and religious liberty and founded Belfast's first Sunday school. In 1795 he joined Samuel Neilson, Robert Simms, Thomas Russell and Theobald Wolfe Tone at the site of MacArt's Fort on the summit of Cave Hill, overlooking Belfast. There they took an oath 'Never to desist in our efforts until we have subverted the authority of England over our country and asserted our independence.'

In 1796 McCracken was imprisoned in Kilmainham Jail for over a year. Released on bail, he planned and led the rising in County Antrim. Defeated at Antrim town (see above), he went on the run in the Slemish mountains. His escape to America was planned when he was captured, court-martialled and hanged at Belfast Market House on 17 June. The song embraces the Protestant nationalist tradition.

An Ulsterman I am proud to be; from Antrim's glens I come.
Although I labour by the sea, I have followed flag and drum.
I've heard the martial tramp of men; I've seen them fight and die.
Brave lads, I well remember when I followed Henry Joy.

I pulled my boat up from the sea and hid my sails away,
I hung my nets on a greenwood tree and I scanned the moonlit bay,
The Boys were out, the Redcoats too; I kissed my wife goodbye,
And in the shade of a greenwood glade, I followed Henry Joy.

Now lads, for Ireland's cause we fought, for home and her we bled.
'Though our pikes were few, our hearts beat true and fifty one lay dead.
Yes, many a lassie missed her lad, and mother mourned her boy;
For youth was strong in the gallant throng that followed Henry Joy.

In Antrim Town the tyrant stood, he tore our ranks with ball,
But with a cheer and a pike to clear we swept them o'er the wall.
Our pikes and sabres flashed that day. We won, but lost. Oh, why?
No matter lads, I fought beside, and shielded Henry Joy.

In Belfast Town they built a tree, and the Redcoats mustered there;
I watched them come as the beat of drum, rolled from the barrack square.
He kissed his sister, then went aloft, as he bade a last goodbye;
My God! he died, sure I turned and cried, 'They have murdered Henry Joy!'

HENRY JOY McCRACKEN
Anon.

This version of the ballad voices the sentiments of Mary Bodle, who had a child by McCracken. She mourns his betrayal and defeat as she anticipates his escape to France (an escape to America was envisaged, however).

Some sources credit P.J. McCall with this version also. It appears in Henry Joy McCracken *by Fred Heatley (Belfast Wolfe Tone Society 1967), where it is attributed to T.P. Cuming.*

It was on the Belfast Mountains I heard a maid complain
And she vexed the sweet June evening with her heart-broken strain,
Saying, 'Woe is me, life's anguish is more that I can dree,
Since Henry Joy McCracken died on the gallows tree.

'At Donegore he proudly rode and he wore a suit of green,
And brave though vain at Antrim his sword flashed lightning keen,
And when by spies surrounded his band to Slemish fled,
He came unto the Cavehill for to rest a weary head.

'I watched for him each night long as in our cot he slept,
At daybreak to the heather to MacArt's fort we crept,
When news came from Greencastle of a good ship anchored nigh,
And down by yon wee fountain we met to say good-bye.

'He says, "My love be cheerful for tears and fears are vain,"
He says, "My love be hopeful our land shall rise again,"
He kissed me ever fondly, he kissed me three times o'er,
Saying, "Death shall never part us my love for evermore."

'That night I climbed the Cavehill and watched till morning blazed,
And when its fires had kindled across the loch I gazed,
I saw an English tender at anchor off Garmoyle,
But alas! no good ship bore him away to France's soil.

'And twice that night a tramping came from the old shore road,
'Twas Ellis and his yeomen, false Niblock with them strode,
My father home returning the doleful story told,
"Alas," he says, "young Harry Joy for fifty pounds is sold."

"'And is it true," I asked her, "Yes it is true," she said,
"For to this heart that loved him I pressed his gory head,
And every night pale bleeding his ghost comes to my side,
My Harry, my dead Harry, comes for his promised bride.'"

Now on the Belfast mountains this fair maid's voice is still,
For in a grave they laid her on high Carnmoney Hill,
And the sad waves beneath her chant a requiem for the dead,
The rebel wind shrieks freedom above her weary head.

RODY McCORLEY
Ethna Carbery

There are two versions of this lively march. They recall a young man who fought at the battle of Antrim and who was hanged at Toomebridge shortly after it ended.

Ethna Carbery (1866-1911) is the pseudonym of Anna Johnston from Bally-mena, who married Seamus MacManus, poet and storyteller. She contributed poems to The Nation, United Ireland *and other nationalist publications and, with Alice Milligan, edited* The Shan Van Vocht. *She published books of short stories.*

Ho! See the fleet-foot host of men
Who speed with faces wan,
From farmstead and from fisher's cot
Upon the banks of Bann;
They come with vengeance in their eyes,
Too late, too late are they,
For Rody McCorley goes to die
On the Bridge of Toome today.

Oh Ireland, Mother Ireland,
You love them still the best;
The fearless brave who fighting fall,
Upon your hapless breast
But never a one of all your dead
More bravely fell in fray,
Than he who marches to his fate
On the Bridge of Toome to-day.

Up the narrow street he stepped
Smiling and proud and young;
About the hemp-rope on his neck
The golden ringlets clung.
There's never a tear in the blue, blue eyes
Both glad and bright are they;
As Rody MacCorley goes to die
On the Bridge of Toome to-day.

Ah! when he last stepped up that street
His shining pike in hand,
Behind him marched in grim array
A stalwart earnest band!
For Antrim town! for Antrim town!
He led them to the fray —
And Rody MacCorley goes to die
On the Bridge of Toome to-day.

The grey coat and its sash of green
Were brave and stainless then;
A banner flashed beneath the sun
Over the marching men —
The coat hath many a rent this noon
The sash is torn away,
And Rody MacCorley goes to die
On the Bridge of Toome to-day.

Oh, how his pike flashed to the sun!
Then found a foeman's heart!
Through furious fight, and heavy odds
He bore a true man's part;
And many a red-coat bit the dust
Before his keen pike-play —
But Rody MacCorley goes to die
On the Bridge of Toome to-day.

Because he loved the Motherland,
Because he loved the Green,
He goes to meet the martyr's fate

With proud and joyous mien,
True to the last, true to the last,
He treads the upward way –
Young Rody MacCorley goes to die
On the Bridge of Toome to-day.

RODY McCORLEY
Anon.

The hero now I speak of, he was proper tall and straight,
Like to the lofty poplar tree his body was complete,
His growth was like the tufted fir that does ascend the air,
And waving o'er his shoulders broad the locks of yellow hair.

In sweet Duneane this youth was born and reared up tenderly,
His parents educated him, all by their industry,
Both day and night they sorely toiled all for their family,
Till desolation it came on by cursed perjury.

'Twas first the father's life they took and secondly the son,
The mother tore her old grey locks, she says 'I am undone
They took from me my property, my houses and my land,
And in the parish where I was born I dare not tread upon.'

'Farewell unto you sweet Drumaul, if in you I had stayed,
Among the Presbyterians I wouldn't have been betrayed,
The gallows tree I'd ne'er have seen had I remained there
For Dufferin you betrayed me, McErlean you set the snare.

'In Ballyscullion I was betrayed, woe be unto the man,
Who swore me a defender and a foe unto the crown,
Which causes Rody for to lie beneath the spreading thorn,
He'll sigh and say 'Alas the day that ever I was born'.'

Soon young Rody was conveyed to Ballymena town,
He was loaded there with irons strong, his bed was the cold ground,
And there young Rody he must wait until the hour has come,
When a court martial does arrive for to contrive his doom.

They called upon an armed band, an armed band came soon,
To guard the clever tall young youth down to the Bridge of Toome,
And when young Rody he came up the scaffold to ascend,
He looked at east and looked at west to view his loving friends.

And turning round unto the north he cried 'O faithless friend,
'Twas you who proved my overthrow and brought me to this end.
Since 'tis upon Good Friday that I'll executed be,
Convenient to the Bridge of Toome upon a Gallows Tree.'

They called on Father Devlin, his reverence came with speed,
'Here's one of Christ's own flock,' he said, 'ye shepherds for to feed.'
He gave to him the Heavenly food, that nourishes the soul,
That it may rest eternally while his body is in the mould.

And looking up unto the Lord he says, 'O Lord receive,
Here is my soul, I do bestow my body unto the grave,
That it may rest in peace and joy without the least surprise,
Till Michael sounds his trumpet loud, and says 'Ye dead arise'.

GENERAL MUNROE
Anon.

A Scottish Protestant linen draper from Lisburn, Henry Munroe was head of the town's Freemasons. He was elected leader of County Down rebels because of his record in speaking for Catholic Emancipation and Parliamentary reform. Tradition tells that, after his defeat at Ballynahinch he was found hiding in a potato field and brought to Hillsborough. Later, he was hanged in Lisburn market place, opposite his own home from where his wife and mother watched. A fellow prisoner acted as executioner and Munroe gave the signal to pull the ladder from under him by dropping his own hand- kerchief. This version of the song appears in Broadside Ballads, *National Library of Ireland.*

My name is George Campbell. At the age of eighteen,
I joined the United men to strive for the Green
And many a battle I did undergo,
With that hero commander, brave General Munroe.

Come all you good people, and listen with woe,
Till I sing a few verses concerning Munroe:
May liberty to Erin thro' this nation down flow,
And the tyrant did suffer for the death of Munroe.

Were you at the battle of Ballynahinch,
When the country arose to stand their defence,
And the army all gathered to prove their overthrow,
When commanded by that hero called General Munroe.

My name is George Clayton, and my age is nineteen,
In many a skirmish and battle I've been,
And many a great hardship I did undergo,
When commanded by that hero called General Munroe.

Long life to Lord Moira, and long may he reign
We fought the last battle within his demesne,
May liberty and freedom thro' this nation flow,
And the tyrants did suffer for General Munroe.

Munroe took the mountains, his men took the field,
They swore that to tyrants they never would yield;
We fought them four hours, and beat them to and fro,
When commanded by that hero called General Munroe.

Munroe being weary, and wanting to sleep,
He gave a woman ten guineas his secrets to keep,
When she got the money the devil tempted her so,
That she sent for the army who surrounded Munroe.

The army did come and surrounded them all,
He thought to escape but he could not at all;
They marched him to Lisburn without more delay,
And put his head on a spear that very same day.

If you had seen the cavalry when they came there,
Their horses did caper and prance in the rear;
The traitor being with them, as you may all know,
'Twas out of a hay-stack they hauled poor Munroe.

Then in came his sister well clothed in green
With a sword by her side, both sharp, long, and keen;
Three cheers she did give them, and away she did go,
Saying, I'll have revenge for my brother Munroe.

Now he being taken, and brought to the tree,
Said, farewell to my comrades, wherever they be;
There's nothing doth grieve me but parting you so —
May the Lord have mercy on brave General Munroe.

Here's a health to each hero, who for freedom will stand,
May their souls rest in peace who died for our land;
Remember the martyrs who were slain by the foe,
Brave Emmet, Fitzgerald, and General Munroe.

ULSTER'S JOAN OF ARC

Bessie/Betsy Grey, one of the legendary figures of the Northern rising, joined the rebel forces in County Down along with her brother, George, and her lover, William Boal, and was prominent in the battle of Ballynahinch, riding a white horse and carrying a green flag. After the defeat of General Munroe's forces all three were killed as they retreated, Bessie allegedly being shot by Thomas Nelson of Anahilt. She quickly became the subject of numerous songs and stories, and of a romantic novel, Betsy Grey or Hearts of Down *by W.G. Lyttle (1888).*

BESSIE GREY
Anon.

If through Killinchy's woods and vales
You searched on a summer day,
The loveliest maiden to be found
Was bonnie Bessie Grey.

The wild flowers shed their sweet perfume
Whene'er she passed them by,
And put their brightest colours on
To meet her gladsome eye.

She gathered pebbles in the brook,
And berries in the dell —

A favourite wheresoe'er she went –
The neighbours loved her well.

And Willie loved her tenderly,
And won her maiden heart;
He loved, and was beloved again,
And nought but death would part.

Alas! alas! Killinchy woods,
Woe worth the summer day
When Willie left his native hills
To join the battle fray!

And Bessie by her brother's side
Rode on in sadden'd glee,
While many a weeping one cried out
'God bless the gallant three!'

'Twas morning when they reached the hill,
And welcome words were said
By many who, before the night,
Lay numbered in the dead.

Fierce looks were quickly interchanged
Between contending foes.
As sound of sharp'ning pike and song
From Ednavady rose.

And shouts of noisy soldiery
From Windmill Hill were heard
As proud defiance lifted up
The Musket and the sword.

Now Bessie on her tiny steed
Bore high her flag of green;
Where'er the battle fiercely raged,
Killinchy's Lass was seen.

Now woe be on thee, Anahilt!
And woe be on the day,
When brother, lover, both were slain,
And with them Bessie Grey.

Mary Balfour (1775-c.1820), daughter of a Derry clergyman, ran a school in Lim-
avaddy and later in Belfast. Her poems, published in 1810, included the following
lament for Bessie Grey.

The star of evening slowly rose,
Through shades of twilight gleaming,
It shone to witness Erin's woes,
Her children's life-blood streaming;
'Twas then sweet star, thy pensive ray,
Fell on the cold, unconscious clay,
That wraps the breast of Bessie Grey,
In softened lustre beaming.

Poor maiden, she, with hope elate,
With fond affection swelling,
To share a lover's, brother's fate,
Forsook her peaceful dwelling;
With them to share her simple store,
O all their griefs a balm to pour,
The field of death she dared explore,
Each selfish thought repelling.

The battle lost, the vanquished fled,
The victors swift pursuing,
And trampling o'er the mighty dead,
With blood their steps bedewing;
They come to where, with fervent zeal,
These friends their Bessie would conceal:
Mark! how they point the gleaming steel,
Their destined victim viewing.

'Oh spare that life!' her brother cries,
With indignation glowing,
Tears tremble in the lover's eyes,
His arms around her throwing;
But lover's, brother's sighs are vain,
Even in their sight the maid is slain,
And now on Erin's ruined plain,
Their mingled blood is flowing.

Of the Imprisoned

The Sheares Brothers, Henry (1753-98) and John (1766-98), were born in Cork, sons of a wealthy banker and Member of Parliament. Both were educated at Trinity College and called to the Bar. Both became members of the United Irishmen and the National Directory. They were informed upon, captured, found guilty of high treason and executed in public outside Newgate Prison on 14 July 1798. Their remains lie in the crypt of St Michan's Church, Dublin.

Henry received a commission in the British army and served for three years. Married, with four children, his wife died in 1791. The children were sent to France and, while visiting them there, Henry became interested in revolutionary strategy.

John visited Henry in France and joined him in pursuing similar tactics in Ireland. He contributed regularly to the nationalist publication, *The Press*.

GOOD TASTE

In 1860 an edition of Richard R. Madden's work The United Irishmen, Their Lives and Times *was published. It contained an anecdote about John Sheares that commends his good taste in certain matters.*

The following little anecdote, related to me by Miss Steele, will show the kind of terms John Sheares was on with her mother. He called one morning and found Lady Steele examining a new bonnet. She was not pleased with the fashion of it, and said it was a 'nonsensical shape – there was no sense in it'. John Sheares differed, 'Now I hope there is some sense in it.'

John Sheares evinced powers of perception of female excellence of no common kind, judgment capable of appreciating qualities in woman, of head and heart of the highest order, when he fixed his affections on and aspired to the hand of Maria Steele. Now that she is gone and many years have passed away since her death, it may be permitted to me to express an opinion of that lady, that in more restricted terms on my first acquaintance with her upwards of twenty years ago I ventured to give utterance to. A person so estimable, so right-minded of intellectual tastes, so well cultured, such refined yet genial feelings and generous sentiments, so truly lady-like, yet so single-hearted, as the woman who engaged the affections of John Sheares, is rarely to be heard of, and still more rarely to be met with, in any country or in any circle. Maria Steele, the daughter of Sir R. Parker Steele, was born at Portobello, Dublin, in 1779. In 1798 (in her twenty-second year), her father being then dead, she resided with her mother,

Lady Steele, at their house No. 11 Merrion Square, South. She married, in 1802, Joshua Smith, Esq., Barrister-at-law, of No. 13 North Great George's Street, called to the Irish bar in 1798. Mrs Smith died in her 63rd year, in September, 1841, at her house No. 31 Upper Fitzwilliam-Street, leaving one son, her only surviving child, Robert Bramston Smith, Esq., an eminent barrister, an amiable and highly intellectual man, well capable of appreciating his mother's fine qualities, and of duly honouring her memory. She had two other children whom she survived – one of them an eminent physician attached to the English embassy in Paris, Sir Francis Smith, a young man of great promise, who died very shortly before her. An elder sister of Mrs Smith, Miss Eliza Steel, who resided in Baggot Street, died in 1845. The remains of Mrs Smith were interred in the family vault of Sir R. Parker Steele, in St George's Church, Dublin.

TO MRS. N.

Samuel Neilson, who was imprisoned for editing the Belfast newspaper The Northern Star, *was a reckless member of the Leinster and National Directory of the United Irishmen. He advocated marching the United Irishmen's armies of the surrounding counties on Dublin. While on a desperate mission to reorganize a depleted Dublin movement, he was arrested but, before his trial in August, he co-operated with the government in return for permission to emigrate to America. On 14 July 1798, he wrote from Newgate to his wife.*

Newgate, 14th July, 1798.
Among all my other calamities it has not been the least, that I was likely to leave this scene of everlasting sorrow and renewed affliction without knowing my dear wife, children, and friends did so much as exist. I need not, therefore, tell you what pleasure I felt on receipt of yours, with your accustomed fortitude. I trust it will not fail you in case of the worst, for which we should, on such occasions, be always prepared. I have had a smart illness these few days past, which vexed me the more as it was likely to affect my head, which at this crisis would be dreadful indeed. I am, however, nearly quite well again. My irons have been taken off, and I get walking in the lobby much earlier and later than formerly, *but alone*. My appetite is still very poor, and my pillow nearly sleepless.

I cannot form the slightest conjecture who is to swear against me, nor is the day of my trial fixed; it may be to-morrow. The Messrs Sheares were tried yesterday, and their trial continued from nine in the morning until half-past seven this morning, when they were found guilty. I understand my name was not implicated in any part of this immensely long trial of twenty-two hours.

The evidence (for me) from Belfast is intended chiefly as a proof of the wickedness of my persecutors and the extent of my sufferings. I have had but a few minutes' conversation with my agent since the return of his son, for whose safety he has been extremely anxious these two days past. Mr Horner has got an order to see me, and he paid his first visit to-day. I think this condescension in Mr Cooke the more extraordinary, as I had been treated with such unexampled severity. You will, perhaps, be astonished when I tell you, that it was for several days the orders to the sentinel to shoot any of my fellow-prisoners who would ask me (across a yard eighty feet wide) how I was, and I locked up in a cage; nay, out of 170 prisoners who have access to a yard from which my cell could be seen, not more than two or three would venture to *look* through the bars into my grating of a morning, to see whether I was alive or dead.

Mr Curran has been with me two or three times, and expresses warm friendship. Mr Crawford, my agent, is very indefatigable – indeed more so than I wish. He has heard that my celebrated friend Bird, *alias* Smith, is once more to be my accuser; but this is too ridiculous and wicked even for the present times ...

The Messrs Sheares got their sentence to-day at four o'clock: they are now here in irons, and will, I believe, suffer to-morrow, but in what part of the town is yet unknown.

My mother and uncle will look after the farm, and your father after the town parks; to these three I advise you to entrust everything out of doors; the children will be sufficient for your care. And oh! let me entreat you once more to rear them hardily, to do everything in the house in turn. To William, reading, writing, English well – no other language, nor dancing; to the girls, the same, with knitting and sewing, but no tambour nonsense. Let their dress be plain and homely, befitting their state; and of all things, labour to form their minds by curbing pride and inciting to virtue and industry, not by scolding and whipping, or cajoling, but by *emulation*, which is by far the safest and surest incentive to exertion.

S. N.

🐜 🐜 🐜

Of Humbert

Most of the fighting in Leinster and in Ulster was over when the French finally set foot on Irish soil. The plan drawn up by Wolfe Tone and the French War and Marine departments envisaged small detachments initially leaving several ports and landing unobtrusively at Irish harbours in advance of the main invasion. To this end, General Humbert waited at Rochelle with 1000 troops; General Hardy commanded a further 3000 at Brest, while the main body, under General Kilmaine, was estimated at 9000. Tone was not pleased; he estimated that 10,000 to 15,000 would be needed initially, with more to follow. James Napper Tandy, more willing than wise and somewhat bumptious, claimed that 30,000 Irishmen would rise in arms on his appearance. But as the rebellion was petering out in Ireland, the French still prevaricated.

Finally, around mid-August, Humbert took the initiative. By extortion, he received from the magistrates, merchants and other wealthy members of the Rochelle community, money for arms and provisions. He set sail for Ireland with a small fleet of transports and frigates, 1099 armed men and as many spare muskets and guineas. With just a few artillery pieces, the expedition was a brave if somewhat desperate venture.

Bartholomew Teeling, Matthew Tone (brother of Theobald), an officer named Sullivan and Humbert's *aide-de-camp*, Captain Byrne, were among the complement. The French landed at Killala, County Mayo, on 22 August 1798.

MISE 'GUS TUSA

Gan anim

A contemporary song (first published by Colm Ó Lochlainn in An Claisceadal I *c.1931) refers to the French at Killala and Castlebar. A translation follows.*

An raibh tú 'g Cill Ala
Nó i gCaisleán an Bharraigh,
Nó 'n bhfaca tú 'n campa
Bhí age na Francaigh.

CÓR
Mise 'gus tusa 'gus ruball na muice
'Gus bacaigh Shíol Aindí, bacaigh Shíol Aindí.

Do bhí mé 'g Cill Ana
'S i gCaisleán an Bharraigh
'S do chonaic mé 'n campa
Bhí age na Francaigh.
CÓR

An raibh tú 'r a' gCruach
Nó 'n bhfaca tú 'n slua
Do bhí ar Chruach Phádraic?
Bhí ar Chruach Phádraic?
CÓR

Do bhí mé 'r a' gCruach
Is do chonaic mé 'n slua
Do bhí ar Chruach Phádraic?
Bhí ar Chruach Phádraic?
CÓR

ME AND YOU
Anon.

Scottish regiments, often referred to as 'Bucky Heelanders' operated in Mayo during the rebellion. The 'bacaigh Shíol Aindí' (cripple of the race of Andrew) in the Irish above probably refers to one of them. Climbing the 'Reek' or Croagh Patrick is a penitential exercise.

Were you in Killala
Or in Castlebar,
Or did you see the camp
The French had there?

CHORUS
Me and you and the pig's tail
And Bucky Heelander, Bucky Heelander.

I was in Killala
And in Castlebar
And I saw the camp
The French had there.
CHORUS

Were you on the Reek
Or did you see the throng
That was on Croagh Patrick
That was on Croagh Patrick.
CHORUS

I was on the Reek
And I saw the throng
That was on Croagh Patrick
That was on Croagh Patrick.
CHORUS

THE MEN OF THE WEST
William Rooney

Humbert wasted valuable time training and drilling local rebels before moving to establish a bridgehead. Taking Ballina without a fight, he moved towards Castlebar where General Hutchinson's defending garrison was reinforced by General Lake's troops. On 27 August Humbert arrived by an unexpected route, a mountain track below Nephin; Hutchinson's outposts waited at Foxford, on the other side of Lough Conn.

Lake was now in command. He had a Royal Artillery troop, the Fraser Fencibles, the Galway yeomen, and the Kilkenny and Longford Militia. In reserve were Lord Roden's Foxhunters with some yeomen and carbineers. Humbert's second-in-command, Sarrazin, charged. The garrison fled, some to Tuam, others to Athlone. Their hasty retreat went down in Irish and British lore as 'The Races of Castlebar'.

Eventually Humbert set out to connect with the United Irishmen in Ulster. He defeated a local garrison at Collooney, County Sligo, but, hearing about the Longford rebels' rising, he swung around and headed south-west. He was defeated at Ballinamuck on 8 September 1798 after a token resistance.

This popular march extols the United Irishmen who joined the long-awaited French under Humbert.

A Dublin man, Rooney (1873-1901) was a classmate of Arthur Griffith's, establishing with him the Celtic Literary Society in 1893 and Cumann na nGaedheal in 1900. He contributed to a number of nationalist publications and, in 1890, revived the title United Irishman *for a new nationalist publication. He appointed Griffith its editor in 1899.*

While you honour in song and in story the names of the patriot men,
Whose valour has covered with glory full many a mountain and glen,
Forget not the boys of the heather, who marshalled their bravest and best,
When Eire was broken in Wexford and looked for revenge to the West.

    CHORUS
    I give you the gallant old West, boys,
    Where rallied our bravest and best
    When Ireland lay broken and bleeding;
    Hurrah for the men of the West!

The hilltops with glory were glowing, 'twas the eve of a bright harvest day,
When the ships we'd been wearily waiting sailed into Killala's broad bay;
And over the hills went the slogan, to awaken in every breast

The fire that has never been quenched, boys, among the true hearts of the
West.
CHORUS

Killala was ours ere the midnight, and high over Ballina town
Our banners in triumph were waving before the next sun had gone down.
We gathered to speed the good work, boys, the true men anear and afar;
And history can tell how we routed the Redcoats through old Castlebar.
CHORUS

And pledge me 'The stout sons of France,' boys, bold Humbert and all his
brave men,
Whose tramp, like the trumpet of battle, brought hope to the drooping
again.
Since Eire has caught to her bosom on many a mountain and hill.
The gallants who fell so they're here, boys, to cheer us to victory still.
CHORUS

Though all the bright dreamings we cherished went down in disaster and
woe,
The spirit of old is still with us that never would bend to the foe;
And Connaught is ready whenever the loud rolling tuck of the drum
Rings out to awaken the echoes and tell us the morning has come.

FINAL CHORUS
So here's to the gallant old West, boys,
Who rallied her bravest and best
When Ireland was broken and bleeding;
Hurrah, boys! Hurray for the West!

ROUSE HIBERNIANS
Anon.

*'Vive!' The cry of the French revolution was popular among the United Irishmen.
When the French actually landed, it took on a new and emotive significance.*

Rouse, Hibernians, from your slumbers!
See the moment just has arrived
Imperious tyrants for to humble,

Our French brethren are at hand.
Vive la United heroes,
Triumphant always may they be!
Vive la, our gallant brethren
That have come to set us free!

Erin's sons, be not faint-hearted,
Welcome, sing then 'Ca ira',
From Killala they are marching
To the bold tune of 'Vive la'.
Vive la United heroes,
Triumphant always may be!
Vive la, our gallant brethren
That have come to set us free!

To arms quickly, and be ready;
Join the ranks and never you flee,
Determined stand by one another
And from all tyrants you'll be free.
Vive la United heroes,
Triumphant always may be!
Vive la, our gallant brethren
That have come to set us free!

Cruel tyrants who oppressed you,
Now with terror we will see their fall!
Then bless the heroes who caress you;
Orange now goes to the wall.
Vive la United heroes,
Triumphant always may be!
Vive la, our gallant brethren
That have come to set us free!

BISHOP STOCK

A vivid eye-witness account of the French landing is contained in Bishop Stock's
Narrative of what passed at Killala in the County of Mayo and the Parts
Adjacent during the Summer of 1798. *The work was published, anonymously, in*

1800. Part of it comments on the behaviour of the rebels. Colonel Charost was appointed as local commandant by Humbert.

Although the cathedral church of Killalla escaped violence in the manner related, there was scarcely another protestant place of worship throughout the united diocese that did not quickly bear evident marks of the religious intolerance of the rebels. But their malice was principally directed against a presbyterian meeting-house between Killalla and Ballina, the only one of the kind, I believe, in the county. It had lately been fitted up and decently ornamented by the unwearied exertions of the minister, the rev. [*sic*] Mr Marshall, whose exemplary character had entitled him to so much respect, that all his protestant neighbours without distinction had contributed to give him a handsome place of worship. In a very short time after the commencement of the rebellion, nothing remained of the meeting-house except the walls. The congregations experienced no better treatment than their temple. They were a colony of very industrious weavers from the North, translated hither some years back by the Earl of Arran to a village of his, called Mullifaragh, where they had flourished so much that they were grown rich and had increased to the number of a thousand persons. The name of Orangemen had but just begun to be heard of in Connaught; and much it were to be wished, that no such society had ever appeared among us, to furnish to the Romanists too plausible a pretext for alarm and hostility against their protestant brethren. The bishop had opposed their establishment with all his might. On the very day when the invasion happened, he was busied in entering a protest, in his primary visitation charge, against the first sentence of the oath by which Orangemen are united together, 'I am not a Roman catholic.' The words sounded in his ears too like those in the prophet, *Stand off, I am holier than thou*; and assuredly they are not calculated to conciliate. The society had originated in the same northern county which some years before had disgraced itself by an infamy new to protestants, an actual expulsion of Roman catholics from their homes. The perpetrators of this lawless deed were supposed to be chiefly presbyterians; and now upon the unoffending people of that persuasion in Connaught were to be retaliated the injuries done to the Romanists in Ulster. The village of Mullifaragh, on pretence of searching for arms, was ransacked in three nocturnal invasions of the rebels, till there was nothing left in it worth carrying away; and this in defiance of a protection under the hand of the commandant, obtained for them and their pastor by the bishop. The poor sufferers came in tears to M. Charost to return him a protection which had done them no good. It shocked him very much. Often did he whisper to the bishop, that no consid-eration should prevail on him again to trust himself to such a horde of savages as the Irish.

THE PRIEST OF ADDERGOOL
William Rooney

This ballad refers to Fr Andrew Conroy, who was parish priest of Addergool, near Dunmore, County Galway. When the French arrived at Killala, he roused his parishioners and led them to the support of Humbert. He also drew maps for the French. He was hanged in Castlebar.

There's some one at the window. Tap! tap! tap anew:
Sharp through the silent midnight it speeds the cottage through.
'Some poor soul speeding onward, some sudden call to go
Unshriven on the footpath we all of us must know.'

Thus muses he, that sagart, as from his couch he flies
And opens full the window where wonder widened eyes
Look into his, and accents with haste all husky spake:
'The French are in Killala, and all the land's awake!

''Twas William Burke that told me as riding he went by
With letters for the Saxons in Castlebar – and I
Came hot upon his footsteps to tell you all I knew
And let you teach the people what's best for them to do!'

There's silence for a second – out speaks the sagart then –
'I'll follow him that told you; you gather all the men;
Keep watch beside the houses till I come back to you –
And God to guide our counsels, we'll then see what to do!'

The priest is in the saddle and down the road he flies,
A while his echoed paces upon the silence rise,
Then melt into the distance, while figures one by one,
Steal out from gloom and shadow and muster in the dawn.

The moonlight floods the mountain, no horseman hies in sight,
No sound comes up the valley to break the hush of night;
Yet on the sagart presses and close beside the town,
Still wrapped in dream and slumber, he runs his quarry down.

A moment more the messenger has yielded up his load,
Another, and a penitent, he's kneeling on the road;

There in the solemn moonlight he pledges hand and heart,
He's knelt a slave – he rises now to do a true man's part.

'Tis done, and ere that noontide pours over hill and glen,
In Ballina they're standing, that sagart and his men;
His part is o'er, he may not lift the brand in bloody fray;
But he hath seen his duty, and shown his flock the way.

A few short weeks, the noonday sun shines over Castlebar,
Triumphant through the country rides ruin near and far;
And on a scaffold proudly a priest stands bound – 'Tis he,
Who rode him through the midnight for Ireland's Liberty!

There's many a lonely hearth-stone tonight in wide Mayo,
There's many a gallant heart content again can never know
But darkest woe and grief from him the saintly, true and tried,
Who on the Saxon scaffold that day for freedom died.

We'll shrine his name and story bright to guide us on,
Till hope has reached its haven, till gloom and grief are gone;
Till free men's hands may fashion the name and fame on high,
Of all who trod that pathway and showed the way to die!

CASTLEBAR COURTESY

Sir Jonah Barrington was impressed by the social graces of the French at Castlebar.

The native character of the French never showed itself more strongly than after this action. When in full possession of the large town of Castlebar, they immediately set about putting their persons in the best order, and the officers advertised a ball and supper that night, for the ladies of the town; this, it is said, was well attended; decorum in all points was strictly preserved; they paid ready money for everything; in fact, the French army established the French character wherever they occupied.

Hearing that Westmeath and Longford had risen, Humbert altered his northward march on 7 September to return and join them in a push towards Dublin. He crossed the Shannon at Carrick-on-Shannon and rested at Cloone village before moving. As it happened, the rebels had been defeated at Wilson's Hospital, County Westmeath.

MARIA EDGEWORTH

The following anecdotal extract by a famous author and her father suggests that the landlord class often looked on the rebellion with some trepidation and not a little puzzlement. It is taken from The Black Book *of Edgeworthstown and Other Edgeworth Memories, 1587-1817 (London 1925).*

Maria Edgeworth (1767-1849) helped her father, Richard Lovell Edgeworth, on his large estate. On his instructions, she prepared moral stories for her siblings. A series of these appeared in 1796 as The Parent's Assistant. *In the rebellion year she and her father published* Practical Education. *Her most famous novel,* Castle Rackrent, *appeared in 1800.*

The French, who landed at Killala, were on the march toward Longford. The touch of Ithuriel's spear could not have been more effectual than the arrival of this intelligence in showing people in their real forms. In some faces joy struggled for a moment with feigned sorrow and then, encouraged by sympathy, yielded to the natural expression. Still my father had no reason to distrust those in whom he had placed confidence; his tenants were steady; he saw no change in any of the men of his corps, though they were in the most perilous situation, having rendered themselves obnoxious to rebels by becoming yeomen, and yet standing without means of defence, their arms not having arrived.

The evening of the day when the news of [their] approach came to Edgeworthstown, all seemed quiet. But early the next morning, September 4, a report reached us that the rebels were up in arms within a mile of the village, pouring in from West Meath, hundreds strong. We could not at first believe the report. An hour afterwards it was contradicted. An English servant, who was sent out to ascertain the truth, brought back word that he had ridden three miles from the village ... and that he had seen only twenty or thirty men with green boughs in their hats and pikes in their hands, who said they were standing there to protect themselves against the Orangemen, who were coming down to cut them to pieces.

Maria goes on to tell how her father sent a despatch to the commanding officer of the garrison in Longford requesting protection and how an officer in charge of an ammunition escort arrived, offering protection if the family wished to evacuate to Longford. Fortunately for them, they declined:

About a quarter of an hour after the officer and the escort had departed, we, who were all assembled in the portico of the house, heard a report like a loud clap of thunder. The doors and windows shook, and a few minutes afterwards the officer galloped into the yard and threw himself off his horse into my father's arms almost senseless. The ammunition cart had blown up, one of the officers had been severely wounded, and the horses and the man leading them killed; the wounded officer was at a farm-

house on the Longford Road at about two miles distance. Mrs Edgeworth went immediately to give her assistance; she left her carriage for the use of the wounded gentleman, and rode back. At the entrance of the village she was stopped by a gentlemen in
great terror who, taking hold of the bridle of her horse, begged her not to attempt to
go further, assuring her that the rebels were coming into town. But she answered that
she must and would return to her family. She rode on and found us waiting anxiously
waiting for her. No assistance could be afforded from Longford; the rebels were
reassembling and advancing towards the village, and there was no alternative but to
leave our home as fast as possible. As we passed through the village, we heard nothing
but the entreaties, lamentations and objurgations of those who could not procure the
means of carrying off their goods or their families; most painful when we could give
no assistance.

THE BATTLE OF BALLINAMUCK

*Pádraig Mac Gréine, from Ballinalee, County Longford, took down the following
account of the battle of Ballinamuck from a nonagenarian, Patrick 'Grey Pat' Gill
from Edenmore, Ballinamuck, in May 1933* (Bealoideas V [1935], pp. 157-9):

My grandmother lived here in the end of her days, and was buried out of this house.
Her own name was Cassidy from Fardromin, between Drumlish and Ballinamuck, and
that's where all the Gills lived until after '98 when my grandfather came over here and
took a big wipe of land here in Edenmore. I often heard her talking of the battle of
Ballinamuck, for she was there that day and had a child on her back, not two years old.

The night before the battle the French and General Blake camped at Cloone [Co.
Leitrim]. They stopped at the house of a man named West, and that night a man called
Larry McGlynn stole the chains out of the cannon they had, and threw them into a
draw-well. The next day the men had to pull the cannon to Ballinamuck, and only for
the chains being gone they'd have got as far as Granard. If they had got that far, it
would have been a different story, but the English caught up with them at Ballinamuck,
and they had to fight. The English had a cannon on Coillte Craobhach hill [N.W. of
Ballinamuck] and the Irish cannon was on the mearin' of Coillte Craobhach and
Graigue [E. of Ballinamuck]. All the men of the whole place were gathered, and the
women were there too with bonnocks of bread and creels of potatoes for the French.
My grandmother was there too, and I heard her say that she come on Frenchmen and
they pullin' rushes and chewin' the roots with solid hunger. She had a few bonnocks of
bread that was after gettin' wet somehow or other, but she gave them to the soldiers,
and they took them and squeezed the water out of them and ate them, even though
they were only like dough.

Well, Gunner Magee was the Irish gunner, and the third shot he fired he blew up
the English magazine. My grandfather Michael Gill was there in the fight with the pike-

men, and his brother Robin was in charge of the third line of pikemen. When the English magazine was blown up General Blake ordered the French and the pikemen up the side of Sean Mullach [a hill to the N. of Ballinamuck] so that they could come down on the English, but before they got to the top the English were there and began to mow them down. Gunner Magee could not use his cannon, for his own men were between him and the English. The poor Croppies had only poor ways of fightin', and they were slaughtered out of a face. They were runnin' in all directions over the country, and the Cavan Orangemen were round about on horseback, and anywhere they saw a man runnin' they sabred him. My grandfather came off safe and sound, but Robin got a scar of a bullet along the hip, and the caipín of his left elbow was knocked off by another bullet. Himself and a man called Sorohan were runnin' away, and they came upon a Frenchman sittin' under a bush with his gun on his knees.

'You have a gun an' can save us', says Sorohan.

'I can't' says he, 'the truce is up [*i.e.* called].'

Up came a dragoon.

'Kneel down, ye Croppy dog an' say your prayers!' says he to Sorohan, ridin' up an splittin' open his skull with his sabre. Robin caught the crook of his pike in his collar and dragged him out of the saddle. He pulled him across the ditch, for he was a powerful man over fourteen stone weight, and put his foot on his neck.

'Spare me and I'll give ye a pass!' says he.

'Wait till I loosen the pike,' says Robin. He loosened the pike and gave him one clout across the forehead that split his head in two.

The English brought the prisoners to Jack Griffin's house in Coillte Craobhach, and the first man they hung was General Blake. They heeled up two spoke-wheeled carts and began hangin' the Croppies out of a face, but there was such a lot of them that they got tired of the job and started to pick them by lottery. Any man who drew 'life' was let go, and anyone who drew 'death' was hanged. Some of the prisoners were brought to Ballinalee, and Cornwallis hanged them without any trial. The very first man he hung was Gunner Magee. They were all buried in Bully's Acre in Ballinalee.

The Irish that were killed in the battle were all buried in big pits that were dug near the top of Sean Mullach, and they were never stirred to this day. The English didn't bury their own dead at all, but put them all on carts and threw them into Cilldre Lough so that no one would see how many of them were killed.

The whole country was plundered and robbed by the English after the battle. They were goin' about for days and slaughtered cattle for themselves, and made the people dig potatoes for them. The Cavan Orangemen drove away all the cattle and horses they could get, and left the whole place beggared. If only the French ship that came into Kilalla waited for more of the other ships that were com' the war would have been different, but Ballinamuck was the biggest beatin' the Irish ever got, or ever will again.

Of Clergymen

We have read of Father Conroy's connection with Castlebar, above. Father John Murphy of Boolavogue, in County Wexford, is one of the most celebrated clergymen of the rebellion. A namesake, Father Michael Murphy, was curate in Ballycanew, also in County Wexford. Father Michael was educated in Bordeaux but returned to Ireland when the French Revolution began. In May 1798, in a local newspaper, he advertised his loyalty to the Crown. On learning of the arming of rebels in the Ballycanew area, Lord Mount Norris and some colleagues visited Catholic churches after Masses and invited men to take this oath:

I do hereby declare upon the Holy Evangelists, and as I hope to be saved through the merits of my blessed Lord and Saviour, Jesus Christ, that I will be true and faithful to his Majesty King George the Third, and to the succession of his family to the throne; that I will support and maintain the Constitution, as by law established; that I am not a United Irishman, and that I never will take the United Irishman's oath; that I am bound, by every obligation, human and divine, to give every information in my power to prevent tumult and disorder; that I will neither aid nor assist the enemies of my King or my country, and that I will give up all sorts of arms in my possession: all the above I voluntarily swear –

So help me God and Redeemer!

Mount Norris, who also signed his name as below, noted on one copy of this oath:

The above oath was taken on this 19th day of January, 1798, before me, by A.B., of Ballycanow [*sic*] parish.

'Mountnorris'

After this incident, some loyalist Catholics met in Ballycanew parish and voluntarily signed a declaration oath which they forwarded through Mount Norris to the Lord Lieutenant, Camden:

May it please your Excellency,

We, the Roman Catholic inhabitants of the parish of Ballycanow [*sic*], this day assembled in the chapel, holding in abhorrence the barbarous outrages lately committed, and seditious conspiracies now existing in this kingdom, by traitors and rebels, styling themselves United Irishmen, think it incumbent on us, thus publicly, to avow and declare our unalterable attachment and loyalty to our most revered Sovereign King George III, and our determined resolution to support and maintain his rights and our happy Constitution. And we do further pledge ourselves to co-operate with our Protestant brethren of this kingdom, in opposing, to the utmost of our power, any foreign or domestic enemy, who may dare to invade his Majesty's dominions, or disturb the peace or tranquillity of this country.

Father Michael Murphy countersigned the declaration. Hearing of the rising at Oulart, however, he led a resistance to Crown cavalry that raided his village. He suffered losses but when his attackers retreated to Enniscorthy, he and the remainder of his force joined Father John Murphy's advance to Enniscorthy. He was killed at the battle of Arklow on 9 June and his corpse mutilated.

Father Philip Roche left Gorey to take over as Commander-in-Chief of the rebel forces. He fought at New Ross and was reprimanded by his bishop for debauchery. A heavy drinker, he was boisterous but humane. At Wexford he tried to prevent outrages on loyalists and, after defeat, attempted to arrange terms with Lake. He was dragged from his horse and beaten before being court-martialled and hanged three days later on Wexford Bridge.

The Enniscorthy priest, Father Clinch, lost his life after retreating from Vinegar Hill. The loyalist Musgrave described him in Memoirs of the Different Rebellions in Ireland (Dublin 1801) as:

a man of huge stature, with a scimitar and broad cross-belts, mounted on a large white horse, with long pistols, and made such a conspicuous figure on the hill during the action, and the day preceding it, as attracted the notice of our troops, particularly as he seemed to be constantly employed in reconnoitring them. The Earl of Roden having singled him out among the fugitives, overtook him after a mile's pursuit, and received his fire, which his Lordship returned, and wounded him in the neck. He then discharged his second pistol at Lord Roden, on which an officer of the regiment rode up and shot him. He wore his vestments under his clothes; had near forty pounds in his pocket, a gold watch, and a remarkable snuff-box; all which, it is presumed, he had acquired by plunder. He had been as active in the cabinet as the field, having constantly sat at the committee at Enniscorthy, and, mounted on his charger and fully accoutred, he daily visited the camp.

Father Mogue Kearns was one of the chief leaders of the rebels in Wexford. Having marched a force of rebels from Three Rocks to Newtownbarry (Bunclody) he took the town, but a counter-attack by its garrison inflicted heavy casualties on his force and dispersed it. He was one of several leaders who pressed into Kildare and Meath in early July 1798. After a failed attack on Clonard he was captured near Edenderry and hanged in late July.

A Dundalk priest, Father Quigley, was a leader of the United Irishmen there. He was with Arthur O'Connor in London when the pair were arrested in May 1798, Quigley posing as 'Colonel Morris', O'Connor as 'Captain Jones'. While on the scaffold at Penendon Heath, early in June, he took a penknife and began peeling an orange.

So the attitude of the Roman Catholic clergy to the rebellion was volatile. The blanket appreciation expressed below by Rev. J.M. Furlong is not representative.

THE PRIESTS OF '98
J.M. Furlong

The story of our native land, from weary age to age,
Is writ in blood and scalding tears on many a gloomy page;
But darkest, saddest page of all is that which tells the fate
Of Erin's noblest martyr-sons, the priests of Ninety-Eight.

The love of father for his flock of helpless little ones –
The love a darling mother wins from true and tender sons –
A love that liveth to the end, defying time and fate –
With such a love they loved their land, the priests of Ninety-Eight.

To heaven in ceaseless dirge ascends the mother's wild despair,
The wail of sorrowing wife and child, the maid's unheeded prayer;
The voice of vengeful blood, that cries up from the reeking sod –
Ah! well may ache your Irish hearts, O patient priests of God!

They drew the green old banner forth and flung it to the light,
And Wexford heard the rallying cry and gathered in her might,
And swore around uplifted cross until the latest breath
To follow where her Sagairt led – to victory or death!

The Sagairt led, the pikemen fought like lions brought to bay,
And Wexford proved her prowess well in many a bloody fray,
Where wronged and wronger, foot to foot, in deadly grip were seen,
And England's hated Red went down before the Irish Green.

Radiant shall their memory live, though dark and sad their doom,
To brighten in our history a page of woe and gloom –
A pillar-fire to guide a nation struggling to be free
Along the thorny, sunless path that leads to liberty.

Honour them – the martyred dead – the fearless, good, and wise,
Who for its sake in evil days made willing sacrifice
Of earthly hope and earthly joy, and dared the felon's fate,
To feed it with their own heart's blood – the priests of Ninety-Eight.

Of Tone

The most celebrated of the United Irishmen, Theobald Wolfe Tone (1763-98) was a Protestant coachman's son, born in Stafford Street, Dublin. He was educated at Trinity College and at London's Middle Temple. He married sixteen-year-old Martha Witherington and they lived for a while at his father's home in Blackhall, Clane, County Kildare. A qualified lawyer, he preferred politics to the bar. In 1791 he published a pamphlet outlining the injustices suffered by Irish Roman Catholics. Enthusiastic about France's revolution, he was a founder-member of the United Irishmen. His ideology, still quoted by republicans, was aimed at breaking the connection with England, 'the never failing source of all our political evils', and substituting 'the common name of Irishman in place of the denominations of Protestant, Catholic and Dissenter'. Dissatisfied with the contents of the 1793 Catholic Relief Act, he looked to France for help. The authorities became aware of this and, under threat of arrest, he and his family left Ireland, sailing from Belfast in June 1795.

In Philadelphia he received an *entrée* to France, travelled there and persuaded its new ruling Directory to accept him into the army and to prepare an invasion of Ireland, joining with its revolutionaries to end British rule. In December 1796 a fraction of a French fleet made it to Bantry Bay, but failed to land due to the absence of General Hoche, whose ship never arrived, and to unfavourable winds in the bay. Later, Tone attempted to raise a Dutch force but was unsuccessful. Further efforts to initiate another major French expedition failed; only Humbert's ill-prepared landing made any impression.

In September 1798 General Bombard commanded a fleet with 3000 men, including Tone, that sailed from Brest. They reached Lough Swilly on 11 October but were captured. At his court martial in Dublin on 10 November, Tone appeared dressed in his French uniform. He was sentenced to death by hanging but, it is said, committed suicide two days later by cutting a neck artery with a knife. He slashed his windpipe instead of his jugular vein, and is alleged to have remarked to his doctor, 'I am sorry I have been so bad an anatomist.' Tone had wished to be shot as a French army officer.

WOLFE TONE

Alice Milligan

From Omagh, County Tyrone, Alice Milligan got a Methodist education but went to Dublin to learn Irish. Organizer of the 1798 centenary celebrations in Ulster, she brought the Fenian John O'Leary to the celebrations. She travelled the country organizing the Gaelic League and received support from W.B. Yeats and George Russell (AE). She was co-founder, with Ethna Carbery, of the newspapers **Northern Patriot** and **Shan Van Vocht.**

The first storm of winter blew high, blew high;
Red leaves were scattering to a gloomy sky;
Rain clouds were lowering o'er the plains of Kildare,
When from Dublin, southward, the mourners came there.

'In the spring', they whispered, 'Lord Edward bled.
And the blood of hosts was in summer shed;
Death in the autumn o'er Connacht passed,
But the loss that is sorest came last, came last.

'Though Fitzgerald died, sure we fought them still.
And we shouted 'Vengeance' on Vinegar Hill,
Knowing our flag would again be flown
If France gave ear to the prayers of Tone.

'Twice', we thought, 'his appealing lips
Brought forth her armies and battleships.
And the storms of God shall not always stay
England's doom, as in Bantry Bay.'

'And oh', we said to the hopeless ones,
Who made count of Ireland's martyred sons,
'The bravest lives; be your mourning dumb,
Ere the snow of winter Wolfe Tone shall come.'

He came – was beaten – we bear him here
From a prison cell on his funeral bier,
And Freedom's hope shall be buried low
With his mouldering corpse 'neath the winter snow.

'Hush', one said, o'er the new-set sod.
'Hope shall endure with our faith in God.
And God shall only forsake us when
This grave is forgotten by Irishmen.'

TONE'S ARREST

Wolfe Tone's eldest son, William Theobald Wolfe Tone, served as a lieutenant under Napoleon. When Bonaparte fell, William left the French army and went to America. He wrote the following account of his father's arrest:

During the action [against the intercepting British fleet in Lough Swilly] my father commanded one of the batteries, and, according to the report of the officers who returned to France, fought with the utmost desperation, and as if he was courting death. When the ship struck, confounded with the other officers, he was not recognized for some time, for he had completely acquired the language and appearance of a Frenchman. The two fleets were dispersed in every direction; nor was it till some days later that the *Hoche* was brought into Loch Swilly, and the prisoners landed and marched to Letterkenny. [Some say he was brought to Buncrana Castle. *Donegal Annual*, vol 2, no 1, p. 350]

Yet rumours of his being on board must have been circulated, for the fact was public at Paris. But it was thought he had been killed in the action; and I am willing to believe that the British officers, respecting the valour of a fallen enemy, were not earnest in investigating the point. It was at length a gentleman well known in the county Derry as a leader of the Orange party, and one of the chief magistrates in that neighbourhood, Sir George Hill, who had been his fellow-student in Trinity College and knew his person, who undertook the task of discovering him. It is known that in Spain grandees and noblemen of the first rank pride themselves in the functions of familiars, spies, and informers of the Holy Inquisition; it remained for Ireland to offer a similar example. The French officers were invited to breakfast with the Earl of Cavan, who commanded in that district. My father sat undisguised amongst them, when Sir George Hill entered the room, followed by police officers. Looking narrowly at the company, he singled out the object of his search, and, stepping up to him, said, 'Mr. Tone, I am *very happy* to see you.' Instantly rising, with the utmost composure, and disdaining all useless attempts at concealment, my father replied, 'Sir George, I am happy to see you; how are Lady Hill and your family?' Beckoned into the next room by the police officers, an unexpected indignity awaited him. It was filled with military, and one General Lavau, who commanded them, ordered him to be ironed, declaring that, as on leaving Ireland to enter the French service he had not renounced his oath of allegiance, he remained a subject of Britain, and should be punished as a traitor. Seized with a momentary burst of indignation at such unworthy treatment and cowardly cruelty to a prisoner of war, he flung off his uniform, and cried, 'These fetters shall never degrade the revered insignia of the free nation which I have served.' Resuming then his usual calm, he offered his limbs to the irons, and when they were fixed he exclaimed, 'For the cause which I have embraced, I feel prouder to wear these chains than if I were decorated with the star and garter of England.' The friends of Lord Cavan have asserted that this extreme, and, I will add, *unmanly* and *ungenerous severity*, was provoked by his outrageous behaviour when he found he was not to have the privileges of a prisoner of war. This supposition is not only contradicted by the whole tenor of his character and his subsequent deportment, but no other instances of it have ever been specified than those noble replies to the taunts of General Lavau. Of the latter I know nothing but these anecdotes, recorded in the papers of the day. If, as his name seems to indicate, he was a French emigrant, the coincidence was curious and his conduct the less excusable.

Another version of this story, which I have seen, for the first time, in the *London New Monthly Magazine*, states that Mr. Tone was recognized by, or, according to another account, had the impudence to make himself known to an old acquaintance at Lord Cavan's table, who speedily informed his lordship of the guest who sat at his board. The first circumstantial account is the one which reached us in France; but, in my opinion, the difference between the two stories is very trifling. It regards only the fashion in which Sir George Hill gave in his information.

From Letterkenny he was hurried to Dublin without delay. In the same Magazine I find that, contrary to usual custom, he was conveyed during the whole route, fettered and on horseback, under an escort of dragoons. Of this further indignity I had never heard before. During this journey the unruffled serenity of his countenance, amidst the rude soldiery, and under the awe-struck gaze of his countrymen, excited universal admiration. Recognizing in a group of females, which thronged the windows, a young lady of his acquaintance: 'There', said he, 'is my old friend Miss Beresford; how well she looks!' On his arrival he was immured in the Provost's prison, in the barracks of Dublin, under the charge of the notorious Major Sandys, a man whose insolence, rapacity, and cruelty will long be remembered in that city, where, a worthy instrument of the faction which then ruled it, he enjoyed, under their patronage, a despotic authority within its precincts.

WHO WOULD BLAME ME
IF I DID CRY MY FILL?

❧ 1798-1803 ❧

Of Victory

Many loyalists felt a sense of triumph at the defeat of the United Irishmen. This is reflected in some of their songs of the period.

THE REBELLION OF 1798
Anon.

The ruthless Fitzgerald stepp'd forward to rule,
His principles formed in the Orleans school,
The torch of rebellion he waved in the air,
And massacre spread thro' the plains of Kildare:
The weakness of L——r abetted his crime,
He fell like a ruffian and died in his prime.
Down, down, Croppies lie down.

In Dublin the traitors were ready to rise,
And murder was seen in their lowering eyes,
With poison, like cowards, they aim'd to succeed,
And thousands were doom'd by assassins to bleed;
But the yeomen advanced, of rebels the dread,
And each Croppy soon hid his dastardly head.
Down, down, Croppies lie down.

The Northerns displayed the merciless steel,
And murder'd in Antrim the high-born O'Neill;
By Clav'ring and Durham assaulted, they ran,
To their fortified camp on the banks of the Bann,
From whence they dispersed and skulked away home,
When they heard of the Orangemen marching to Toome.
Down, down, Croppies lie down.

The innocent rebels of Ballynahinch,
With tears in their eyes when they thought of the Prince,
To treason's head-quarters their thousands they bring,
To pay no more rents and to pull down the King;
But soon as bold Nugent advanced to attack,
The innocent Croppies were thrown on their back.
Down, down, Croppies lie down.

In Wexford they made a most desperate stand,
And with fire and rapine disfigured the land,
Their massacred captives they cast to the flood,
The Slaney ran crimson with Protestant blood!
But vengeance pursued them with death and despair,
And the carcase of Harvey soon tainted the air.
Down, down, Croppies lie down.

Defeated by Lake, they rallied their force,
And into Kilkenny directed their course,
By Murphy led on, o'er the Barrow they pour,
But hundreds were fated to pass it no more,
For Asgill attacked them again and again,
And three times five hundred lay dead on the plain.
Down, down, Croppies lie down.

Priest Murphy declared to the fanatic crew,
Who believed all his words as the Gospel were true,
No bullet could hurt a true son of the Church;
But the devil soon left the poor saint in the lurch;
For by some sad mistake, through a hole in the skin,
A heretic bullet just chanced to pop in.
So down, down, the Croppies fell down.

THE ORANGE LILY
Anon.

The Emmet referred to in stanza three is Thomas Addis, brother of Robert, and Arthur is Arthur O'Connor.

My dear Orange brothers, have you heard of the news,
How the treacherous Frenchmen our gulls to amuse,
The troops that last April they promised to send,
At length to Killala they ventured to land.

CHORUS
Good Croppies, but don't be too bold now,
Lest you should be all stow'd in the hold now,
Then to Bot'ny you'd trudge, I am told now,
And a sweet orange lily for me.

But now that they're landed they find their mistake,
For in place of the Croppies they meet the brave Lake;
He soon will convince them that our orange and blue
Can ne'er be subdued by their plundering crew.
CHORUS

That false traitor Emmet, more ungrateful than hell,
With McNevin and Arthur, though fast in their cell;
What they formerly swore they have dar'd to deny,
And the Secret Committee have charg'd with a lie!
CHORUS

But as, by this falsehood, it is clear they intend
To induce us poor peasants the French to befriend;
We shall soon, I hope, see them high dangling in air,
'Twould be murd'ring the loyal such miscreants to spare.
CHORUS

On the trees at the camp Crop Lawless intended,
To hang up all those who their country defended;
As the scene is reversed, a good joke it will be,
In the place of dear Camden to put up those three.
CHORUS

Judgment being entered on that bloody Bond,
Execution should follow, the people contend;
Why stay it, say they, when engagements they've broken?
The Direct'ry deny ev'ry word they had spoken.
CHORUS

Then gird on you sabres, my brave Orangemen all,
For the Croppies are down, and the Frenchmen shall fall;
Let each lodge sally forth, from one to nine hundred.
Those freebooters ere long with the dead shall be numbered.
CHORUS

DE GROVES OF DE POOL
Richard A. Milliken

*This song, also called 'The Groves of Blackpool', celebrates the Cork City Militia's role
in suppressing the rising. Its last stanza, clearly a later interpolation, is thought to be
by John Lander, a Cork solicitor who wrote many popular songs in the early nine-
teenth century.*

*Richard Alfred Milliken (1767-1815) was born in Castlemartyr, County Cork,
and became an attorney in Cork, where he devoted most of his time to literary and
artistic pursuits – his best-known work being the burlesque 'The Groves of Blarney'. A
staunch loyalist, he joined the Royal Cork Volunteers at the outbreak of the rebellion.
Blackpool is a suburb on the north side of Cork city. Milliken probably intended the
title to echo his most famous piece of verse.*

Now de war, dearest Nancy, is ended,
And de peace is come over from France;
So our gallant Cork City Militia
Back again to head-quarters advance.
No longer a beating dose rebels,
We'll now be a beating de bull,
And taste dose genteel recreations
Dat are found in de groves of de Pool.

CHORUS
Right fol didder rol didder rol, didder rol,
Right fol didder rol dae.

Den out came our loving relations,
To see whether we'd be living or no;
Besides all de jolly ould neighbours,
Around us who flocked in a row,
De noggins of sweet Tommy Walker
We lifted according to rule,
And wetted our necks wid de native
Dat is brewed in the groves of de Pool.
CHORUS

When de regiment marched into de Commons,
'Twould do your heart good for to see;
You'd tink not a man nor a woman
Was left in Cork's famous city.
De boys dey came flocking around us,
Not a hat nor wig stuck to a skull,
To compliment dose Irish heroes
Returned to de groves of de Pool.
CHORUS

Wid our band out before us in order,
We played coming into de town;
We up'd wid de ould 'Boyne Water',
Not forgetting, too, 'Croppies lie down'.
Bekase you might read in the newses
'Twas we made dose rebels so cool,
Who all tought, like Turks or like Jewses,
To murther de boys of de Pool.
CHORUS

Oh, sure dere's no nation in Munster
Wid de groves of Blackpool can compare,
Where dose heroes were all edicated.
And de nymphs are so comely and fair.
Wid de gardens around entertaining,
Wid sweet purty posies so full,
Dat is worn by dose comely young creaturs
Dat walks in de groves of de Pool.
CHORUS

Oh, many's de time, late and early,
Dat I wished I was landed again,
Where'd I'd see de sweet watercourse flowing,
Where de skinners dere glory maintain;
Likewise dat divine habitation,
Where dose babbies are all sent to school.
Dat nebber had fader nor moder,
But were found in de groves of de Pool.
CHORUS

Come all you young youths of dis nation,
Come, fill up a bumper all round;
Drink success to Blackpool navigation,
And may it wid plenty be crowned.
Here's success to the jolly hoop-coilers;
Likewise to de shuttle and de spool;
To de tanners and worthy glue-boilers,
Dat lives in de groves of de Pool.
CHORUS

🐝 🐝 🐝

Of Hardship, Trial and Censure

THE GALLANT MEN OF NINETY-EIGHT
Bernard McGuinness

A typical rebel song, this work recalls some celebrated battles in County Wexford during the rebellion. In true tradition, it also calls for a further strike for freedom.

The spirit of our fathers bright inspires our hearts to firm unite,
And strike again for God and Right, as did the Men of Ninety-Eight,
When Wexford and New Ross could tell, and Tubberneering and Carnew,
Where many a Saxon foreman fell, and many an Irish soldier, too.

CHORUS
Hurrah, brave boys, we vow to stand together for our Fatherland,

As did that bold devoted band, the gallant men of Ninety-Eight.

Their altars and their homes they rose to guard from ruthless tyrant foes,
Who reeled beneath the vengeful blows for freedom dealt in Ninety-
Eight,
The patriots' blood that reddened deep the soil where fell they in their
gore,
Their mem'ry green and fresh shall keep within our bosoms' inmost
core.
CHORUS

Then let us here give three times three for those who fought for liberty,
As slaves could never bend the knee the free-born men of Ninety-Eight,
Not they that bondsmen's yoke could bear while one stout pike could deal
a blow,
Then by their memory let us swear to meet once more the hated foe!
CHORUS

CROPPIES LIE DOWN
Anon.

*The 'Soldiers of Erin' reference in this Orange poem's opening line demonstrates the
nationalism that existed among many Protestants. Their humour is obvious too in its
satirical lines. This is one of the best-known Orange songs.*

We soldiers of Erin, so proud of the name,
Will raise upon Rebels and Frenchmen our fame;
We'll fight to the last in the honest old cause,
And guard our religion, our freedom, and laws;
We'll fight for our country, our king, and his crown,
And make all the traitors and Croppies lie down.

Down, down, Croppies lie down.

The rebels so bold – when they've none to oppose –
To houses and hay-stacks are terrible foes;
They murder poor parsons, and also their wives,
But soldiers at once make them run for their lives;

And wherever we march, thro' the country or town,
In ditches or cellars, the Croppies lie down.
Down, down, Croppies lie down.

United in blood, to their country's disgrace,
They secretly shoot whom they dare not to face;
But when we can catch the sly rogues in the field,
A handful of soldiers make hundreds to yield,
And the cowards collect but to raise our renown,
For as soon as we fire the Croppies lie down.

Down, down, Croppies lie down.

While they, in the war that unmanly they wage
On woman herself turn their blood-thirsty rage,
We'll fly to protect the dear creatures from harms,
And shelter them safely when clasp'd in our arms:
On love in a soldier no maiden will frown,
But bless the dear boys that made Croppies lie down.

Down, down, Croppies lie down.

Should France e'er attempt, or by fraud or by guile,
Her forces to land on our emerald isle,
We'll shew that they ne'er can make free soldiers slaves,
And only possess our green fields for their graves;
Our country's applauses our triumph will crown,
While low with the French, brother, Croppies lie down.

Down, down, Croppies lie down.

When wars and when dangers again shall be o'er,
And peace with her blessings revisit our shore;
When arms we relinquish, no longer to roam,
With pride will our families welcome us home,
And drink, as in bumpers past troubles we drown,
A health to the lads that made Croppies lie down.

Down, down, down, Croppies lie down.

Of Patriots

THE DYING SOLDIER
'Sean'

The maudlin device of a dying soldier's sentiments expressed to his mother appears in songs of every struggle for freedom. This example, published by Joseph Clarke's Irish Book Bureau, concerns the 1798 Rebellion.

Mother Eire I have walked with you
Along the roads of happiness and pain;
Oft have I drank the chalice of your sweetness –
Sweetness ne'er touched by avaricious gain.

Like you the world has oftimes called me fool,
To cast away my years and gifts on you –
How men would laugh and scorn to see me dying here,
Here on the hillside in the morning dew.

Before I proffered you my arm and heart
They greeted me as fellow-friend;
But now no more they speak my name,
No longer seek my honour to defend.

Fair Mother; thou hast been the kindest friend of all
'Tis you who taught me how to live and die;
In golden threads your love is wreathed on my heart,
And on my dying lips your name I'll often sigh.

Here amid your mantle green I'll sleep,
Contented that I'm sleeping on your breast –
You who bore and daily nursed me
I know, will seek from God my rest.

THE MEMORY OF THE DEAD
John Kells Ingram

This poem was first published anonymously in The Nation. *As a ballad, the work is better known as 'Who Fears to Speak of Ninety- Eight'. Despite the poem's sentiments, Ingram was never overtly nationalistic; indeed, he became a strong unionist in later years.*

John Kells Ingram (1823-1907), from Temple Carne, County Donegal, was not quite twenty years of age when he wrote the poem that became a popular song. Three years later he became a Fellow of Trinity College, Dublin, and went on to become its Professor of Oratory, Professor of Greek, Librarian, Senior Lecturer and Vice-Provost. He was also President of the Royal Irish Academy from 1892 to 1896.

Who fears to speak of Ninety-Eight? Who blushes at the name?
When cowards mock the patriot's fate who hangs his head in shame?
He's all a knave or half a slave who slights his country thus;
But true men, like you, men, will fill a glass with us.

We drink the memory of the brave, the faithful and the few!
Some lie far off beyond the wave, some sleep in Ireland, too;
All, all are gone, but still lives on the fame of those who died;
All true men, like you, men, remember them with pride.

Some on the shores of distant lands their weary hearts have laid,
And by the stranger's heedless hands their lonely graves were made;
But, though their clay be far away beyond th' Atlantic foam,
In true men, like you, men, their spirit stays at home.

The dust of some is Irish earth – among their own they rest;
And that same land that gave them birth has caught them to her breast;
And we will pray that, from their clay, full many a race may start,
Of true men, like you, men, to act as brave a part.

They rose in dark and evil days to right their native land;
They kindled here a living blaze that nothing shall withstand;
Alas! that Might can vanquish Right – they fell and passed away;
But true men, like you, men, are plenty here today.

Then here's their memory – may it be for us a guiding light
To cheer our strife for liberty and teach us to unite!
Through good and ill, be Ireland's still, thought sad as theirs your fate:
And true men, be you, men, like those of Ninety-Eight.

THE LAMENTATIONS OF PATRICK BRADY,
OR, THE HEROES OF NINETY-EIGHT
Anon.

Although the chronology of the action is not precise, this lament refers to most of the episodes in the rebellion outside those in the north.

Ye true born heroes I hope you will now lend an ear
To a few simple verses, the truth unto you I'll declare.
My name is Pat Brady, the same I will never deny
In Ross I was born, and in Naas condemned to die.

I once had a home, and a shelter from want and from woe,
But I'm now among strangers where no person does me know,
Condemned for high treason, to die on a gallows tree,
For seeking the rights of poor Erin my dear country.

My father, God rest him, was taken without any crime,
And marched off a prisoner, and hanged in one hour's time,
Myself and two brothers to the wood were forced to fly
We vowed for revenge or else by the sword we'd die.

It was early next morning to Gorey we all marched away,
Where the drums they did rattle, and our fifes so sweetly did play,
Full twelve thousand heroes, nine hundred and forty-three,
We took all the cannon that day from their artillery.

It was early next morning to Wicklow we all marched away,
Our hearts most glorious with liberty shining that day.
But entering of Ferns we were attacked by the yeomanry,
We fought them for four hours till we gained a complete victory.

We fought in New Ross, and we fought upon Vinegar Hill,
And in sweet Castlecomer where the Colliers joined us with free will,

Out of fourteen engagements we received not a wound or a scar,
Till I lost my two brothers at the battle of sweet Castlebar.

To march with the Frenchmen it left me much troubled in mind,
To think I should go and leave my two brothers behind,
Through the sweet county Leitrim to Granard our way we took,
And were attacked by the army at the village of Ballinamuck.

We fought with good courage but defeated we were on that day,
We were forced to retreat, no longer our heroes could stay,
But the brave Longford heroes to fly from us they never could,
They never could yield till they'd lose the last drop of their blood.

When forced to retreat for refuge we thought for to fly,
For all that was taken was certain and sure for to die,
To the sweet County Wicklow for refuge we thought for to face,
We were taken in Rathangan and twelve were hanged in Naas.

Come all you brave heroes the truth unto you I'll relate,
From powder or ball poor Brady has ne'er met his fate,
So all you good Christians who hear of my sorrowful fate,
You'll pray for Pat Brady, the hero of '98.

THE THREE FLOWERS
Norman G. Reddin

Two of the flowers in Norman Reddin's song represent Michael Dwyer, for whom see 'Of Persistence' below, and Wolfe Tone. The third flower is Robert Emmet. Emmet (1778-1803) was the younger brother of Thomas Addis Emmet, the Secretary of the Supreme Council of the United Irishmen and executive member of its Leinster Directory. Robert, the son of the Viceroy's physician, led the United Irishmen's Trinity College cell. When the Lord Chancellor, Lord Clare, visited the college to assess the strength of the cell, it had already broken up. In protest at the visit, however, Robert Emmet discontinued his studies there and escaped to France where, no doubt, he began planning his own later rebellion of 1803.

One time when walking down a lane,
When night was drawing nigh,

I met a cailín with three flowers,
And she more young than I.
'St Patrick bless you, dear,' said I,
'If you will be quick and tell
The place where you did find these flowers,
I seem to know so well.'

She took and kissed the flower once,
And sweetly said to me:
'This flower comes from the Wicklow hills,
Dew wet and pure,' said she,
'Its name is Michael Dwyer –
The strongest flower of all;
But I'll keep it fresh beside my breast
'Though all the world should fall.'

She took and kissed the next flower twice
And sweetly said to me:
'This flower I culled in Antrim fields.
Outside Belfast,' said she.
'The name I call it is Wolfe Tone –
The bravest flower of all;
But I'll keep it fresh beside my breast
'Though all the world should fall.'

She took and kissed the next flower thrice,
And softly said to me:
'This flower I found in Thomas Street,
In Dublin fair,' said she.
'It's name is Robert Emmet,
The youngest flower of all;
But I'll keep it fresh beside my breast,
'Though all the world should fall.

Then Emmet, Dwyer and Tone I'll keep,
For I do love them all;
And I'll keep them fresh beside my breast
'Though all the world should fall.'

Of Tone, In Memory

BODENSTOWN

Maeve Cavanagh McDowell

It is almost obligatory for organizations claiming assorted shades of republicanism to affirm their cause at the grave of Wolfe Tone, in Bodenstown, County Kildare.

In 1916 James Connolly declared Maeve Cavanagh (later Cavanagh McDowell) the 'poetess of the revolution'. She served on the first committee of the Gaelic League and was active in national and labour movements.

The lush grass hides forgotten graves,
The elders are abloom
An ivied wall stands sentinel
Beside a lonely tomb.
And here, while summer holds her sway,
Linnet and blackbird throng,
And blend their sweetest songs o'er him
Who loved the battle song.

No gleaming marble rises tall
Above that sacred dust,
But simple words on modest stone
Tell of his freedom lust.
Enough – they bear his message on;
Methinks could be but know,
No other monument he'd crave
While Ireland's flag lies low.

Could he the grave's deep silence break,
Not sculptured stone he'd ask –
But men and guns, and gleaming swords,
To consummate his task.
Then let us in this holy place
Kneel down and breathe a prayer –
A vow to carry on the work
Of him who slumbers there.

SUICIDE LETTERS

Tone, allegedly, could see soldiers erecting a gallows from his cell. Before using a pen-knife to cut his throat, he wrote two letters to his wife.

Provost Prison — Dublin Barracks,
Le 20 Brumaire, an 7 [10 November 1798].

Dearest Love,

The hour is at last come when we must part. As no words can express what I feel for you and our children, I shall not attempt it; complaint of any kind would be beneath your courage and mine; be assured I will die as I have lived, and that you will have no cause to blush for me.

I have written on your behalf to the French Government, to the Minister of Marine, to General Kilmaine, and to Mr Shee; with the latter I wish you especially to advise. In Ireland I have written to your brother Harry, and to those of my friends who are about to go into exile, and who, I am sure, will not abandon you.

Adieu, dearest love: I find it impossible to finish this letter. Give my love to Mary; and, above all things, remember that you are now the only parent of our dearest children, and that the best proof you can give of your affection for me will be to preserve yourself for their education. God Almighty bless you all.

Yours ever,

T.W. TONE

November 11th

Dearest Love,

I write just one line to acquaint you that I have received assurances from your brother Edward of his determination to render every assistance and protection in his power; for which I have written to thank him most sincerely. Your sister has likewise sent me assurances of the same nature, and expressed a desire to see me, which I have refused, having determined to speak to no one of my friends, not even my father, from motives of humanity to them and myself. It is a very great consolation to me that your family are determined to support you; as to the manner of that assistance, I leave it to their affection for you, and your own excellent good sense, to settle what manner will be most respectable for all parties.

Adieu, dearest love. Keep your courage, as I have kept mine; my mind is as tranquil this moment as at any period of my life. Cherish my memory; and especially preserve your health and spirits for the sake of our dearest children.

Your ever affectionate,

T. WOLFE TONE

TONE'S GRAVE
Thomas Davis

In Bodenstown churchyard there is a green grave,
And wildly around it the winter winds rave;
Small shelter I ween are the ruined walls there
When the storm sweeps down o'er the plains of Kildare.

Once I lay on that sod – it lies over Wolfe Tone –
And thought how he perished in prison alone,
His friends unavenged and his country unfreed –
'Oh, bitter,' thought I, 'is the patriot's meed.'

'For in him the heart of a woman combined
With a heroic life and a governing mind –
A martyr for Ireland, his grave has no stone –
His name seldom named, and his virtues unknown.'

I was woke from my dream by the voices and tread
Of a band who came into the home of the dead;
They carried no corpse, and they carried no stone,
And they stopped when they came to the grave of Wolfe Tone

There were students and peasants, the wise and the brave,
And an old man who knew him from cradle to grave.
And children who thought me hard-hearted; for they
On that sanctified sod were forbidden to play.

But the old man, who saw I was mourning there, said
'We come, sir, to weep where young Wolfe Tone is laid,
And we're going to raise him a monument, too –
A plain one, yet fit for the simple and true.'

My heart overflowed, and I clasped his old hand,
And I blessed him, and blessed every one of his band;
'Sweet, sweet 'tis to find that such faith can remain
To the cause and the man so long vanquished and slain.'

In Bodenstown churchyard there is a green grave,
And freely around it let winter winds rave –
Far better they suit him – the ruin and the gloom –
Till Ireland, a nation, can build him a tomb.

YOUNG WOLFE TONE
Felimy Fidileir

Where on the skyline Muckish lies
Like a great boar asleep,
I wandered under sunset skies
Past flocks of browsing sheep,
And heard a boy's voice, loud and bold,
Breaking the silence lone,
Singing a country ballad old
In praise of Young Wolfe Tone.

It seemed as if a hundred throats
Chorused the rousing strain
As from the hollow cliffs the notes
Rang proudly back again.
What King or Caesar drunk with power
Has such sweet tribute known
As this boy pays at twilight hour
To honour Young Wolfe Tone?

Where sotted George's grave is made
What man would stop to pray?
Where Norbury's vile dust is laid
Who knows or cares to-day?
But whether on Kildare's green meads
The snows or flowers are strewn,
Well-trodden is the path that leads
To thy grave, young Wolfe Tone!

For he, who all to Ireland gives,
Dies not while songs are sung –
He in her heart enshrined lives
Forever brave and young.
Time blurs renown, but his abides,
Though crowded years have flown,
As fresh as the Atlantic tides
The fame of Young Wolfe Tone.

Still forth his clarion message rings
When Freedom's mighty breath

Whirls from their thrones the puppet kings
Down to unhonoured death
And Freedom's flower from his grave starts,
And far its seeds are blown
To bloom anew in boyish hearts
That honour Young Wolfe Tone.

A SONG OF TONE
Brian na mBanban

No craven dirge of sorrow
Our hearts will sing to-day,
No whinings for the morrow
Or for ages passed away;
But a song of bold rejoicing
That the seed by our martyrs sown
Has sprung to bloom by the lonely tomb
Of our own unconquered Tone!

His fame is in your keeping,
To hold without a stain,
Till freedom's fires are leaping
From every hill and plain;
Till Ireland's battle slogan
Shall reach to the despot's throne,
And swords aflame shall trace the name
Of our own unconquered Tone!

TONE IS COMING BACK AGAIN
Anon.

This paean for Wolfe Tone also mentions Michael Dwyer of Wicklow and Thomas Russell. 'The scions of Lord Clare's Brigade' are the descendants of Lord Clare, whose Irish regiment captured Marlborough's colours at the battle of Ramillies on 23 May 1705, in the War of the Spanish Succession.

Cheer up, brave hearts, to-morrow's dawn will see us march again
Beneath old Erin's flag of green that ne'er has known a stain.
And ere our hands the sword shall yield or furled that banner be —
We swear to make our native land from the tyrant's thraldom free!

CHORUS
For Tone is coming back again with legions o'er the wave,
The scions of Lord Clare's Brigade, the dear old land to save;
For Tone is coming back again with legions o'er the wave
The dear old land, the loved old land, the brave old land to save!

Though crouching minions preach to us to be the Saxon's slave,
We'll teach them all what pikes can do when hearts are true and brave.
Fling Freedom's banner to the breeze, let it float o'er land and sea —
We swear to make our native land from the tyrant's thraldom free!
CHORUS

Young Dwyer, among the heat-clad hills of Wicklow leads his men;
And Russell's voice stirs kindred hearts in many an Ulster glen;
Brave Father Murphy's men march on from the Barrow to the sea —
We swear to make our native land from the tyrant's thraldom free!
CHORUS

Too long we've borne with smouldering wrath the cursed alien laws,
That wreck our shrines and burn our homes and crush our country's
    cause;
But now the day has come at last; revenge our watchword be!
We swear to make our native land from the tyrant's thraldom free!
CHORUS

Of Love for the Brave

Songs of the pride of women for their martyred menfolk are common in all
struggles. The mother weeps for her son but is proud and welcomes death
rather than the shame of cowardice. The maiden must, in her heart of
hearts, wish that her lover would live rather than die, for whatever cause.

She cannot express this, however. She must state her willingness to see him give his blood for his country.

THE PATRIOT MOTHER
Eva Mary Kelly

This is another of the poems issued by Joseph Clarke's Irish Book Bureau. It tells of a mother exhorting her son not to inform, despite her knowledge that he will hang if he does not. It therefore stresses the absolute abhorrence held for informers.

For her writings in the celebrated publication edited by Thomas Davis, Mary Kelly (1826-1910) of Headford, County Galway, became known as 'Eva' of The Nation. *She was engaged to the Dublin nationalist Kevin Izod O'Doherty when, in 1849, he received a ten-year sentence in Tasmania (Van Diemen's Land) for treason. He offered to release her from her promise of marriage but she refused. She married him in 1855, one year after he received a pardon, and they lived in Australia.*

> Come, tell us the name of the rebelly crew
> Who lifted the pike on the Curragh with you;
> Come, tell us the treason, and then you'll be free,
> Or right quickly you'll swing from the high gallows tree.
>
> A leanbh! a leanbh! the shadow of shame
> Has never yet fallen on one of your name,
> And, oh! may the food, from my bosom you drew
> In your veins, turn to poison if you turn untrue.
>
> The foul words! Oh let them not blacken your tongue!
> That would prove to your friends and your country a wrong,
> Or the curse of a mother, so bitter and dread,
> With the wrath of the Lord – may they fall on your head!
>
> I have no one but you in the whole world wide,
> Yet false to your pledge you'd ne'er stand by my side;
> If a traitor you lived, you'd be farther away
> From my heart than, if true, you were wrapped in the clay.
>
> Oh! deeper and darker the mourning would be
> For your falsehood so base than your death proud and free:

Dearer, far dearer, than ever to me,
My darling, you'll be on the brave gallows tree!

'Tis holy, a ghradh, from the bravest and best —
Go, go from my heart and be joined with the rest,
A leanbh, mo chroidhe! O, a leanbh mo chroidhe!
Sure, a 'stag' and a traitor you never will be!

There's no look of a traitor upon the young brow
That's raised to the tempters so haughtily now;
No traitor e'er held up the firm head so high —
No traitor e'er showed such a proud flashing eye.

On the high gallows tree, on the brave gallows tree,
Where smiled leaves and blossoms, his sad doom met he!
But it never bore blossom so pure or so fair
As the heart of the martyr that hangs from it here.

THE PATRIOT MAID

Anon.

An Irish girl in heart and soul,
I love the dear old land;
I honour those who in her cause
Lift voice or pen or hand.
And may I live to see her free
From foreign lord and knave,
But Heaven forbid I'd ever be
The mother of a slave.

God bless the men who take their stand
In Ireland's patriot host;
I'd give the youth my heart and hand
Who serves his country most;
And if he fell, I'd rather lie
Beside him in the grave
Than wed a wealthy loon and be
The mother of a slave.

Thro' many a blood-red age of woe
Our Nation's heart has bled;
But still she makes her tyrants know
Her spirit is not dead.
God bless the men who for her sake
Their life and genius gave;
God bless the mothers of those sons,
They nursed no dastard slave!

Some on the scaffold place of doom
For loving Ireland died;
And others to the dungeon-gloom
Are torn from our side.
But God the Just, who ne'er designed
His image for a slave,
Will give our country might and mind
And raise the true and brave.

     🜲   🜲   🜲

Of Resignation

The 1798 rebellion secured support from influential establishment members for a union of the parliaments of Ireland and Great Britain. On 9 December 1798 there was a meeting of the Bar at the Exhibition Room, William Street, Dublin. By 166 votes to 32, it opposed the Union.

BARRINGTON

Shortly after the meeting, Sir Jonah Barrington wrote a letter of resignation to Captain Saurin, Barristers' Cavalry. Saurin later resigned as Attorney-General, fearing that the Union would lead to Catholic Emancipation.

Merrion Square, January 20th, 1799
Permit me to resign, through you, the commission which I hold in the Lawyers' Cavalry; I resign it with the regret of a soldier, who knows his duty to his King, yet feels his duty to his country, and will depart from neither but with his life.

That blind and fatal measure proposed by the Irish Government, to extinguish the political existence of Ireland, to surrender its Legislature, its trade, its dearest rights, and proudest prerogatives, into the hands of a British Minister, and a British Council, savours too much of that *foreign* principle, against the prevailing influence of which the united powers of Great Britain and Ireland are at this moment combating, and as evidently throws open to the British Empire the gate of that seductive political innovation, which has already proved the grave of half the Governments of Europe.

Consistent, therefore, with my loyalty and my oath, I can no longer continue subject to the indefinite and unforeseen commands of a military Government, which so madly hazards the integrity of the British Empire, and existence of the British Constitution, to crush a rising Nation, and aggrandize a despotic Minister.

Blinded by my zealous and hereditary attachment to the established Government and British connexion, I saw not the absolute necessity of national unanimity, to secure constitutional freedom. I see it now, and trust it is not yet too late to establish both.

I never will abet a now developed system, treacherous and ungrateful, stimulating two sects against each other, to enfeeble *both*, and then making religious feuds a pretext for political slavery.

Rejecting the experiment of a reform, and recommending the experiment of a revolution.

Kindling Catholic expectation to a blaze, and then extinguishing it for ever.

Alternately disgusting the rebel and the royalist, by indiscriminate pardon, and indiscriminate punishment.

Suspending one code of laws, and adjudging by another without authority to do either; and when the country, wearied by her struggles for her King, slumbers to refresh and to regain her vigour, her liberty is treacherously attempted to be bound, and her pride, her security, and her independence, are to be buried alive in the tomb of national annihilation.

Mechanical obedience is the duty of a soldier, but active uninfluenced integrity, the indispensable attribute of a legislator, when the preservation of his country is in question. And as the same frantic authority, which meditates our *civil* annihilation, might in the same frenzy meditate *military* projects from which my feelings, my principles, and my honour might revolt, I feel it right to separate my civil and military functions; and, to secure the honest uninterrupted exercise of the one, I relinquish the indefinite subjection of the other.

I return the arms I received from Government – I received them pure, and restore them not dishonoured.

I shall now resume my civil duties with zeal and with energy, elevated by the hope, that the Irish Parliament, true to itself, and honest to its country, will never assume a power extrinsic of its delegation, and will convince the British Nation that we are a people equally impregnable to the attacks of intimidation, or the shameless practice of corruption.

Yours, &c.

Jonah Barrington,   To William Saurin Esq.
Lieut. L Cavalry.   Commandant Lawers' Corps

Of Persistence

Michael Dwyer (1771-1826) was known as 'The Man They Couldn't Capture'. He was born in the Glen of Imaal in County Wicklow. He participated in the rising and led the authorities a merry dance during and after it. As late as 1799 soldiers surrounded him and his colleagues in a cottage at Derrynamuck. One, Sam MacAllister, drew British fire to allow Dwyer and the others to escape. MacAllister was shot dead. Dwyer remained free. He supported Robert Emmet's abortive rising of 1803 but surrendered himself to William Hoare Hume at Humewood, Kiltegan, the following year.

Dwyer was imprisoned in Kilmainham under the tyrannical *de facto* governor, Edward Trevor. Because he had surrendered himself, however, he was not executed but transported in the convict ship *Tellicherry* to a penal colony in New South Wales, Australia, in 1805. Twelve years after his arrival, Dwyer became Chief Constable of Liverpool (Sydney.)

TWENTY MEN FROM DUBLIN TOWN
Arthur Griffith

This popular song tells the unfounded story of how, after the failure of the 1798 rebellion, twenty Dublin men left the city to join Michael Dwyer in the Wicklow mountains, where they hoped to continue the struggle.

Arthur Griffith (1871-1922), Dubliner, was a member of the Gaelic League and of the Irish Republican Brotherhood. He edited the United Irishman *and wrote pamphlets advocating passive resistance to English rule. He led the Irish delegation that negotiated the Treaty of 1921 and became President of the Dáil.*

Twenty men from Dublin Town
Riding on the mountain side,
Fearless of the Saxon frown,
Twenty brothers true and tried.
Blood flows in the City streets,
There the Green is lying low;
Here the emerald standard greets
Eyes alike of friend and foe.

CHORUS
Fly the city, brothers tried;
Join us on the mountain side,
Where we've England's power defied,
Twenty men from Dublin Town.

Twenty men from Dublin Town,
Full of love and full of hate.
Oh! our chief, our Tone is down –
Soul of God, avenge his fate!
Joy it is whene'er we meet
Redcoats in the mountain track –
Ah! as deer they must be fleet
If they get to Dublin back.
CHORUS

Twenty men from Dublin Town,
Every night around the fire
Brimming methers toss we down
To our captain, Michael Dwyer.
Slainte, Michael, brave and true,
Then there rings the wild 'Hurray!'
As we drink, dear land, to you.
Eire Slainte geal go brath!
CHORUS

WICKLOW PERSISTS

Charles Dickson's The Life of Michael Dwyer *(Dublin 1944) tells how resistance continued among Michael Dwyer and his followers in the Wicklow mountains for some time after the main rebellion ended. As late as October 1800, a reward of 200 guineas was offered for taking Andrew Thomas. The report from the* Courier *newspaper of 5 January 1801 is given below.*

Dickson (1886-1978) was born in Down and served with RAMC in the Great War. He joined the Irish Civil Service in 1912 and became became CMO in Dublin. He edited the Irish Journal of Medical Science *from 1962-70. He also wrote* The Wexford Rising in 1798 *(1955) and* Revolt in the North *(1960).*

On the 22nd inst Lieut. Tomlinson and eight of the Rathdrum cavalry, discovered at Castle Kevan, near Rathdrum, three of Dwyer's associates concealed in a cavity under a clump of turf, in an outhouse from whence they rushed on the Lieutenant and one of his troop (the rest being dispersed in other parts adjacent, on the search); on the instant they fired on Mr Tomlinson and his companion, but without effect, and then with precipitancy ran for the open country, which they reached by reason of the scattered state of the troop. The discharge of musketry, however, having collected them, a pursuit began, during which the pursued kept up a sharp fire, being well armed and provided with ammunition, and priming and loading with surprising alacrity; their knowledge of the country too gave them an advantage, as they kept to the bogs and heights, which the yeomen perceiving, some dismounting, dislodged them from their strongholds and after a time Andrew Thomas was killed … The house where they were discovered was consumed and during the conflagration upwards of 100 rounds of cartridge exploded from the thatch. There were also 46 rounds found on the proclaimed persons.

At the subsequent Wicklow inquest:

Mary Healy of Anamoe … single woman maketh oath that the Body now lying dead in the Flannel Hall at Rathdrum with a gunshot wound thro' the hand and another thro' the thigh is the Body of Andrew Thomas late of Anamoe aforesaid and for the taking of whom a reward of Two hundred guineas was offered by Government sayeth she is half sister of the sd Andrew Thomas [who] was born and reared in the same house with Depon. and that she cannot be mistaken as to his person

> Sworn before me this 24th December 1800
> her
> Mary X Healy
> mark

THE MOUNTAIN MEN
William Rooney

Mrs O'Toole of Ballinglen, County Wicklow, gave a folk account of Michael Dwyer entering Glenmalure Barracks in disguise and blowing it up. Commentators have doubted her authenticity. Her story re-echoes through the first stanza of Rooney's poem of Dwyer's Wicklow exploits.

> Did you mark e'er a smoke-drift go sailing
> A while ago down by yon wood?
> Did you hear in the glen the wind wailing
> Where a barrack a week ago stood?

Did you hear the yeos boasting to trap us,
And hang us like dogs on a tree?
Why, then, we're not strangers, and maybe
You'll join in this chorus with me.

CHORUS
Sing ho! for the boys of the mountain;
And hey! for the boys of the glen!
Who never show heel to the sojers –
Here's slainte to Dwyer and his men!

We're not given much to parading;
There's not many guns in the throng;
But he that comes spying our quarters
Won't bother the world for a-long.
The troopers come seeking us daily,
To drive us to hell, so they say;
But the road's a bit long, so we send them
Before us to show us the way.
CHORUS

There's many a white-livered villain
That dreads to awaken our ire,
And tries to be civil, for treason
We visit with steel, lead and fire.
The people all bless us, for many
A cabin's left safe and secure
For fear of the men of the mountain
Whose guns are the guard of the poor.
CHORUS

We laugh at their offers of money
And scorn their power. If we fail
It won't be the sojers or traitors
Who'll bring us to grief, I'll go bail.
We're only a few, but the valleys
And mountains are ours – every hill,
And while God leaves the strength in our sinews
We'll keep the old cause living still.
CHORUS

MICHAEL DWYER

T.D. Sullivan

T.D. Sullivan (1827-1914) was born and educated in Bantry, County Cork. He was co-manager with his brother A.M. Sullivan of The Nation. *A Nationalist MP for Westmeath and, later, Dublin in the 1880s, he wrote many poems and songs including 'God Save Ireland', and edited the popular anthology* Speeches from the Dock.

The soldiers searched the valley, and towards the dawn of day
Discovered where the outlaws, the dauntless rebels, lay.
Around the little cottage they formed into a ring
And called out: 'Michael Dwyer! surrender to the King'.

Thus answered Michael Dwyer: 'Into this house we came
Unasked by those who own it – they cannot be to blame.
The let these peaceful people unquestioned pass you through,
And when they're placed in safety, I'll tell you what we'll do.'

'Twas done. 'And now,' said Dwyer, 'your work you may begin:
You are a hundred outside – we're only four within.
We've heard your haughty summons, and this is our reply –
We're true United Irishmen, we'll fight until we die.'

The burst the war's red lightning, then poured the leaden rain,
The hills around re-echoed the thunder peals again.
The soldiers falling round him brave Dwyer sees with pride;
But, ah! one galland comrade is wounded by his side.

Yet there are three remaining good battle still to do:
Their hands are strong and steady, their aim is quick and true –
But hark that furious shouting the savage soldiers raise!
The house is fired around them; the roof is in a blaze!

And brighter every moment the lurid flame arose,
And louder swelled the laughter and cheering of their foes;
Then spoke brave MacAllister, the weak and wounded man:
'You can escape my comrades, and this shall be your plan:

'Place in my hands a musket, then lie upon the floor:
I'll stand before the soldiers and open wide the door;
They'll pour into my bosom the fire of their array;
Then, whilst their guns are empty, dash through them and away.'

He stood before their foemen, revealed amidst the flame;
From out their levelled pieces the wished-for volley came;
Up sprang the three survivors for whom the hero died,
But only Michael Dwyer broke through the ranks outside.

He baffled his pursuers, who followed like the wind;
He swam the river Slaney and left them far behind;
But many an English soldier he promised should soon fall
For these, his gallant comrades, which died in wild Immal.

❦   ❦   ❦

Of Grattan and Government

Henry Grattan (1746-1820) was a Dublin lawyer and MP for the borough
of Charlemont in the Irish Parliament, where he was leader of the Opposition. He campaigned successfully for repeal of restriction on Irish trade
and pressed for legislative independence for Ireland. Although a Protestant,
he campaigned for Catholic Emancipation.

THE INDEPENDENT IRISH PARLIAMENT
Denis Florence McCarthy

*From 1782 to 1800 there was a separate Irish Parliament in Dublin. Although
Grattan refused office, it was known as 'Grattan's Parliament'.*

*Denis Florence McCarthy (1817-82) was a Dublin lawyer and journalist who
contributed to* The Nation *and other nationalist publications. He became Professor
of Literature at Catholic University, Dublin. He published his poems and also translated Pedro Calderó's classical comedies, philosophical and religious plays.*

A dazzling gleam of evanescent glory
Had passed away, and all was dark once more.
One golden page had lit the mournful story
Which ruthless hands with envious rage out-tore.

One glorious sun-burst, radiant and far reaching,
Had pierced the cloudy veil dark ages wove,
When full-armed Freedom rose from Grattan's teaching

As sprang Minerva from the brain of Jove.
Oh! in the transient light that had outbroken,
How all the land with quickening fire was lit!
What golden words of deathless speech were spoken,
What lightning flashes of immortal wit!

Letters and arts revived beneath its beaming,
Commerce and Hope outspread their swelling sails,
And with 'Free Trade' upon their standard gleaming,
Now feared no foes and dared adventurous gales.

Across the stream the graceful arch extended,
Above the pile the rounded dome arose;
The soaring spire to heaven's high vault ascended,
The loom hummed loud as bees at evening's close.

And yet 'mid all this hope and animation
The people still lay bound in bigot chains,
Freedom that gave some slight alleviation
Could dare no panacea for their pains.

Yet faithful to their country's quick uprising,
Like some fair island from volcanic waves,
They shared the triumph though their chains despising,
And hailed the freedom though themselves were slaves.

But soon had come the final compensation,
Soon would the land one brotherhood have known,
Had not some spell of hellish incantation
The new-formed fane of Freedom overthrown.

On one brief hour the fair mirage had faded,
No isle of flowers lay glad on ocean's green;
But in its stead, deserted and degraded,
The barren strand of slavery's shore was seen.

LAMENT FOR GRATTAN
Thomas Moore

Although a friend of Robert Emmet, Moore (1779-1852) did not join the United Irishmen, preferring to study law in London and become popular among its socialites.

Shall the Harp then be silent, when he who first gave
To our country a name is withdrawn from all eyes?
Shall a Minstrel of Erin stand mute by the grave
Where the first – where the last of her Patriots lies?

No – faint tho' the death-song may fall from his lips,
Tho' his Harp like his soul may with shadows be crost,
Yet, yet shall it sound, 'mid a nation's eclipse
And proclaim to the world what a star hath been lost –

What a union of all the affections and powers
By which life is exalted, embellish'd, refined,
Was embraced in that spirit – whose centre was ours
While its mighty circumference circled mankind.

Oh! who that loves Erin, or who that can see
Through the waste of her annals, that epoch sublime,
Like a pyramid raised in the desert – where he
And his glory stand out to the eyes of all time:

That one lucid interval, snatch'd from the gloom
And the madness of ages, when fill'd with his soul
A nation o'erleap'd the dark bounds of her doom,
And for one sacred instant touch'd Liberty's goal.

Who that ever hath heard him – hath drunk at the source
Of that wonderful eloquence, all Erin's own,
In whose high-thoughted daring, the fire and the force,
And the yet untamed spring of her spirit are shown –

An eloquence rich, wheresoever its wave
Wander'd free and triumphant with thoughts that shone thro'
As clear as the brook's 'stone of lustre,' and gave
With the flash of the gem, its solidity, too.

Who that ever approach'd him, when free from the crowd
In a home full of love he delighted to tread
'Mong the trees which a nation had giv'n and which bow'd
As if each brought a new civic crown for his head —

Is there one, who hath thus, through his orbit of life
But at distance observed him — through glory, through blame,
In the calm of retreat, in the grandeur of strife,
Whether shining or clouded, still high and the same —

Oh no, not a heart that e'er knew him but mourns
Deep, deep o'er the grave, where such glory is shrined
O'er a monument Fame will preserve, 'mong the urns
Of the wisest, the bravest, the best of mankind!

THE UNION
Sliabh Cuilinn

The Act of Union came into force on 1 January 1800, thus ending 'Grattan's Parliament'. This poem appeared first in a publication by Sliabh Cuilinn titled England's Ultimatum *(1801). In his* Poetry History of Ireland *(1927) Stephen J. Brown fails to identify the author. Note the reference to the pitchcap. This was a bowl-shaped container full of hot tar or pitch placed on a rebel's head. In another form, pitch was rubbed thickly on the victim's head and sprinkled with gunpowder before being lit. Its origin was attributed to a militia sergeant known as 'Tom the Devil'.*

How did they pass the Union?
By perjury and fraud;
By slaves who sold their land for gold
As Judas sold his God;
By all the savage acts that yet
Have followed England's track —
The pitchcap and the bayonet,
The gibbet and the rack,
And thus was passed the Union
By Pitt and Castlereagh;
Could Satan send for such an end
More worthy tools than they?

How thrive we by the Union?
Look round our native land:
In ruined trade and wealth decayed
See slavery's surest brand;
Our glory as a nation gone;
Our substance drained away;
A wretched province trampled on
Is all we've left to-day.
Then curse with me the Union,
That juggle foul and base,
The baneful root that bore such fruit
Of ruin and disgrace.

And shall it last, this Union,
To grind and waste us so?
O'er hill and lea from sea to sea
All Ireland thunders, No!
Eight million necks are stiff to bow,
We know our might as men;
We conquer'd once before and now
We'll conquer once again,
And rend the cursed Union
And fling it to the wind

How did they pass the Union?
By perjury and fraud;
By slaves who sold their land for gold
As Judas sold his God;
By all the savage acts that yet
Have followed England's track –
The pitchcap and the bayonet,
The gibbet and the rack,
And thus was passed the Union
By Pitt and Castlereagh;
Could Satan send for such an end
More worthy tools than they?

How thrive we by the Union?
Look round our native land:

In ruined trade and wealth decayed
See slavery's surest brand;
Our glory as a nation gone;
Our substance drained away;
A wretched province trampled on
Is all we've left to-day.
Then curse with me the Union,
That juggle foul and base,
The baneful root that bore such fruit
Of ruin and disgrace.

And shall it last, this Union,
To grind and waste us so?
O'er hill and lea from sea to sea
All Ireland thunders, No!
Eight million necks are stiff to bow,
We know our might as men;
We conquer'd once before and now
We'll conquer once again,
And rend the cursed Union
And fling it to the wind –
And Ireland's laws in Ireland's cause
Alone our hearts shall bind!

Of Emmet

Robert Emmet (1778-1803) joined with his brother, Thomas Addis, in encouraging a French invasion. A warrant for his arrest in 1799 was not enforced. He remained in France during the rebellion and attempted another rising in Dublin on 23 July 1803. He was hanged in Thomas Street, Dublin, on 20 September 1803.

ARBOUR HILL
Robert Emmet

Bodies of 1798 rebels were interred in the cemetery at Arbour Hill in Dublin, and in another, later rebellion, the executed men of 1916 similarly found a last resting-place there. This is believed to be one of the few poems of Emmet's extant, published in R.R. Madden's biography of 1846.

No rising column marks the spot
Where many a victim lies;
But Oh! the blood which here has streamed
To Heaven for justice cries.
It claims it on the oppressor's head
Who joys in human woe,
Who drinks the tears by misery shed
And mocks them as they flow.

It claims it on the callous judge,
Whose hands in blood are dyed,
Who arms injustice with the sword,
The balance throws aside.
It claims it for his ruined isle,
Her wretched children's grave;
Where withered Freedom droops her head,
And man exists – a slave.

O Sacred Justice! Free this land
From tyranny abhorred;
Resume thy balance and thy seat
Resume but sheathe thy sword.

No retribution should we seek
Too long has horror reigned;
By mercy marked may freedom rise,
By cruelty unstained.

Nor shall a tyrant's ashes mix
With those our martyred dead;
This is the place where Erin's sons
In Erin's cause have bled.
And those who here are laid at rest,
Oh! Hallowed be each name;
Their memories are for ever blest
Consigned to endless fame.

Unconsecrated is this ground,
Unblest by holy hands;
No bell here tolls its solemn sound,
No monument here stands.
But here the patriots' tears are shed,
The poor man's blessing given;
These consecrate the virtuous dead,
These waft their fame to heaven.

LAST LETTER

Before his execution, Emmet wrote to his brother and sister-in-law:

My dearest Tom and Jane,

I am just going to do my last duty to my country. It can be done as well on the scaffold as on the field. Do not give way to any weak feeling on my account, but rather encourage the proud ones that I have possessed fortitude and tranquillity to the last.

God bless you, and the young ones that are growing up around you. May they be more fortunate than their uncle, but may they preserve as pure and ardent an attachment to their country as he has done. Give the watch to little Robert. He will not prize it the less for having been in possession of two Roberts before him. I have one dying request to make to you. I was attached to Sarah Curran, the youngest daughter of your friend [John Philpot Curran]. I did hope to have her my companion for life. I did hope that she would not only constitute my happiness, but that her heart and understanding would have made her one of Jane's dearest friends. I know that Jane would have loved her on my account and I feel also that had they been acquainted she must have loved her for her own. No one knew of the attachment until now, nor is it now generally known, therefore do not speak of it to others. She is living with her father and brother, but if these protectors should fall off and that no other should replace them, treat her as my wife, and love her as a sister. God Almighty bless you all. Give my love to all my friends.

SPEECH FROM THE DOCK

Robert Emmet's speech from the dock of 19 September 1803 was once the choice of nationalist performers at concerts and parlour gatherings. Those who heard it praised the speaker's loud, beautifully modulated delivery that reached the outside of the courtroom building. It was censored, and later attempts to reconstruct it led to a number of published versions. The following is Richard Madden's.

The Clerk of the Crown then, in the usual form, addressed the prisoner, concluding in these words: 'What have you, therefore, now to say why judgment of death and execution should not be awarded against you, according to law?'

Mr Emmet, standing forward in the dock, in front of the bench, said:

'My lords, as to why judgment of death and execution should not be passed upon me, according to law, I have nothing to say; but as to why my character should be relieved from the imputations and calumnies thrown out against it, I have much to say. I do not imagine that your lordships will give credit to what I am going to utter; I have no hopes that I can anchor my character in the breast of the court, I only wish your lordships may suffer it to float down your memories until it has found some more hospitable harbour to shelter it from the storms with which it is as present buffeted. Was I to suffer only death, after being adjudged guilty, I should bow in silence to the fate which awaits me but the sentence of the law which delivers over my body to the executioner, consigns my character to obloquy. A man in my situation has not only to encounter the difficulties of fortune, but also the difficulties of prejudice. Whilst the man dies, his memory lives and that mine may not forfeit all claim to the respect of my countrymen, I seize upon this opportunity to vindicate myself from some of the charges alleged against me. I am charged with being an emissary of France: it is false – I am no emissary. I did not wish to deliver up my country to a foreign power, and least of all, to France. Never did I entertain the remotest idea of establishing French power in Ireland.

'From the introductory paragraph of the address of the Provisional Government, it is evident that every hazard attending an independent effort was deemed preferable to the more fatal risk of introducing a French army into this country. Small, indeed, would be our claim to patriotism and to sense, and palpable our affection of the love of liberty, if we were to sell our country to a people who are not only slaves themselves but the unprincipled and abandoned instruments of imposing slavery on others. And my lords, let me here observe, that I am not the head and life's blood of this rebellion. When I came to Ireland I found the business ripe for execution. I was asked to join in; I took time to consider; and after mature consideration I became one of the

Provisional Government; and there then was, my lord, an agent from the United Irishmen and Provisional government of Ireland at Paris negotiating with the French Government, to obtain from them an aid sufficient to accomplish the separation of Ireland from Great Britain, the preliminary of which assistance has been a guarantee to Ireland similar to that which Franklin obtained for America; but the intimation that I, or the rest of the Provisional Government, meditated to put our country under the domain of a power which has been the enemy of freedom in every part of the globe, is utterly false and unfounded. Did we entertain any such ideas, how could we speak of giving freedom to our countrymen? How could we assume such an exalted motive? If such an inference is drawn from any part of the proclamation of the Provisional Government it calumniates their views, and is not warranted by the fact.

'Connection with France was, indeed, intended, but only as far as mutual interest would sanction or require. Were they to assume any authority inconsistent with the purest independence, it would be the signal for their destruction. We sought aid, and we sought it – as we had assurance we should obtain it – as auxiliaries in war, and allies in peace.

'Were the French to come as invaders or enemies uninvited by the wishes of the people, I should oppose them to the utmost of my strength. Yes! my countrymen, I should advise you to meet them upon the beach with a sword in one hand and a torch in the other.

'My lords, will a dying man be denied the legal privilege of exculpating himself in the eyes of the community from a reproach thrown upon him during his trial, by charging him with ambition, and attempting to cast away for a paltry consideration, the liberties of his country, why then insult me, or rather, why insult justice, in demanding of me why sentence of death should not be pronounced against me? I know, my lords, that the form prescribes that you should put the question, the form also confers a right to answering. This, no doubt, may be dispensed with, and so might the whole ceremony of the trial, since sentence was already pronounced at the Castle before your jury was impanelled. Your lordships are but the priests of the oracle, and I submit, but I insist on the whole of the forms.'

(Here Mr Emmet paused, and the court desired him to proceed.)

'My lords, you are impatient for the sacrifice. The blood which you seek is not congealed by the artificial terrors which surround your victim – it circulated warmly and unruffled through its channels, and in a little time it will cry to heaven – be yet patient! I have but a few words more to say – I am going to my cold and silent grave – my lamp of life is nearly extinguished – I have parted with everything that was dear to me in this life, and for my country's cause with the idol of my soul, the object of my affections. My race is run – the grave opens to receive me, and I sink into its bosom. I have but one request to ask at my departure from this world, it is the *charity of its silence*. Let no man write my epitaph; for as no man who knows my motives dare now vindicate them, let not prejudice or ignorance asperse them. Let them rest in obscurity and peace, my memory be left in oblivion, and my tomb remain untouched, until other times and other men can do justice to my character. When my country takes her place among the nations of the earth, *then*, and not till *then*, let my epitaph be written. I have done.

BOLD ROBERT EMMET
Thomas Maguire

One of the great nineteenth-century ballads on Ireland's single most popular insurgent hero. It was written by Thomas Maguire, an authentic balladeer who sang and sold his own songs at fairs and on street corners, and survived into the twentieth century.

The struggle is over, the boys are defeated,
Old Ireland's surrounded with sadness and gloom;
We were defeated and shamefully treated,
And I, Robert Emmet awaiting my doom.
Hung, drawn and quartered, sure that was my sentence,
But soon I will show them no coward am I;
My crime is the love of the land I was born in,
A hero I lived and a hero I'll die.

CHORUS
Bold Robert Emmet, the darling of Erin,
Bold Robert Emmet will die with a smile;
Farewell companions both loyal and daring,
I'll lay down my life for the Emerald Isle.

The barque lay at anchor awaiting to bring me
Over the billows to the land of the free;
But I must see my sweetheart for I know she will cheer me,
And with her I will sail far over the sea.
But I was arrested and cast into prison,
Tried as a traitor, a rebel, a spy;
But no one can call me a knave or a coward,
A hero I lived and a hero I'll die.
CHORUS

EMMET'S DEATH
S.F.C.

'He dies to-day,' said the heartless judge,
Whilst he sat him down to the feast,
And a smile was upon his ashy lips
As he uttered a ribald jest;

For a demon dwelt where his heart should be
That lived upon blood and sin,
And oft as that vile judge gave him food
The demon throbbed within.

'He dies to-day,' said the gaoler firm,
Whilst a tear was in his eye;
'But why should I feel so grieved for him?
Sure I've seen many die!
Last night I went to his stony cell
With scanty prison fare –
He was sitting at a table rude,
Plaiting a lock of hair!
And he looked so mild, with his pale, pale face,
And he spoke in so kind a way
That my old breast heav'd with a smothering feel,
And I knew not what to say.'

'He dies to-day,' thought a fair, sweet girl –
She lacked the life to speak,
For sorrow had almost frozen her blood,
And white were her lip and cheek –
Despair had drank up her last wild tear
And her brow was damp and chill,
And they often felt at her heart with fear
For its ebb was all but still.

SHE IS FAR FROM THE LAND
Thomas Moore

A song in honour of Sarah Curran, daughter of John Philpot Curran and Emmet's sweetheart. Emmet was captured at her house in Harold's Cross by Major Sirr, who earlier had taken Lord Edward Fitzgerald.

Thomas Moore (1778-1852) was born in Aungier Street, Dublin, and educated at TCD, where he befriended the Emmet brothers, and went on to study law in London. He became Ireland's 'greatest songster' with the publication of his Irish Melodies *(1803-34) based on airs recorded by Edward Bunting.*

She is far from the land where her young hero sleeps
And lovers around her sighing;
But coldly she turns from their gaze and weeps
For her heart in his grave is lying.

She sings the wild song of her dear native plains,
Ev'ry note which he lov'd a-waking;
Ah! little they think who delight in their strains,
That the heart of the minstrel is breaking.

He had liv'd for his love, for his country he died,
They were all that to life had entwin'd him;
Nor soon shall the tears of his country be dried,
Nor long will his love stay behind him.

O make her a grave where the sunbeams rest,
When they promise a glorious morrow
They'll shine o'er her sleep, like a smile from the West,
From her own lov'd island of sorrow.

OH BREATHE NOT HIS NAME
Thomas Moore

Deriving from Emmet's speech from the dock.

Oh! Breath not his name – let it sleep in the shade
Where cold and unhonour'd his relics are laid!
Sad, silent, and dark, be the tears that we shed,
As the night-dew that falls on the graves o'er his head!

Night dew that falls, tho' in silence it weeps,
Shall brighten with verdure the grave where he sleeps,
And the tear that we shed, tho' in secret it rolls,
Shall long keep his mem'ry green in our souls.

Of Recollection

BY MEMORY INSPIRED

Anon.

This street ballad appeared when John Mitchel (1815-75) was deported in 1848. The devastation that resulted from the Famine of 1845-47 prompted Mitchel to found the United Irishman *as an organ for advancing republicanism and passive resistance by small farmers. The paper was suppressed in 1848. The ballad recalls events of 1798.*

John McCann, the Secretary of the Leinster Directory, favoured an early rebellion. He was arrested at Oliver Bond's home. Sentenced on the evidence of Thomas Reynolds, he was hanged in July 1798.

An officer of the King's County Militia, Captain John Warnford Armstrong wormed his way into the confidence of rebel leaders, mainly through a reputation that, as a student at Trinity College, he had offered to behead the King. He befriended and duped the Sheares Brothers. While arranging Henry's arrest, he dined at his home and played with his child as Mrs Sheares played the harp for him.

Oliver Bond (1760-98), a Donegal-born Dublin woollen merchant, was a leader of the United Irishmen. In an upstairs room of his home at 9 Lr Bridge Street on the night of 12 March 1798, Major Sirr arrested eighteen members of the Leinster Directory and of the Supreme Executive of the movement. Bond was sentenced to death on 20 July. He and others – McNevin, O'Connor, Neilson and Thomas Addis Emmet – co-operated with the authorities and were later exiled to Fort George in Scotland. Bond died in prison in September.

By memory inspired, and love of country fired,
The deeds of men I love to dwell upon;
And the patriotic glow of my spirit must bestow
A tribute to the heroes that are gone, boys, gone –
Here's a health to John Mitchel that is gone!

In October, 'Ninety-Seven – may his soul find rest in heaven –
William Orr to execution was led on;
The jury, drunk, agreed that Irish was his creed,
For perjury and threats drove them on, boys on –
Here's the memory of the friends that are gone!

In 'Ninety-Eight – the month, July – the informer's pay was high
When Reynolds gave the gallows brave McCann:
But McCann was Reynolds' first – one could not allay his thirst –
So he brought up Bond and Byrne that are gone, boys, gone –
Here's the memory of the friends that are gone.

We saw a nation's tears shed for John and Henry Sheares.
Betrayed by Judas, Captain Armstrong;
We may forgive, but yet we never can forget
The fate of Tone and Emmet that are gone, boys, gone.
Of all the fearless heroes that are gone.

How did Lord Edward die? Like a man, without a sigh,
But he left his handiwork on Major Swan!
But Sirr, with steel-clad breast, and coward heart at best,
Left us cause to mourn Lord Edward that is gone, boys, gone –
Here's the memory of our friends that are gone!

September, Eighteen-three, closed this cruel history.
When Emmet's blood the scaffold flowed upon.
Oh, had our men been wise they then might realize
Their freedom – but we drink to Mitchel that is gone boys, gone –
Here's the memory of the heroes that are gone!

THE MEN OF NINETY-EIGHT
Anon.

A song that originated in Ulster during the centenary year of the rebellion.

A hundred years have passed and gone since Irishmen, they stood
On the green hillsides of Erin and for freedom shed their blood.
The Irish race is called upon for to commemorate
Those bold United Irishmen who died in Ninety-Eight.

Then hurrah for the flag, the dear bold flag of green,
And Hurrah for the men who, beneath its folds are seen.
Hurrah for the heroes, we now commemorate;
Those brave United Irishmen who died in Ninety-Eight

FORGET NOT THE FIELD
Thomas Moore

This lamentation for his friends was published in Moore's Irish Melodies *in 1818.*

Forget not the field where they perish'd,
The truest, the last of the brave,
All gone – and the bright hope they cherish'd
Gone with them, and quench'd in their grave.

Oh! Could we from death but recover
Those hearts, as they bounded before,
In the face of high Heaven to fight over
That combat for freedom once more –

Could the chain for an instant be riven
Which Tyranny flung round us then,
Oh! 't is not in Man nor in Heaven,
To let tyranny bind it again!

But it is past – and, though blazon'd in story
The name of our Victor may be,
Accursed is the march of that glory
Which treads o'er the hearts of the free.

Far dearer the grave or the person,
Illumed by one patriot name,
Than the trophies of all who have risen
On liberty's ruins to fame!

Selected Reading

DOCUMENTS, JOURNALS AND PAMPHLETS

An t-Óglách, Vol. III, No. 1, January 1930.

Bartlett, Thomas, 'Defenders and Defenderism in 1795', *Irish Historical Studies,* XXIV (1984-85).

Béaloideas, The Journal of the Irish Folklore Society, Vol. 4, No. 4, Nollaig 1934; Vol. 5 No. 2, Nollaig 1935.

Broadside Ballads, National Library of Ireland Collection.

Broadside Ballads, White Collection, Trinity College, Dublin.

Clarke, Joe, Irish Book Bureau Publications.

Donegal Annual, Vol. 2, No. 2.

Journal of the Cork Historical and Archaeoleogical Society, Vol. III, 1894.

McCall Collection of Irish Ballads, National Library of Ireland.

McDonagh, Bernard, *Lough Gill,* Sligo n.d.

Mackey, Patrick, *Selected Walks Through Waterford,* Waterford n.d.

Madden Collection of Irish Ballads, National Library of Ireland.

Oughterany: Journal of the Donadea Local History Group, Vol. 1, No. 1, 1993.

Rebellion Papers, National Archives.

The Irish Sword, Vol. VIII, No. 33.

The Irish Sword, Vol. XIII, No. 50.

BOOKS

Barrington, Sir Jonah, *Personal Sketches of his Own Times,* 3 vols, London 1827-32.

—, *Rise and Fall of the Irish Nation,* Dublin 1833.

Bartlett, Thomas (ed.), *Life of Thebald Wolfe Tone,* Dublin 1998.

Bodkin, M. McDonnell, *Lord Edward Fitzgerald,* Dublin n.d.

Boylan, Henry, *Wolfe Tone,* Dublin 1981.

Brophy, John, *Sarah,* London, 1948.

Brown, Stephen J., *Ireland in Fiction,* Dublin 1915.

— (ed.), *Poetry of Irish History,* Dublin & Cork 1927.

Bryce, Right Hon. James and contributors, *Two Centuries of Irish History, 1690-1870,* London 1888.

Byrne, Miles, *Memoirs,* 2 vols, Paris 1863. New edn Dublin 1906.

—, *Notes of An Irish Exile of 1798,* Dublin n.d.

Carty, James, *Ireland from Grattan's Parliament to the Great Famine,* Dublin 1966.

Chart, D.A., (ed.), *The Drennan Letters 1776-1819,* Belfast 1931.

Clarke, Joseph, (ed.), *128 Songs & Ballads of Ireland*, Dublin n.d..

Cloney, Thomas, *A Personal Narrative of These Transactions in the County of Wexford … during the Period of 1798*, Dublin 1832.

Corish, Patrick J., *The Catholic Community in the Seventeenth & Eighteenth Centuries*, Dublin 1981.

Corrigan, S.L., *History of the Rebellion in Ireland, 1798*, Belfast 1844.

Costello, Con, *Botany Bay*, Cork & Dublin 1987.

Cullen, Rev. Br. Luke, *Personal Recollections of Wexford and Wicklow Insurgents of 1798*, Enniscorthy 1959.

Curry, J., *Historical and Critical Review of the Civil Wars in Ireland*, ed. C. O'Conor. Dublin 1810.

Curtin, Nancy J., *The United Irishmen: Popular Politics in Belfast and Dublin 1790-98*, Oxford 1994.

De Latocnaye, *A Frenchman's Walk Through Ireland 1796-7*, Belfast 1984.

Dickson, Charles, *The Life of Michael Dwyer*, Dublin 1944.

—, *The Wexford Rising in 1798: Its Causes and its Course*, Tralee 1955.

Dickson, D., D. Keogh and K. Whelan (eds), *The United Irishmen: Republicanism, Radicalism and Rebellion*, Dublin 1993.

Edgeworth, Maria, *Memoirs of Richard Lovell Edgeworth*, 2 vols, London 1820.

Edgeworth, Maria and Richard Lovell, *The Black Book of Edgeworthstown and other Edgeworth Memories, 1587-1817* (ed. Butler & Butler), London 1925.

Elliott, Marianne, *Partners in Revolution: The United Irishmen and France*, London 1982.

—, *Wolfe Tone, Prophet of Irish Independence*, New Haven & London 1989.

Faly, Patrick C., *Ninety-Eight*, London 1897.

Farrell, Hugh, *Farrell Clann – A brief History*, Longford n.d.

Farrell, James P., *Historical Notes and Stories of the County Longford*, Longford (1886) 1979.

—, *History of the County Longford*, Longford (1891) 1980.

Farrell, William, *Carlow in '98: The Autobiography of William Farrell of Carlow*. (ed. Roger J. McHugh), Dublin 1949.

Fitzpatrick, W.J., *The Sham Squire, and the Informers of 1798*, Dublin 1866.

Fogra Failte, *Ireland Guide*, Dublin n.d.

Folley, Terence, (ed.), *Eyewitness to 1798*, Cork 1996.

Freyer, Grattan, (ed.), *Bishop Stock's 'Narrative' 1798 of the Year of the French*, Ballina 1982.

Froude, James Anthony, *The English in Ireland in the Eighteenth Century*, 3 vols, London 1895.

Furlong, Nicholas, *Fr John Murphy of Boolavogue*, Dublin 1991.

Gahan, Daniel, *Rebellion! Ireland in 1798*, Dublin 1997.

—, *The People's Rising*, Dublin 1996.

Glassie, Henry, *Irish Folk History*, Dublin 1982.

Gordon, Rev. James Bentley, *History of the Rebellion in Ireland in the Year 1798, etc.*, Dublin 1801.

Gough, Hugh, and David Dickson (eds), *Ireland and the French Revolution*, Dublin 1996.

Graves, Alfred P., *Irish Songs and Ballads*, Dublin 1880.

Harwood, Philip, *History of the Irish Rebellion of 1798*, London 1848.

Hassencamp, R., *The History of Ireland, from the Reformation to the Union* (trans. E.A. Robinson), London 1888.

Haughton, Joseph, *Narration of Events during the Irish Rebellion in 1798*, n.p. n.d.

Hay, Edward, *History of the Insurrection of the County of Wexford, A.D. 1798*, Dublin 1803.

Hayes, Richard, *The Last Invasion of Ireland*, Dublin 1937.

Hayes-McCoy, G.A., *Irish Battles*, London 1969.

Hayley, Barbara, and Christopher Murray (eds), *Ireland and France – A Bountiful Friendship*, Gerrards Cross 1992.

Holland, Lord, *Memoirs of the Whig Party during my Time* (ed. by his son, Henry Edward, Lord Holland), 2 vols, London 1852.

Holt, J., *Memoirs of J. Holt, General of the Irish Rebels in 1798* (ed. from original MS by T. Crofton Croker), 2 vols, London 1838.

Jones, John, *An Impartial Narrative of each Engagement which took place between his Majesty's Forces and the Rebels, during the Irish Rebellion, 1798*, Dublin 1800.

Kavanagh, Rev. Patrick F., *A Popular History of the Insurrection in 1798*, Dublin n.d.

—, *A Popular History of the Insurrection of 1798: derived from every available Record and reliable Tradition*, Cork 1898.

Kelly, Freida, *A History of Kilmainham Gaol*, Cork & Dublin 1988.

Kennedy, Patrick J. (ed.), *Senior Poetry: An Anthology of Matriculation & Leaving Certificate Poetry*, Dublin 1961.

Keogh, Dáire, *'The French Disease', The Catholic Church and Radicalism in the 1790s*, Dublin 1993.

—, & Furlong, N. (eds), *The Mighty Wave: The 1798 Rebellion in Wexford*, Dublin 1996.

Kiely, Benedict, *And As I Rode By Granard Moat*, Dublin 1996.

Killen, John, *The Decade of the United Irishmen – Contemporary Accounts*, Belfast 1997.

Kinsella, Thomas, *The New Oxford History of Irish Verse*, Oxford, 1990.

Latimer, W.T., *Ulster Biographies, relating chiefly to the Rebellion of 1798*, Belfast 1897.

Lecky, W.E.H., *History of Ireland in the Eighteenth Century Vol. IV*, London 1913.

McDonnell, John (ed.), *Songs of Struggle & Protest*, 1986 Cork/Dublin.

McDonnell, Randal, *Kathleen Mavourneen*, Dublin 1898.

McDowell, R.B., *Ireland in the Age of Imperialism and Revolution, 1760-1801*, Oxford 1979.

McMahon, Sean, *A Book of Irish Quotations*, Dublin 1984.

—, *Rich & Rare – A Book of Ireland*, Dublin 1984.

—, & Jo O'Donoghue, *Taisce Duan*, Dublin 1992.

McNeill, Mary, *The Life and Times of Mary Ann McCracken 1770-1866*, Dublin 1960.

Mac Suibhne, Peadar, *Kildare in '98*, Naas 1978.

Madden, Richard.R. (ed.), *Literary Remains of the United Irishmen of 1798*, Dublin 1887.

—, *The United Irishmen, their Lives and Times*, Dublin 1860.

—, *Antrim and Down in '98*, Dublin n.d.

—, *The Life and Times of Robert Emmet*, Dublin 1846.

Magee, Malachy, *1000 Years of Irish Whiskey*, Dublin 1980.

Maxwell, William Hamilton, *History of the Irish Rebellion in 1798*, London 1845.

Moody, T.W., and F.X. Martin, *The Course of Irish History*, Cork 1984.

Moore, Desmond, *Dublin's Yesterdays*, Portlaoise n.d.

Moore, Thomas, *The Life and Death of Lord Edward Fitzgerald*, 2 vols, London 1831.

Morgan, Edward, *A Journal of the Movements of the French Fleet in Bantry Bay*, Cork 1797.

Mulcahy, Michael, and MarieFitzgibbon, *The Voice of the People: Songs & History of Ireland*, Dublin 1982.

Murphy, John A., ed., *The French Are in the Bay: The Expedition to Bantry Bay*, Cork 1997.

Musgrave, Sir Richard, *Memoirs of the Different Rebellions in Ireland*, Dublin 1801.

O'Brien, R. Barry (ed.), *The Autobiography of Theobald Wolfe Tone*, Dublin n.d.

O'Dálaigh, Pádraig (ed.), *A Ballad History of Ireland for Schools*, Dublin & Cork n.d.

O'Donnchu M.F., *Leo*, Baile Átha Cliath 1981.

O'Donnell, Ruan, *Rebellion in Wicklow 1798*, Dublin 1998.

Ó Duilearga, Séamus (ed.), *Béaloideas, The Journal of the Folklore of Ireland Society,* Iml I, Uimh. IV, Nollaig 1928.

—, *Béaloideas,* Iml I, Uimh IV, Nollaig 1934.

—, *Béaloideas,* Iml V, Uimh. II, Nollaig 1935.

—, *Béaloideas,* Iml XXXII, 1964.

O'Farrell, Padraic, *Irish Rogues, Rascals & Scoundrels*, Cork/Dublin 1992.

O'Kelly P., *General History of the Rebellion of 1798 &c*, Dublin 1842.

O'Kelly, Seamus G., *Sweethearts of the Irish Rebels*, Dublin 1968.

Oram, Hugh, *The Newspaper Book*, Dublin 1983.

Pakenham Thomas, *The Year of Liberty*, London 1969, 1997.

Sheedy, Kieran, *Upon the Mercy of Government*, Dublin 1988.

Smyth, Jim, *The Men of No Property: Irish Radicals and Popular Politics in the Late Eighteenth Century*, Dublin 1992.

Stewart, A.T.Q. *A Deeper Silence: The Hidden Origins of United Irishmen*, London 1993.

—, *The Summer Soldiers: The 1798 Rebellion in Antrim and Down*, Belfast 1995.

Stock, Bishop Joseph, *A Narrative of … The French Invasion in the Summer of 1798*, Dublin & London 1800.

Taylor, George, *A History of the Rise, Progress and Suppression of the Rebellion in the County of Wexford in the Year 1798*, Dublin 1829.

Taylor, W.C., *A History of the Civil Wars in Ireland*, London 1826.

Teeling, C.H., *History of the Irish rebellion of 1798 – A Personal Narrative*, Glasgow 1828.

—, *Sequel to the Personal Narrative of the Irish Rebellion.* London 1832.

Thuente, Mary Helen, *The Harp Re-Strung: The United Irishmen and the Rise of Irish Literary Nationalism*, Syracuse 1990.

Toomey & Greensmyth, *An Antique and Storied Land*, Limerick 1991.

Weber, Paul, *On the Road to Rebellion*, Dublin 1997.

Wheeler, H.F.B., and A.M Broadley, *The War in Wexford*, London 1910.

Whelan, Kevin, *The Tree of Liberty. Radicalism, Catholicism and the Construction of Irish Identity 1760-1830*, Cork 1996.

Wilsdon, Bill, *The Sites of the 1798 Rising in Antrim and Down*, Belfast 1997.

Woods, C.J. (ed.), *The Journals and Memoirs of Thomas Russell,* Dublin 1992.

Woods, James, *The Annals of Westmeath*, Dublin 1907.

Wright, Thomas, *The History of Ireland,* London 1821.

Zimmerman, George-Denis, *Songs of Irish Rebellion – Political Street Ballads and Rebel Songs 1780-1900*, Dublin 1967.

Chronology
⚜ 1778-1803 ⚜

1778

Feb. 7. Henry Grattan moves a parliamentary address to the Crown. It states that conditions in Ireland can not be endured any longer. He is defeated, 143 to 66.

March 17. Volunteer companies are established in Belfast. Lord Charlemont becomes leader of the Northern Volunteers. The Duke of Leinster commands the Leinster Volunteers.

April 13. An American War of Independence veteran and privateer, Scottish-born John Paul Jones, attacks Scottish and English ports. On board the *Ranger*, he carries out two raids on Belfast Lough. When he captures H.M.S. *Drake*, the Lord Lieutenant, Buckinghamshire, calls for resistance.

April 16. The Jones escapade, above, gives impetus to the Volunteer movement. Meetings take place in Belfast's Donegall Arms and elsewhere. Recruitment is substantial.

Aug. 14. Luke Gardiner's First Catholic Relief Bill allows Catholics to inherit property and to contract leases for 999 years, bringing rights into line with those of other religions.

1779

March 17. The Irish Volunteers take part in New York St Patrick's Day Parade.

March 28. Rev. William Steel Dixon calls for the enlistment of Catholics in the Volunteers.

July 15 *c.* The Lord Lieutenant allows the arming of Volunteers with infantry weapons.

Nov. 4. The Volunteers parade in College Green, Dublin. They demand the removal of restrictions on Irish trade.

1780

Feb. 24. An Act of British Parliament authorizes Ireland to trade with British colonies on similar terms to Great Britain. It also lifts other trade sanctions.

April 19. In the House of Commons, Henry Grattan moves resolutions favouring Irish legislative independence. After a long debate the resolutions are deferred indefinitely.

July 11. Grattan and Lord Charlemont attend a parade of Volunteers in Dublin.

1781

July 20-22. A gathering of over 230,000 witness a weekend of Volunteer military exercises in Belfast.

Dec. 28. Lord Charlemont reiterates the demand for legislative independence and calls for a Volunteer Convention in Dungannon on Feb. 15, 1782.

1782

Feb. 15. The Volunteer Convention at Dungannon approves the relaxation of the Penal Laws but resolves that it is unconstitutional for any but the King, Lord and Commons of Ireland to legislate for Ireland.

Feb. 22. Grattan moves to have the Declaratory Act of 1720 repealed but again fails in his bid for legislative independence.

May 4. Catholics' rights to purchase and inherit freehold lands assured in Luke Gardiner's Second Catholic Relief Act. The Attorney General, John Scott, is dismissed for insisting that it is wrong for Great Britain to enact Acts of Parliament for Ireland.

May 27. Independence of the Volunteers is announced, prompting Napper Tandy to parade them on the approaches to Parliament.

June 21. The Declaratory Act of 1720 is repealed due to an earlier (May 17) initiative by Charles James Fox in the British House of Commons and Lord Shelbourne in the House of Lords.

July 27. Luke Gardiner's Third Catholic Relief Act allows Catholics to become schoolmasters and guardians and to own horses valued over £5. Poyning's Law of 1494 is amended by the Yelverton Act. This allows bills approved by both houses of Irish Parliament to be transmitted unaltered to Whitehall. The Irish Mutiny Act sets down conditions for the raising of an army in Ireland for two years.

1783

April 17. The Renunciation Act is passed. It recognizes the exclusive right of the Irish Parliament to legislate for Ireland. It also acknowledges the exclusive jurisdiction of the Irish courts.

Sept. 8. The Second Dungannon Convention urges Volunteers in the provinces to press for parliamentary reform.

Nov. 10. The Volunteer movement estimated at 150,000 strong. Lord Charlemont presides over 300 delegates seeking parliamentary reform at Dublin's Rotunda. The move is stymied by Sir Boyle Roche, MP for Tralee, who, improperly claiming to speak for the Catholic Committee's Lord Kenmare, states that Catholics have no wish for the franchise.

Nov. 29. By 157 to 77, the Irish House of Commons defeats the Parliamentary Reform Bill.

1784

May 13. No 1. Company of Belfast Volunteers invites people of every religious persuasion to enlist in its ranks. This represents the first public call for Catholics to join. The Volunteers begin a collection for a mass house and attend its opening on May 30. Protestants collect half of its cost.

June 7. The High Sheriff of Dublin calls a reform meeting that resolves on the rights of Irish people to frequent elections, equitable representation and suffrage.

June 21. James Napper Tandy and reformers petition King George III to dissolve Parliament.

July 4. A dispute in Markethill, County Armagh, leads to the immediate formation of a secret agrarian society of Protestants, the Peep O'Day Boys, and eventually (see Sept. 1794) the Catholic Defenders.

Oct. 25-27. First Session of Radical Reform congress takes place in William Street, Dublin. Convened by the High Sheriff and led by Napper Tandy, only a small number of delegates arrive. Lacking popular support, they make little impact.

1785

Jan. 20-Feb. 4. Second session of Radical Reform conference held in William Street, Dublin. Still not successful.

Feb. 7. In the Irish House of Commons the Chief Secretary, Thomas Orde, introduces Prime Minister William Pitt's proposal to allow free trade between Ireland and Great Britain.

Feb. 22. Pitt himself introduces amended proposals for free trade in the British parliament.

April 20-30. Third session of Radical Reform conference held in William Street, Dublin. A failure.

Aug. 12. Henry Grattan says that Pitt's proposals for free trade are fatal to the Irish Constitution. After discussion, they are abandoned.

Sept. Munster Whiteboys, called Rightboys, cause disturbances. Defenders movement, prominent in Armagh, spreads (see July 4, 1784).

1786

May 8. The Irish Parliament passes a Bill calling into existence a small police force under three magistrates, called Commissioners of Police.

1787

Jan.-March. Whiteboy dissent aggravated by rack-rents, tithes and church rates.

March 26. The Tumultuous Risings Act introduced in Ireland to curb the administration or taking of illegal oaths and interference with tithe collection.

May 21. New powers granted to the Lord Lieutenant and to Grand Juries to appoint chief constables and sub-constables, respectively.

Dec. 16. The Marquis of Buckingham, George Grenville, becomes Lord Lieutenant, heralding a period of corruption in Ireland.

1788

Nov. 5. King George III displays insanity, leading to a parliamentary decision for a regency in Great Britain, but not immediately in Ireland.

1789

Feb. 16-20. Houses of Commons and of Lords approve Henry Grattan's motion to declare the Prince of Wales Regent of Ireland but Whitehall announces the King's recovery. Both Houses still feel that an Irish Regent would underline legislative independence but the Lord Lieutenant, Buckingham, refuses to issue the invitation to the Prince. Parliament censures him and despatches the Duke of Leinster and the Earl of Charlemont, bearing the invitation. The King's recovery is confirmed before their arrival.

May 5-Oct. 15. Revolution at Versailles. When, due to Louis XIV's bankruptcy,

the Estates General meet at Versailles, France, the Third Estate seeks recognition as a National Assembly. This opens the way to revolution and the fall of the Bastille to the workers of Faubourg St Antoine (July 14). The gesture of defiance to despotism found approval in Ireland. where radicals despaired of reforming a corrupt establishment. They began to regard France as a potential ally.

June 20. The Attorney-General, John Fitzgibbon (Lord Clare a year later), becomes Lord Chancellor of Ireland.

June 26. Henry Grattan, John Ponsonby, John Philpot Curran and the Earl of Charlemont form a Dublin Whig Club to pursue internal reform and the 'purification' of Parliament.

1790

Feb. 28. A Northern Whig Club is formed in Belfast.

March 11. The government issues a Proclamation against Volunteers.

July 2. Parliament votes £200,000 towards defence and voices support for war against Spain. Alluding to the war, Grattan emphasises that the interests of England and Ireland were inseparable. Wolfe Tone published a pamphlet arguing that Ireland had no quarrel with Spain and that 'the good of the Empire' advocated by Grattan was specious.

Aug. Edmund Burke's son Richard becomes adviser to the Catholic Committee.

Nov. 1. Edmund Burke's *Reflections on the Revolution in France* is published.

1791

March 13. Part One of Thomas Paine's *The Rights of Man* is published.

April 1. In Barclay's Inn in Crown Entry, Belfast, Samuel McTier chairs a meeting that decides to form an association to unite all Irishmen and pledge themselves to their country (see Oct. 14).

July 14. The second anniversary of the fall of the Bastille is celebrated in Belfast by the Northern Whig Club. In Dublin, Napper Tandy heads a Volunteer commemoration. There are minor commemorative events elsewhere in Ireland.

Aug. 22 c. Wolfe Tone anonymously publishes *An Argument on Behalf of the Catholics of Ireland*. It espouses electoral and parliamentary reform, Catholic Emancipation and the end of England's influence in Ireland.

Oct. 14. Wolfe Tone visits Belfast, where the Society of United Irishmen is founded (see April 1). Main support comes from Ulster Presbyterians and Protestant liberals seeking parliamentary reform. Tone and others favour emulating events in France by pursuing a republic. The religious and political establishments disapprove of the organization.

Nov. 9. First formal meeting of the Dublin Society of United Irishmen at Eagle Tavern, Eustace Street. It adopts the resolutions of the Belfast meeting (above). Napper Tandy becomes secretary.

Dec. 27. The Catholic Committee splits. John Keogh heads the majority radical element. Lord Kenmare and 67 fellow aristocrats secede and seek relief for Catholics at the discretion of Parliament.

1792

Part Two of Thomas Paine's *The Rights of Man* is published. Lord Edward Fitzgerald, officially still in the British army, meets Paine in Paris and attends debates. At a dinner of British residents he joins a toast to abolish hereditary titles and is cashiered from the service. Wolfe Tone becomes adviser to the Catholic Committee, replacing Richard Burke (see Aug. 1790).

Jan. 4. First issue of *Northern Star*, organ of Belfast's United Irishmen, edited by Samuel Neilson.

Feb. 20. Napper Tandy is prosecuted for challenging Solicitor-General, John Toler, over a personal slight and charged with breach of parliamentary privilege. Imprisoned, he escapes three days later.

April 18. A Catholic Relief Act entitles Catholics to practise at the Bar and hold state appointments below King's Council. Napper Tandy surrenders himself (see Feb. 20), is re-imprisoned for some hours before being released. Tone and Tandy attend Bastille Day celebrations at Belfast Linen Hall. Rev. Steel Dickson secures unanimous agreement from 800 Volunteers to press for total Catholic Emancipation.

July 25. Tone becomes assistant secretary and agent of the Catholic Committee.

Aug. 13. Louis XVI and his family imprisoned.

Dec. 3-8. Catholic Convention at Tailors' Hall, Dublin. Tone and Keogh selected as delegates to petition Pitt and the King on abolishing outstanding Penal Laws. They are to do so directly, avoiding the Dublin parliament.

Dec. 9. John Fitzgibbon, Lord Chancellor, proclaims the bearing of arms by unauthorized organizations.

Dec. 16. Dublin Volunteers state that the defence of their country from internal or external aggression is their aim.

Dec. 22. In Paris, Lord Edward Fitzgerald marries Pamela, ward of Madame de Genlis and allegedly her daughter by the Duke of Orleans.

1793

Jan. 2. The King receives Tone and Keogh (see 3-8 Dec. 1792).

Jan. 10. At the opening of Parliament, the King urges Catholic relief.

Jan. 21. Louis XVI is executed.

Feb. 1. France declares war on England and Holland. This leads to a slump that cripples the Irish economy and increases Irish disapproval of the war. It also makes the French revolutionary cause more popular.

Wishing to forestall further conflict, England adopts a more conciliatory approach to Ireland.

Feb. 15-16. An Ulster Volunteer Convention at Dungannon demands reforms.

Feb. 25. Parliament passes an Act banning importation of arms and gunpowder.

March 11. The Ulster Volunteers are proclaimed.

April 9. Hobart's Catholic Relief Act allows Catholics parliamentary franchise and removes remaining disabilities except exclusion from parliament, judgeships and named high public appointments. The Militia Act allows for the raising of borough and county militias to a strength of almost 15,000 who will undergo 28 days training annually.

July 11. At Taghmon, Co. Wexford, 80 peasant agitators are killed by the 56th Regiment of Infantry in an anti-militia riot.

1794

March 4. Second reading of bill for parliamentary reform.

April *c*. A French Government agent, Anglican Rev. William Jackson, meets Tone and other United Irishmen in Dublin. Tone gives him a document outlining conditions in Ireland and advocating a French invasion. Unknown to Jackson, a colleague, Cockayne, is a British spy who inform on him.

April 28. Jackson is arrested.

May 2. Prominent United Irishman, Archibald Hamilton Rowan, arrested on a charge of distributing seditious material. Fined £500 and imprisoned for two years, but escapes to France from where he goes to America.

May 23. The United Irishmen are proscribed following a raid on Tailors' Hall in Dublin by government forces.

June 25. William Drennan charged with seditious libel. Acquitted following defence by John Philpot Curran.

1795

Feb. 2. Protestants in Belfast petition parliament to repeal Penal Laws against Catholics.

Feb. 12. Henry Grattan introduces the Catholic Relief Bill.

Feb. 17. British Cabinet rejects Grattan's Relief Bill and moves to dismiss Lord Lieutenant Fitzwilliam.

Feb. 23. Fitzwilliam is dismissed.

March 31. Lord Camden becomes Lord Lieutenant of Ireland. Catholic Emancipation supporters riot. (John Jeffreys Pratt Camden, the second Earl of Camden, remained Viceroy of Ireland from 1795 to 1798. He led a corrupt cabinet. While as Viceroy he was responsible to the Prime Minister and to the King, in effect his cabinet or 'Junto' made the decisions. His prevarication and incompetence in dealing with the rebellion led to his recall.)

April 9. Emancipation supporters meet in Dublin, protesting the removal of Fitzwilliam and demanding a new Relief Bill.

April 21. Grattan's parliamentary proposal for an inquiry into the state of Ireland is defeated by 158 to 84.

April 30. William Jackson (see 1794) is tried for treason. He dies in the dock, having taken arsenic at breakfast.

May 5. By 155 to 84, the House of Commons defeats Grattan's Relief Bill.

May 10. National Executive Directory of the United Irishmen is formed and it becomes an oath-bound secret society advocating an Irish Republic separated from Britain.

June 13. Tone leaves for America.

Sept. 14. In Tentaraghan, Co. Armagh, Defenders attack and plunder Protestant holdings, provoking retaliation.

Sept. 18-20. Shooting at The Diamond, Loughgall, Co. Armagh, when a group of Protestants known as The Wreckers come from Portadown and Rich Hill. Skirmishes and house-burnings continue for two days between Defenders and Peep o'Day Boys.

Sept. 21. The Wreckers are leaving Loughgall when a party of Defenders from Cavan, Tyrone and Monaghan arrive and break the windows of a Protestant home. This leads to the 'Battle of the Diamond'. After the fracas, at the home of James Sloan, the Peep O' Days form the Orange Society that later becomes the Orange Order.

1796

Jan. *c.* The Royal Black Perceptory or Royal Black Institution is formed in Loughgall, Co. Tyrone. It dedicates itself to maintaining the 'pure evangelical truth' written in the Bible.

Feb. 1. After a 31-day voyage from America, Tone lands at Havre de Grace in France.

Feb. 15. Having arrived in Paris three days earlier, Tone meets the French Minister for Foreign Affairs.

March 24. The Insurrection Act authorizes magistrates to proclaim areas within their jurisdiction. Administering illegal oaths becomes a capital offence.

May 5. Tone meets the President of the Directory, Carnot, and is disappointed at his merely advising him to write a memorial desiring leave to stay.

July *c.* Arthur O'Connor and Lord Edward Fitzgerald support Tone in France. They visit Switzerland and Germany also.

July 12. Members of the Orange Order, representing ninety Lodges, hold their first 'Twelfth of July' parades. In Lurgan, Co. Armagh, one member strikes a soldier and is killed in retaliation.

Sept. 16. Samuel Neilson, Charles H. Teeling and Thomas Russell and other United Irishmen leaders are arrested and charged with high treason.

Oct. 10. Henry Joy McCracken is arrested and imprisoned in Kilmainham Jail for almost fourteen months.

Oct. 26. The *Habeas Corpus* Suspension Act, to last until June 1799, aims at tackling

unrest brought about by the United Irishmen, the Defenders and the Orange Order.

Nov. 9. An Act regulates raising of yeomanry corps of armed volunteers by landlords.

Dec. 15. General Lazare Hoche commands a fleet of forty-five ships and 13,975 men that leave Brest for Ireland. Tone is on board the *Indomptable*. The fleet evades the British squadron blockading the port. The intention is to invade Ireland and join with the United Irishmen in driving out the British and establishing an Irish Republic. This would be a prelude to the conquest of England.

Dec. 21. Separated from Hoche and part of the fleet, fifteen French ships, bearing 6400 troops, arrive in Bantry Bay. A calm sea makes conditions for landing perfect, but in the absence of Hoche no landing takes place.

Dec. 22. Snow and sleet fall and winds separate the waiting fleet in Bantry Bay.

Dec. 24. A raging storm blows. A council of war decides to land the force, but a worsening gale prevents this.

Dec. 26-29. One by one, the French fleet raises anchor and leaves Bantry Bay.

1797

Jan 7. Lord Edward Fitzgerald joins the United Irishmen' military committee.

Feb. *c.* Thomas Reynolds joins the United Irishmen and becomes a member of the Leinster Directory against which he later informs (see Feb. 19 & March 12, 1798).

March 13. Lieutenant General Gerard Lake, commanding the northern portion of the country, introduces martial law. This partly succeeds in disarming Ulster.

May 15. Ponsonby's reform resolution defeated 117 to 30 in the House of Commons. Grattan and other opposition leaders leave parliament.

May 17. Lord Camden, the Lord Lieutenant, places parts of Ireland under martial law. The United Irishmen are proclaimed.

May 21. Orange Lodge Masters meet in Armagh. They pledge support to the King, the Constitution, the Protestant ascendancy and the Established Church.

July 12. Members of Belfast's Orange Order parade. Lake reviews Orange parades at Lurgan and Lisburn. Militia and regular troops clash in Stewartstown, Co. Tyrone. Seven militia lose their lives and seven are wounded.

Oct. 14. William Orr hanged in Carrickfergus for administering illegal oaths. Because his execution aroused indignation, the call 'Remember Orr' became a common one in rousing rebels to action during 1798.

Dec. 8. Henry Joy McCracken is released from prison on bail. He returns to organize Antrim rebels.

1798

Jan. 6-13. Tone meets Napoleon in Paris and discusses possible involvement of exiled United Irishmen in another French expedition to Ireland.

Jan. 9. Opponent of the Union, John Foster, is re-elected Speaker of the House of Commons.

Feb. 1. Friction becomes obvious between Tone and Napper Tandy in Paris.

Feb. 15. The Orangemen of Ulster present Lord Camden with an address of loyalty.

Feb. 19. United Irishmen in Leinster resolve that Parliament should not interfere with their plans. Thomas Reynolds informs on them.

March 3. Tone criticizes the Parisian press for describing Napper Tandy as 'an Irish general to whose standard 30,000 United Irishmen would fly as soon as he displayed it'.

March 12. As a result of betrayal by Thomas Reynolds (see Feb. 19), most of the Provincial Directory of Leinster (United Irishmen) are arrested at the house of Oliver Bond.

March 30. Lord Camden directs the Commander-in-Chief, Sir Ralph Abercromby, to suppress the rebellion.

April 20 c. Hostilities at Holy Cross, County Tipperary. Rebels dispersed by Cashel Fencible Cavalry and Louth Militia. Three rebels killed, twenty wounded and some prisoners taken.

April 23. Abercromby resigns. General Gerard Lake becomes Acting Commander-in-Chief (see June 20).

April 27. A conference of magistrates gathered at Gorey, Co. Wexford, places part of the county under legal restriction.

May 15. Dublin Castle issues a Proclamation: 'The Lord Lieutenant and Privy Council of Ireland have issued a Proclamation declaring that they have received information upon oath, that Lord Edward Fitzgerald has been guilty of High Treason.' They offer a reward of £1000 sterling to 'any person who shall discover, apprehend or commit him to prison'.

May 17. A newly appointed National Directory of the United Irishmen (Fitzgerald, the Sheares brothers, Lawless and Neilson) meets in Dublin and decides on a rebellion. His Under-Secretary informs Major Sirr that Lord Edward Fitzgerald is residing at the home of a feather-merchant in Thomas Street, Dublin.

May 19. Lord Edward Fitzgerald is wounded and captured. In the struggle, R.M. Swan and Captain Ryan, guard commander, are seriously injured.

May 21. The Sheares brothers, Henry and John, are arrested, having been betrayed by Captain Armstrong of the King's County militia. Lord Edward Fitzgerald is despatched to Newgate Prison. Francis Higgins is suspected of claiming the reward for information leading to Fitzgerald's arrest.

May 23-24. The 1798 Rebellion proper begins with a successful rebel attack on Cork Militia and Ancient British Cavalrymen at Prosperous, Co. Kildare. Beauchamp Bagenal Harvey, Edward Fitzgerald and John Colclough are arrested and imprisoned in Wexford.

May 24. Insurgents are repulsed at Clane, Monasterevin, Naas and Kilcullen (which they burn), Co. Kildare; at Lucan, Fox and Geese Commons, Rathfarnham, Tallaght and Lusk, Co. Dublin; at Baltinglass, Co. Wicklow and at Slane, County Meath. They have some successes at Barrettstown, Co. Kilkenny; Rathangan and Old Kilcullen, Co. Kildare and at Dunboyne, Co. Meath. At Dunlavin, Co.Wicklow, the Wicklow Militia allegedly kill over 40 rebel prisoners. There was never any official confirmation of these atrocities. All general officers are empowered by Proclamation to inflict the death penalty on rebels or known collaborators. General Lake orders General Loftus not to take prisoners.

May 25 c. 400 rebels killed at Carlow; 50 at Castledermot, Co. Kildare. Rebels are publicly lashed in Nenagh, Co. Tipperary.

May 26. The rebellion in Meath ends with defeat at Tara. Throughout this and the following day, houses in Wexford are fired and ransacked. Boolavogue church burned by North Cork Militia. Lieutenant Bookey of the Camolin Cavalry is killed at the Harrow.

May 27. Rebels are defeated at Kilthomas, Co.Wexford, but Father Murphy leads his men in routing yeomen and militia at Oulart Hill.

May 28. Father Murphy leads rebels in taking Enniscorthy. They kill, pillage and loot. Rebel prisoners are shot in Carnew, Co. Wicklow..

May 29. At Gibbet Rath, on the Curragh, Co. Kildare, Major-General Sir James Duff slaughters 350 rebels after they agreed an end to hostilities with General Dundas and surrendered their arms to him. A large gathering of Wexford rebels collect at Vinegar Hill.

May 30. Wexford rebels successful at Three Rocks, where they capture artillery, but are defeated at Ballymenane Hill, near Gorey and at Newtownbarry (Bunclody). They seize Wexford town. They appoint Beauchamp Bagenal Harvey, released from custody in Wexford, as their leader.

June 2-3. Major General Duff and his Cork Militia defeat rebels at Kilcock, Co.Kildare. In the press, the National Directory (a) calls on all Irish exiles to return or send funds for the struggle; (b) calls on Irishmen serving in the British service to quit or forfeit their rights as Irish citizens. If they refuse, and are seen bearing arms, they will be shot on sight; (c) promises to recompense all soldiers and sailors who desert the enemy and join the insurgents. They will be given first consideration in sharing out the national property and all ships brought in by them will become their property.

June 4. Lord Edward Fitzgerald dies in Newgate. Colonel Walpole and scores of his troops killed in action against rebels at Tubberneering. Rev. William Steel Dickson and others arrested. Government forces withdraw from Arklow.

June 5. Major General Henry Johnson fends off an attempt by Beauchamp Bagenal Harvey to seize New Ross and open a way towards Kilkenny and Waterford. Fr Philip Roche replaces Harvey. John 'Kelly the Boy from Killane' and Lord Mountjoy killed in action. Over 100 loyalist prisoners, mainly Protestant, are massacred by rebels at Scullabogue, Co. Wexford.

June 6. Rebellion begins in Antrim.

June 7. After a successful attack on Antrim town by Henry Joy McCracken, a counter-attack succeeds. Lord O'Neill is killed and McCracken is captured.

June 9. Linen merchant Henry Munroe leads insurrection of Co. Down United Irishmen. Major-General Francis Needham defeats the north Wexford/ south Wicklow rebels at Arklow. Father Michael Murphy killed in action.

June 10. Rebels are repulsed at Portaferry, Co. Down. William Aylmer of Painstown,

Kilcock, Co. Kildare, leads 500 rebels to Maynooth and routs its garrison. Munroe and his rebels occupy Saintsfield, Co. Down, displacing the York Fencibles.

June 11. Munroe and his forces seize and hold the Montalto Heights, around Bally-nahinch, Co. Down.

June 12. General Nugent counter-attacks at Ballynahinch (above) and drives rebels six miles south-west to Slieve Croob, captur-ing Munroe. Carlow town is burned after rebels are driven from it.

June 13. Nugent's troops pillage Bally-nahinch, Co. Down. This ends resistance in Ulster.

June 14 *c.* Father Quigley of Dundalk is hanged in London.

June 15. Munroe is hanged at the front door of his home in Lisburn, Co. Antrim.

June 16. Troops arrest Luke Teeling, father of Charles Hamilton and Bartholomew. No charge is made against him but he is held for four years.

June 17. Rebels burn Tinahely, Co.Wicklow.

June 18. At Ovidstown , Kilcock, Co. Kil-dare, General Dundas defeats William Aylmer's rebels.

June 19. Wexford rebels retreat from Lack-en Hill to Three Rocks.

June 20. Wexford rebels under Father Philip Roche are defeated at Foulke's Mill by Major General Sir John Moore. Lord Camden is replaced as Lord Lieutenant by Charles, Marquis Cornwallis. Corn-wallis takes over as Commander-in-Chief, ending Lake's acting appointment.

June 21 *c.* Wolfe Tone is called to the Min-istries of War and the Marine in Paris. He discusses a new expedition to Ireland. General Johnson recaptures Enniscorthy from rebels who also abandon Wexford town. At Vinegar Hill, General Lake wins the day. Some rebels fall back to Three Rocks.

June 22. Fr John Murphy leads his men from Three Rocks and marches inland.

June 24. Father Murphy's rebels reach Castlecomer, Co. Kilkenny. They decide

to return to Wexford. *En route*, they sur-prise yeomen and supporters at Gorey, killing 37.

June 25-6. Rebels capture Hacketstown, Co. Carlow. The authorities hang Father Roche and Matthew Keogh at Wexford. Father Murphy reaches Kilcomney Hill, Co. Carlow, close to Scollagh Gap, and is heavily attacked.

June 26. Father Murphy allegedly subjected to rack torture before burning in a tar barrel in Tullow, Co. Carlow.

July 2. Rebels under Garret and Billy Byrne disperse yeomen from Ballyrahan Hill, between Tinahely and Carnew, Co. Wick-low.

July 4. Yeomen force rebels from their stronghold at White Heap mountain, Co. Wexford, making further effective resis-tance in the county impossible.

July 14. When the Wexford force under Anthony Perry and Fitzgerald march into Kildare in July, they make contact with William Aylmer in Timahoe. Aylmer does not join them in their march northward. In Meath, along with the forces of Garret Byrne and Father Kearns, they cross the Boyne but are encircled by government forces at Knightstown, Co. Louth. They attempted to draw the enemy into a pitched battle, but Generals Wemys and Meyrick wait until they have artillery in place. After a heavy bombardment, the rebels disperse. They try to escape across a bog and suffere severe casualties. Found guilty of high treason, the Sheares broth-ers, Henry and John, are executed in public outside Newgate Prison.

July 17. Henry Joy McCracken is executed in Belfast. In the House of Commons Lord Castlereagh reads the King's Mes-sage of Mercy. Lord Cornwallis, Lord Lieutenant, announces an amnesty for rebels who were not leaders. At the trial of John McCann, Thomas Reynolds is publicly revealed as an informer.

July 20. On the evidence of Reynolds, Oliver

Bond and William Michael Byrne are convicted of high treason. (See March 12 and July 25.)

July 24. John McCann, secretary of the Leinster Directory of the United Irishmen, is hanged. Other prisoners sign a round robin, offering to give information on the structure and plans of the United Irish movement, but not names. In return, they seek and receive permission to emigrate.

July 25. William Michael Byrne is executed.

Aug. 4-16. A secret House of Lords Committee examines statements on the United Irishmen received from Bond, Thomas Addis Emmet, Samuel Neilson, William James MacNeven and Arthur O'Connor.

Aug. 12. Rev. William Steel Dickson is moved to a prison ship where he is detained until March 1799.

Aug. 22. General Jean Humbert, accompanied by Matthew Tone and Bartholomew Teeling in a small fleet of transports and frigates, 1000 armed men and as many spare muskets, lands at Kilcummin, Killala, Co. Mayo. The force storms and occupies Killala.

Aug. 25-6. Irish rebels, including deserters from Longford Militia, join Humbert's force for a march via Ballina and Nephin mountain, to Castlebar.

Aug. 26. General Lake's force reaches Castlebar in time to reinforce the garrison commanded by General Francis Hely-Hutchinson.

Aug. 27. Humbert and his Irish allies are victorious at Castlebar. Bartholomew Teeling bears a flag of truce to General Lake. His escort is fired upon and killed. Teeling is taken prisoner but General Hutchinson apologizes for the action and returns Teeling to the French lines.

Aug. 31. Humbert announces the Provisional Republic of Connaught. He installs John Moore as its President. Lord Cornwallis calls on his officers to stop their men inflicting harm on peasants.

Aug. 31 to Sept. 2. Humbert is advised to move to strongholds of the United Irishmen in Ulster but he wastes time drilling local rebels who joined his force.

Sept. 3-4. Humbert moves east from Castlebar with the intention of reaching Dublin. Government forces re-occupy the town.

Sept. 4. Lord Cornwallis and his forces arrive in Hollymount and prepare to advance to Castlebar. On board the *Anacreon*, Napper Tandy leaves Dunkirk with a small force.

Sept. 4-6. Rebels rise in Westmeath and Longford. They are defeated in actions at Wilson's Hospital, Multyfarnham, and at Granard.

Sept. 5. Humbert's Franco-Irish force defeats Colonel Charles Vereker's militia at Collooney, Co. Sligo.

Sept. 7. Humbert changes his plan of moving north. Hearing that Longford and Westmeath have risen, he decides to return and join with them in a push towards Dublin. He crosses the Shannon at Carrick-on-Shannon and rests at Cloone village. His cannon chains are stolen and he is forced to abandon some.

Sept. 8. Lord Cornwallis and General Lake force the surrender of Humbert's force at Ballinamuck, Co. Longford. Bartholomew Teeling is captured. Irish rebels are massacred.

Sept. 16. Napper Tandy lands on Rutland Island, off Burtonport, Co. Donegal. He learns of Humbert's defeat, leaves some proclamations and departs for Norway. Having heard of Humbert's initial success, the French Directory despatches from Brest a small fleet of ten craft under Commodore Bombart. General Hardy commands the complement of 3000 men. Wolfe Tone is on board the flagship, *Hoche*.

Sept. 23. General Trench routs the Irish rebels holding Killala.

Sept. 24. Convicted by court martial in Dublin, Bartholomew Teeling is hanged.

Sept. 29. Matthew Tone is hanged in Dublin. Oliver Bond dies in prison.

Oct. 6. Acts pardon certain categories of sedition, offering banishment, instead of execution, in return for surrender. Failure to accept leaves rebels open to charges of high treason. The Irish Parliament is prorogued.

Oct. 10. Due to adverse weather conditions, only the *Bische*, *Hoche*, *Loire* and *Resolue* of the French fleet reach Lough Swilly.

Oct. 11. Sir John Borlase Warren's squadron of six sail of the line, two frigates and one razee of 60 guns intercept Bompart's ships. A boat is despatched from the *Bische* to take Tone on board and effect an escape. He refuses. The *Bische* manages to escape.

Oct. 12 The *Hoche* is taken to Buncrana. Lord Cavan invites its officers to breakfast. Tone is recognized by Sir George Hill. He is taken into custody and is despatched to Dublin.

Nov. 3. Robert Stewart, Viscount Castlereagh, is appointed Chief Secretary when Pelham becomes ill.

Nov. 8. Tone is escorted to Dublin and incarcerated in the Provost's Prison under Major Sandys.

Nov. 10. A Dublin court martial convicts Wolfe Tone of high treason. He is sentenced to hanging.

Nov. 12. Tone allegedly cuts his throat in a suicide attempt.

Nov. 19. Tone dies.

Dec. 9. William Saurin assembles Dublin lawyers. By 166 votes to 32, a motion is carried stating that it would be dangerous and improper to propose a legislative union between Great Britain and Ireland.

Dec. 18. Dublin merchants and bankers also rule out a legislative union but confirm their loyalty to the Crown.

Dec. 27. *Anti-Union* newspaper publishes its first issue.

1799

Jan. 5. The Grand Orange Lodge of Ireland forbids its members taking sides on legislative union of Great Britain and Ireland.

Jan. 22. The King's speech at opening of Parliament includes proposals for legislative union.

Jan. 31. Pitt puts the case for legislative union before the British Commons.

March 19. Samuel Neilson, Rev. Steel Dickson, Thomas Addis Emmet, Thomas Russell, Robert Simms and other prominent United Irishmen who were arrested in March 1798 give 'honourable information' and consent to exile. They are deported to Scotland and imprisoned in Fort George.

March 25. The Indemnity Act introduces court martial for offences committed during the rebellion but exonerates unlawful activities engaged in for suppressing it and ensuring the safety of the realm.

1800

Jan. 15. The Irish Parliament opens. It passes writs for elections to endorse proposals for union with Great Britain. This is to be the final session of an Irish Parliament (see Aug. 2).

Feb. 6. The largest division ever recorded in the Irish House of Commons (158 to 115) carries the King's recommendation for legislative union.

March 1. A meeting of 31 Orange Lodges at the Maze, Co. Down, resolves that legislative union will lead to ruin.

March 12. A meeting of 36 Orange Lodges in Armagh resolves to protest against the union.

March 28. The Irish House of Commons agrees on Articles for Union.

May 26. Grattan makes his final speech against the Union in the House of Commons and retires.

June 7. The Irish House of Commons passes the Bill for Union by 65 votes. The House of Lords passes it by 69 votes.

Aug. 1. The Act of Union receives Royal Assent.

Aug. 2. The Irish House of Commons sits for the last time.

Sept. 12. A charge of High Treason against Napper Tandy fails. He is then charged with his action at Rutland Island on 16 September 1798. Napoleon intercedes and Tandy is banished.

1801

Jan. 1. The Irish and British parliaments merge as the Act of Union comes into force.

March 14. Henry Addington, Viscount Sidmouth (1757-1844), becomes Prime Minister after Pitt resigns, after failing to achieve Catholic Emancipation.

1802

March 15. John Freeman Mitford, an opponent of Catholic Emancipation, becomes Lord Chancellor of Ireland.

June 30. Peace of Amiens between Britain, France, Spain and Holland. Arthur O'Connor, Thomas Addis Emmet and William James MacNeven released from prison but forced into exile.

Oct. The remnants of United Irish movement, sensing a resumption of hostilities between Britain and France, once again looks to French assistance. Robert Emmet

(1778-1803), the younger brother of Thomas Addis, returns from France to plan a new rebellion.

1803

May 16. Britain refuses Napoleon's offer for Russian mediation; war resumes between Britain and France.

July 16. One killed and three injured in an explosion of Emmet's munitions. This necessitates an earlier rebellion than anticipated.

July 23. In Thomas Street, Dublin, Emmet issues a Proclamation of the Provisional Government of an Irish Republic. Excited followers kill Lord Kilwarden, his son-in-law, Rev. Richard Wolfe and Colonel Browne of the 21 Scottish Fusiliers. A completely disorganized rebellion fails.

August 25. Having lain low as 'Mr Ellis' in Harold's Cross, Emmet, attempting to meet his fiancée, Sarah Curran, is captured.

Sept. 19. Emmet is tried at Green Street Courthouse and convicted of high treason. He delivers his celebrated speech from the dock.

Sept. 20. Emmet is hanged in Thomas Street.

Oct. 20. At Downpatrick, Thomas Russell is convicted of high treason.

Oct. 21. Thomas Russell is executed.

Dec. 14. Michael Dwyer, who continued to defy government forces in Co. Wicklow, surrenders.

Index

208

Index